Praise for Sky Ranch

"With a backdrop of vivid ranch gives the reader visceral ... it is like for a child and a family when a parent is mentally ill and cannot or will not get the care they need—a problem as relevant today as it was decades ago. This book is an absorbing and insightful read, a must for any family touched by mental illness."
—PATRICIA GRAYHALL, author of *Making the Rounds: Defying Norms in Love and Medicine*

"*Sky Ranch* is a deeply moving modern western memoir. The starkly beautiful Okanogan Highlands serve as the place where a young ranch girl comes of age, learning to navigate life's challenges, including bucking horses, deadly rattlesnakes, and the tragic mental illness of her mother. Highly recommended!"
—NICHOLAS O'CONNELL, journalist, author, and founder of *The Writer's Workshop Review*

"Against the backdrop of the Pacific Northwest, Lockwood locks down a tale of survival of the fittest—one woman vs. one family. Well written, well plotted, and well told, *Sky Ranch* records the author's lifelong quest for purchase—a place to stand, a need to compromise, a chance to heal."
—ROBERT J. RAY, author of *Play or Die: Senior Tennis and the Art of Spin*

"*Sky Ranch* is the setting for a family secret, one that haunted the author's childhood. Just as she rode her horse through the hills rounding up the family's sheep and cattle, as an adult she discovered and brought together the elements of a gripping story about her mother's mysterious illness."
—CHRISTINE HEMP, author of *Wild Ride Home: Love, Loss, and a Little White Horse—A Family Memoir*

"A poignant tribute to the joys and hardships of a caring but troubled ranching family that must navigate the rocky terrain of mental illness. *Sky Ranch* is an intimate portrayal of a young woman's vulnerability and tenacity as she comes to terms with an arduous physical and emotional upbringing. A deeply engaging and thought-provoking read."
—TERESA H. JANSSEN, author of
The Ways of Water

"The ranch's isolation provides a metaphor for the lonely journey loved ones of the mentally ill must traverse to find their way to truth and acceptance. A profound read for those who care for and about the mentally ill."
—LINDA MOORE, author of *Attribution*
and *Five Days in Bogotá*

"Linda Lockwood's memoir is a personable, heartwarming tale of life on a ranch—and a woman's vividly told search for her disappearing mother who vacillated between psychotic paranoia and extreme depression. A richly rewarding read."
—SCOTT T. DRISCOLL, author of
Better You Go Home

SKY
RANCH

SKY RANCH

Reared in the High Country

Linda M. Lockwood

SHE WRITES PRESS

Published 2024
Printed in the United States of America
Print ISBN: 978-1-64742-634-7
E-ISBN: 978-1-64742-635-4
Library of Congress Control Number: 2024909902

For information, address:
She Writes Press
1569 Solano Ave #546
Berkeley, CA 94707

Interior Design by Tabitha Lahr

She Writes Press is a division of SparkPoint Studio, LLC.

Names and identifying characteristics have been changed to protect the privacy of certain individuals.

*For my daughters Deanna and Rosemary,
the lights of my life,*

*and for my brother Bill and cousins Nan and
Kathy, who lived parts of this journey with me.*

AUTHOR'S NOTE

This book is a memoir and reflects current recollections of my life many years ago. In writing this book, I've endeavored to be as factual as possible, turning to journals, letters, scrapbooks, photo albums, report cards, newspaper articles, and other records of my personal and familial history. Allowing for the indulgences of my adult memory, this is a work of nonfiction, except for a handful of names and identifying details I have changed to respect individual privacy. I've recalled dialogue to the best of my memory. Memory is never perfect, and others may recall things differently. This is what I remember, and I have layered it with new understanding to make meaning in the present.

PRELUDE

To say that life on Sky Ranch was hard would be an understatement bigger than the ranch itself. My childhood was a wild and thrilling and sometimes terrifying series of adventures that included roaming isolated hills, taking on a bucking horse and deadly rattlesnakes, and navigating the mysteries of Mother Nature and human nature with very little guidance and almost no supervision. I'll share many of those tales in these pages, but much of my life has found me engaged in a search for truth, and this story won't be the whole truth if I don't include an exploration of the schizophrenia that plagued my mother's mind and perplexed those who loved her. Some estimates claim that schizophrenia strikes one in one hundred people, which means that millions of folks have experienced schizophrenia themselves, and far more have lived with it under the same roof. But not many have talked or written about it because of the stigma it carries.

I certainly understand that stigma. I grew up in an era and a household in which mental illness simply wasn't talked about. Yet every five years or so, my mother blamed all her troubles on my father, and day after day, I watched her verbally attack him. One day, she was sent away to a strange hospital nowhere near where we lived, and even then, I had no one to help me understand what was wrong with my mother. When it came to learning to survive wilderness and weather and wild animals, I was on my own. And when it came to figuring out how to endure and maybe even thrive despite my mother's condition and its destructive effect on my family, I was on my own. That's just the way it was. I learned early that a girl had to do for herself. But ranch life made me strong, very strong. In the end, that's probably what saved me.

It was 1954, and I had just turned eight when my family moved to an isolated ranch in eastern Washington state. At first, I had no idea how rough ranch life could be. I was just a girl who'd lived in a small town and played dolls and card games with the girls in my neighborhood. If you'd seen me then, you probably wouldn't have looked twice. Timid and shy, I wanted to blend in. But if you visited Sky Ranch in 1956 and looked up the hillside to the skyline, you might have caught sight of a skinny, long-legged ten-year-old girl sitting astride a reddish-brown horse. If you could have zoomed in closer, you'd have seen freckled cheeks and, beneath a rumpled straw Stetson, her eyes, made keen by bifocal glasses, watching over the grazing sheep. She would have been sitting tall, tipping her head a bit to listen for the quiet rustle of a slithering rattlesnake. She would have spent all day with her collie companion and hundreds of sheep, riding to keep the flock away from the neighbor's land and out of her father's ripening wheat crop. At day's end, she would have been seen gathering the flock and singing them home before the hungry coyotes began their nighttime attack.

With great speed, life on Sky Ranch propelled me beyond girlish things. It showed me what loneliness means. Compounding the loneliness of shepherding was my lack of playmates outside of school hours, an isolation intensified by my family's desire to keep my mother's mental problems private. We didn't speak of them outside the family or even among ourselves. I was twenty-five years old when I first heard that my mother had been diagnosed as schizophrenic, which is to say that for the better part of three decades, my family chose to look away, ignore, adapt, compensate—to do just about anything other than speak of it. We stayed silent, like the deer that roamed our land, treading quietly, ears and eyes alert and wary. But as it turns out, deer have a voice. I heard one once.

Riding my horse across a flat field on a spring day, I heard a single high-pitched cry, unlike any sound I'd heard from an animal. My searching eyes caught the movement of a lone doe striding in silence across the bunchgrass hillside above us, her eyes and ears focused on the hillock she walked toward. Later that morning, I saw her in the nearby field, bounding away, her spotted fawn running at her side. The mother had left her baby hidden on the hillock while she went away to graze. I hadn't heard the mother grunt, signaling her return, but I heard the waiting fawn's answering cry.

Like the mother deer, I return to the Sky Ranch and its wild places to claim my secrets and give voice to my stories. My mother held the biggest secrets, and decades passed before I began to find answers by following the clues, clues she wrote herself and then hid from us all.

CHAPTER ONE

On the cool spring evening of April 13, 1972, after a long day of coding medical charts at the University of Washington Medical Center, I was home cooking Hamburger Helper and waiting for my husband Tony to arrive for dinner. The phone rang, and Dad's voice startled me. He rarely called. Dad wasn't much of a talker.

"I have some bad news, Cookie."

He'd pinned this childhood nickname on me before I could talk, and I could always hear his fondness in it. But that didn't soften the impact of what he said next. He'd always been direct, never delicate, except by avoidance of things he kept private.

"Your mother is dead," he blurted.

I was so stunned that I barely managed to utter, "Oh, no."

I stumbled into the nearest chair, my pulse thundering in my ears. Long seconds passed as my thoughts raced. *I should have called her this week. What did she do?*

When I'd recovered from my shock enough to ask what happened, Dad said, "Looks like she shot herself. She was found by a couple of Mormon missionaries."

The idea of my mother wanting to end her life wasn't a complete surprise. She'd survived an overdose of sleeping pills six years earlier. Since I left home, Dad had tried to watch, hoping to prevent another attempt, but most of the time, she was by herself all day until Dad went home for dinner. Now this.

I can't let him be alone with this. I swallowed hard and found my voice. "I'll drive over tomorrow, Dad."

"It would sure be nice to have your company right now, Cookie."

"I'll be there by suppertime."

I jammed the green wall phone into its cradle, turned off the skillet, and collapsed into the nearest chair. Mom was gone. And with no goodbye.

All my life, she'd been gradually withdrawing from me, but I wasn't prepared for this. The finality of it began to sink in, and then came the flood of guilt. I felt my forehead flush as my throat constricted. *Why didn't I call her last weekend when I learned I was pregnant? Would the news of her first grandchild have given her something to live for? Now, I'll never know.*

I placed my hands on my stomach and sobbed.

When Tony drove into the carport and slid open the back door, I rose and said, "Mom is dead. Dad just called me."

"Oh, no!" he said. "I'm sorry, honey." He took me in his strong arms as I sobbed.

We sat down to talk, and he agreed that I should go to my father for the weekend. He offered to go with me, but I said no—the next day was Friday, a workday he shouldn't miss. My job at the university provided paid leave for illness and family emergencies. His job as a teamster didn't.

The next morning, I began the five-hour drive east over the Cascade Mountains to the ranch that had been my home for sixteen years. As I climbed to the craggy peaks of Stevens Pass, the climate transitioned from cool and moist with dense greens on the coastal side to hot and dry across the sparse browns of the high desert on the eastern side. At the Columbia River, I turned north to follow the green ribbon of irrigated orchards and alfalfa fields through the arid hills. This intimately familiar drive traced my life in reverse from a college-educated working wife in urban Seattle back to my first days as a ranch girl in the Okanogan Highlands. I was used to the drive feeling like a homecoming, but now I was going back to something different, something very painful. My mother wouldn't be there.

Where the Columbia River veered eastward, I headed north, following its tributary, the Okanogan River, to my homeland with its rugged mountains, verdant river valleys, and high arid plateaus. When I turned from the river and wound up Chiliwist Road, the dejected brown slopes awaiting the new grass of springtime ushered me into the Chiliwist Valley and the Sky Ranch I knew so well and missed so much.

Driving up our lane to the house beside the creek, I smelled charcoal burning in the outside grill, the smell of home. Dad rose from the back porch steps to greet me with a wan smile. I folded into his arms and dwelled in his long hug as I choked back the lump in my throat. He was fifty-six, just four months older than my mother had been. Strong—six feet tall with a red farmer's tan darkening his pale skin outside the neck and short sleeves of his shirt. His light brown hair was fading toward the gray of his eyes, which looked serious behind silver-rimmed bifocals. He'd been waiting for me with steaks and foil-wrapped baked potatoes ready to slap on the grill. Dad had relied on Mom to do the cooking, and I knew he was preparing the best meal he could offer me, his favorite as well. He sipped scotch as he tended the barbecue.

"I really need this tonight," he said, gesturing with his glass and making the ice clink in the brown liquid.

Neither of us was ready to talk, so I sat quietly beside him on the back steps, thinking of the long, hard journey that had led us to this moment.

We ate at the kitchen table in the silence of shared grief. Then we moved to the dining room, where paperwork covered the mahogany table. I pulled out a chair and sank into it, already weary. I knew I had more long days ahead. Dad slid open the lid of the Franklin woodstove that heated the house in winter and dropped in the wrapping from a Raleigh's cigar. He bit off the cigar tip, spat it into the cold stove, then closed the stovetop. He clenched the unlit cigar in his teeth or twirled it between his lips and, every few minutes, spat dark tobacco-laden saliva into the stove. I wasn't crazy about the cigar-sucking, but I preferred it to the idling cigarette that had dangled from the corner of his mouth in my younger years. His three-pack-a-day habit had given him an explosive cough that seemed to miraculously disappear when he gave up his unfiltered Pall Malls. Dad's constant smoking had seemed emblematic of his life of taking risks and surviving them, and though I admired the way he pushed the limits for himself and his machines, I was thrilled when he stopped smoking. With the unlit cigars, he figured he might get lip or throat cancer but probably *not* that fatal case of lung cancer he'd been headed for, and for that, I was grateful. I couldn't bear to lose him too.

With his cigar ready, he turned to me. "Guess you have some questions, Cookie."

I had a lot of questions, most of them about my mother's illness. Nobody in the family had ever talked to me about these things. Mom's psychotic episodes began before I was born, and I'd always wanted to know what was wrong with her that caused her meltdowns every five years or so. This was my chance.

"What was Mom's diagnosis?"

"The doctors at the hospital called it *schizophrenia*."

My fears were confirmed. That dreaded word had never been used in my presence, but I'd suspected it since I took a psychology course during my freshman year of college.

"Dad, when did you first know Mom was sick?"

He rolled the cigar in his mouth as he considered his answer. "Everything seemed fine until she was pregnant with your brother. Zelma grew restless in bed at night and had trouble sleeping. When her labor pains started, I took her to the hospital, and when the doctor came at her with a mask to give her anesthesia, she started screaming and struggling."

Dad paused and looked into the distance before he continued. "I waited outside the delivery room for a long time. At first, I could hear her screaming. Then it got quiet in there. Finally, the doctor came out to say that things were not going well. He told me they had to put her out and try to deliver the baby with forceps. At this point, the doctor wasn't sure if they could save them both. He told me they might have to choose between my wife and my child. I told him, 'Save my wife. We can have another child.' Then he went back to the delivery room, and I waited and waited until he finally came out again to tell me they'd saved them both."

Dad twirled his cigar in his mouth, frowning, before he went on. "When the drugs wore off, Zelma woke up screaming and fighting her restraints, and she couldn't be calmed." He paused and looked at the stove beside him as if he wanted to spit into it, but then he met my eyes and said, "They had to use shock treatments to bring her back."

My brother William had been delivered at Sacred Heart Hospital in Eugene, Oregon, and prior to his birth, my parents had gone to stay with Dad's mother in nearby Corvallis in case Zelma needed help with the baby. Fortunately for them, the Eugene hospital had a psychiatric unit.

So that was when it began. I sat quietly, trying to absorb this news, trying to make sense of the violence of it and what this early episode might have signaled. Shouldn't it have been addressed after all that? Didn't anybody understand that an event like that indicated something seriously wrong that wouldn't just go away? Dad remained standing, his eyebrows drawn down, a faraway look in his eyes.

The shock treatments apparently brought my mother back to her right mind. Only a few months after my brother was born, Mom wrote a lovely poem that I've kept ever since she first showed it to me.

MY HEAVEN
Zelma Carson Lockwood

No, it isn't any mansion
    And the street's not paved with gold;
But it's my heaven here on earth
    Where three happy lives unfold.

There was a time when other things
    Filled all my life with joy.
Now it's my husband and a home
    And a darling baby boy.

A little brown house to dust and keep,
    A baby who takes much care,
A golden cocker spaniel dog,
    A husband these things to share.

Yes, God has been so very good,
    He's blessed my life since birth,
And loaned a bit of heaven itself
    For me to enjoy on earth.

I have counted all my blessings,
    And as the days go by,
I'll love and share my little heaven,
    With guidance from on high.

This poem is the only evidence I have of what my mother thought about this time in her life. She was twenty-eight years old, enjoying her new family as her "bit of heaven" and expressing her satisfaction—even delight—through poetry. She wrote poems throughout her life, but only during her good times, and she often included them in her Christmas letters. I consider these upbeat poems blessings from the creative personality she was. Even more important, they offer a window into the heart of a mother who rarely shared her feelings openly.

The little brown house in the poem was a rental on the shore of Lake Sammamish, east of Seattle, where my father worked at the Boeing Aircraft Company. As Billy grew from the "darling baby" in Mom's poem into a toddler who wanted to roam, the unfenced lakeshore became a source of stress for her. In my childhood, I often heard Mom tell her friends about the day she went to wake Billy from a nap and found his bed empty. She searched the lakeshore with dread for long, torturous minutes until a neighbor brought home the missing two-year-old. Billy had been seen walking alone, following the nearby railroad track.

Because of that experience, the family moved away from the dangerous lakeshore and into a modest home where Issaquah Creek splashed by the backyard. This is where my family lived when I was born in 1946, two years after my brother.

—◆—

Dad and I sat at the dining room table, talking, quietly thinking, and talking again. It was easy to be with him. We were both comfortable with silence, so the air didn't always have to be filled with sound, and as a result, I was able to sit with my thoughts. I found the ease especially merciful following my mother's death. But I was still full of questions.

"What about my birth? Did Mom experience the same kind of drama or upheaval?"

Dad answered with his usual brevity. "Nothing happened with you," he said. "She was fine."

That was good news for her and for newborn me, I thought. Then another thought struck me. I was now in the second month of my first pregnancy. If Mom's illness had a genetic component, could she have passed it to me? Was I headed for the same fate?

I recalled the terrible times in our family when Mom seemed to go crazy, screaming and raging against my father. Learning about my brother's birth told me Dad must have endured twenty-eight years of turbulence with Mom's psychotic episodes.

After several quiet minutes, I asked the question I'd grown up wondering about. "How did you manage to stand by her all those years, to stay married and take care of her, even when she blamed you for her troubles?"

He looked into my eyes. "The first five years of our marriage were heaven. And as things started to turn dark, I kept hoping that someday the doctors would discover some medicine or treatment that would give me back my sweetheart."

My parents-to-be, Zelma and Alferd (his unusual name, often misspelled, honored his uncle Alf and his uncle Ferd), became sweethearts in high school. I learned this at sixteen when I admired a ring I'd found in Mom's jewelry box. She told me it was the "sweetheart ring" Dad had given her. The large oval stone was a brown moss agate, a kind often found along the nearby Oregon coast where they used to walk together. When I held it up to the light, I could see the dark, delicate webs of moss that gave the translucent stone its name. The stone seemed a fitting emblem of their beach walks, their sweethearts' pledge, and maybe even some dark secrets.

Years later, in my mid-twenties, I pieced together the history of their relationship and was delighted to learn that their early years were happy ones despite the hardships of the Depression. After the sweethearts finished high school in 1934, their struggle to find work separated them, except for occasional visits, until Zelma found work on the Oregon State College campus in Corvallis, where Alferd was studying for a degree in civil engineering.

They married in October 1940. By then, Alferd had his private pilot's license and wanted to make flying his career. In 1941, needing two difficult math classes to finish his degree, he left college to join the Army Air Corps, hoping to fly the fighter planes. His need for strong eyeglasses disqualified him from combat flying, but he was assigned the position of ground instructor for the fighter pilots. After his army service, he worked for the Boeing Aircraft Company in Seattle as a trainer on B-29s and B-17s but, again, wasn't given the pilot's seat he desired.

Disappointed with the Boeing corporate world and frustrated he wasn't allowed to pilot their planes, my father left the company in 1945 and found work as a private pilot, skywriting, pulling banners, and performing aerobatics with his two-seater plane at air shows and hydroplane races. Then he and a partner bought and managed the small Issaquah airport and restaurant, and there he instructed new pilots, dropped parachutists, and established the first smoke jumper training base in the Pacific Northwest.

Despite all his efforts, Dad struggled to find enough aerial work to make ends meet, so these were lean years for the family, which, by 1946, included me. During his army and Boeing years, Mom had been used to a regular income, but after he quit the Boeing job, he never again brought home a steady paycheck. I've often wondered if that jolt to their financial security was the beginning of my parents' troubles. Was it after that when Mom began to complain about the lack of money and criticize how he ran his business?

After talking late into the night, Dad and I fell silent. My father wasn't one to offer his thoughts unless asked, and I'd run out of questions. He saw me glance past him to the rifles standing in the corner next to the back door. On a ranch like ours, guns were used to hunt deer and game birds and to protect our livestock from predators. Mom and I had each ridden with a saddle gun to protect the sheep from coyotes; one time, she bagged a buck deer, and now and then, a pheasant for the dinner table.

"I didn't think Zelma would use a gun to kill herself," Dad said, "but I removed the rifle shells from the ranch as a precaution after she took the sleeping pills." He shook his head as if he wanted to shake off the memory. "I didn't even think about the loaded clip for my automatic pistol. She never used the pistol."

I nodded. "She always carried the bolt-action rifle when she rode to herd the sheep."

Dad frowned as he said, "The clip was always removed from my pistol for safety. She must have found it."

The sheriff had ruled my mother's suicide an accident, but I could see my father felt at least partly to blame, and that caused an ache in my chest. How awful if guilt was compounding his grief.

"You tried your best to keep her safe, Dad. Don't blame yourself. She was going to find a way, somehow."

Dad stared out the window, shaking his head. Then he checked his watch and said, "It's midnight. We have a lot to do tomorrow. We'd better turn in."

"Okay, Dad. Good night," I said, and then we shared the long hug of two survivors.

I crawled into the familiar bed of my teen years and tried to fall asleep. It was so dark outside that even the comforting frogs and howling coyotes had gone quiet on the hillside outside my bedroom. In the silence, I missed Tony, who knew just how to hold me and let me talk when I needed to work out something painful. But at the same time, I wanted to be alone with no audience for my thoughts.

I wondered what Dad's life would be like now. Would he feel free? Would he be plagued with guilt? Would his heart start to heal from the wounds he suffered so long ago when he lost his sweetheart to that horrible affliction? Lying in the darkness, I kept hearing my father's words: "The first five years of our marriage were heaven." I was comforted to know that my parents began very much in love, that they married for love, and that my brother and I were born from love. I hadn't often seen their love expressed during our ranch years, but his words gave me a warm feeling, and I clung to them, hoping they'd lull me to sleep.

Then Dad's sweet, nostalgic words collided with the dark bloodstain I'd seen earlier that night on our faded red davenport. I pictured the Mormons finding Mom slumped on that couch just yesterday. Hot tears welled in my eyes and slipped down my cheeks. I turned to my logical mind to distract myself rather than surrendering to weeping, which doesn't solve anything, or so I believed. Years of deducing that emotions were for the weak taught me to quickly change the channel and get on with it. I began to sort through everything Dad had told me that night and tried to piece together what might have happened the day before when my mother ended her life.

◆◆◆

Yesterday, with spring arriving in the Okanogan, two Mormon men had driven up the muddy lane to our house and walked up the long stairs leading to the front door. It was one of their periodic unannounced visits to a Mormon sister who lived on a lonely ranch with a Christian husband. Dad respected Mom's religious beliefs but wouldn't let her raise their children in the Mormon Church because he wanted us to make our own choices on the subject of what to believe about God. As a child, he'd rebelled against his Southern Baptist parents, and insisted on freedom of religious choice for his kids.

Mormons provided home visits to stay in contact with their people who weren't attending church, and when they visited during my childhood, Mom always invited them in to talk. If I was home at the time, I'd dash outside to play in the swampy pasture. I sensed she wanted privacy, and I knew from experience that if I stayed inside, I'd be bored and uncomfortable.

On the day of my mother's suicide, I imagined the two visitors knocking on the varnished maple door. No answer. Peering through the three small windows in the upper part of the door, they saw a figure slumped on the couch. One man rushed around to the back door and found it unlocked. He hurried past the bloodied couch to let the other man enter through the front. They phoned the sheriff.

When the county sheriff arrived, he saw the small automatic revolver near my mother's right hand, the empty .22 shell, and the quarter-inch round hole between her eyebrows. He noted the powder burns around the hole from a muzzle pressed close. He located my father in Okanogan, where Dad had gone to work after having breakfast with Mom that morning.

When my father powered his truck up the muddy driveway, my mother's body was already in the ambulance. The sheriff told him how she'd been found, and Dad headed to the ambulance to see for himself her bloody face and the hole in her forehead.

The sheriff knew both my parents, and he knew about Mom's mental illness. He probably thought calling her death a suicide would embarrass the family, so after discussing it with my father, he noted the cause of death as an "accident," and the newspapers quoted his report. With his decision, the case was closed, and my mother could be laid to rest.

◆━◆

Knowing full well those thoughts were more vivid in the dark, I lay there and let my mind race. Then I thought about my last phone call with Mom two weeks earlier. She was irritated by the red-shafted flicker that was trying again, for another spring, to peck a hole into the corner of the house to attract a mate or make a nest.

"I get awful tired of that darn flicker tapping away on my bedroom wall. It's hard to sleep in the morning with that *rat-a-tat-tat* going on."

"Can't you shoo it away?"

"I've tried. I go out around the house, but it hears me coming and flies away. Pretty soon, that darn thing comes back and starts in again. It echoes through the whole house."

I knew exactly what she meant. I remembered the loud, incessant pecking I'd heard every spring on that same corner of our ranch home. Mom and I used to talk about shooting the pesky bird—to kill it or at least scare it away.

The flicker would have kept on with its pecking for days, and she must have searched for shells for the .22. At some point since we'd talked about the pecking bird, she'd found the automatic pistol in the kitchen cupboard and its loaded clip, which rested on a nearby shelf.

Dad said the sheriff found her tracks going out the kitchen door, past the basement entrance, toward that rear corner of the house, and then back. She may have come in, sat down on the couch, and decided to turn the gun on herself.

That's how I put the pieces together, still wide-awake in my dark room.

Ranch life taught me to intellectually assess a situation first and acknowledge feelings second, if at all. A potentially heart-wrenching occurrence might call for quick action, so allowing emotions to have their way too early could lead to an unfortunate, maybe even fatal, delay. After I walked myself through what must have happened and then accepted what my mother did to herself, I let the tears flow. I cried not only for my own loss but for all she'd lost over the years. In midlife, she couldn't develop friendships, couldn't enjoy social events, couldn't be consistent for her kids, and, for the last ten years, couldn't feel the kind of joy or lightheartedness that had once defined her life and filled her poems. She'd been too numbed by an advancing brain disorder and the meds she had to take every day.

For the past five years, she hadn't been able to write poems, read books, or maintain focus on anything creative to relieve the monotony of her days, not even planting the primroses as she'd always done to welcome another spring. Eventually, it all became too much, and in a cloud of depression and despair, she found a way to end her pain at last.

That was it, the story laid out. I tried to find something positive in it, something to grab onto, maybe shift my focus to the fact that my mother was out of pain now, that her anguish was finally over. I couldn't imagine living with the kind of psychological pain she must have endured. I knew I couldn't live like that, so how could I blame her for putting an end to her suffering? Exhausted, I fell asleep on my tear-soaked pillow.

CHAPTER TWO

The next morning, after Dad made coffee and fried eggs and bacon for breakfast, he asked me to pick out clothes to dress Mom in for the funeral. I felt surprised at first, then honored. Sorting through Mom's closet, I selected the two-piece lavender suit she'd worn for my wedding nearly three years earlier, remembering how nice she'd looked in it. Dad agreed. Then he drove us to Okanogan, where we met with the undertaker and gave him the clothing. Dad asked me to help choose the casket. I expected he'd go with a plain, inexpensive one, but he surprised me by choosing the pretty one with feminine pink ruffles. For his sweetheart.

Once Mom's body was prepared for viewing, Dad and I went in to see her. After fifteen minutes of shared silence, Dad moved closer, held her folded hands in his, and then stepped away to leave me alone with my mother. I moved nearer to her, slowly, and leaned in close to her face. I was struck by how peaceful and serene she looked after such a violent death. The wrinkles around her eyes and the frown that had taken hold between her eyebrows had now been smoothed and her beauty restored by the undertaker's skill. Her best features weren't visible, the big brown eyes I'd always admired and the straight, white teeth I envied, yet in her serenity, she was beautiful. I didn't want to touch her, not even her hands, resting at last. I was grateful her struggle was over, and as I stood there in the quiet of our last moments together, I wished I could have known her as the girl who'd attracted my father. She must have been vivacious and joyful then, camping and mountain climbing with her sweetheart.

I thought about how Dad's grieving must have begun many years ago. How did he lose his sweetheart—in how many phases, during how many angry confrontations, across how many seasons? And my own grieving, which was beginning to seep its way into my bones, was now presenting itself more clearly. I was hurting, not only because my mother had just chosen to die at the age of fifty-six but also because of the way I'd lost her over the years, sometimes in a slow burn and other times in fits and starts. I grieved for the way she'd slipped away from me, couldn't open herself emotionally to me, didn't mother me. Her suicide ended forever any chance she might have had to make up for it, either with me or with her grandchild.

I looked for the bullet entry. The only evidence of the gunshot was a slight round depression, a quarter inch in diameter, between and slightly above her eyebrows. It wasn't completely hidden by the heavy makeup. I stood there absorbing the reality of her deed. I wished I could have been there in her final moments to plead, "Don't do it, Mom. Don't leave me!" My tears fell again for her, and for me.

Back at the ranch, Dad asked me to help notify her four brothers and three sisters. Mom was the third-oldest of the eight Carson siblings but the first of them to die. I didn't want to make those calls, and my thoughts spun crazily. What was I supposed to say if they asked questions? But he was calling all the other friends and relatives, so I steeled myself to do it for him.

I dialed Mom's younger sister, Eva. Aunt Eva and her husband Jimmy were the only relatives who lived in our state and the ones Dad always called on when he needed help with my mother. During her three-week hospitalization in 1951, Eva and Jimmy took my brother to their home in Shelton, Washington, while I stayed with my grandmother in Oregon. In 1955, Eva and Jimmy came to the ranch, drove Mom to the Spokane hospital, and convinced her to sign herself in for psychiatric care. Of all her siblings, Eva was the only one who'd seen my mother when she was psychotic and refusing treatment.

Dad later shared with me his feeling that some in her family blamed him for her illness because she told them *he* was the problem. In my childhood, when we visited her relatives, I sometimes overheard them asking about her recent hospitalization, but she said she was fine, nothing was wrong with her, he was working her too hard, and she just needed a rest and to get away from him. I suppose she didn't want them asking a bunch of questions, and she didn't want to admit to mental illness. Maybe she simply couldn't accept what was happening to her.

Aunt Eva picked up the phone after the first ring. She was shocked by my news despite her previous firsthand experience with Mom's psychotic behavior. She asked, "*What* happened?"

I said, "Mom shot herself." Then, after hesitating, I added, "We think it was an accident."

She didn't ask any questions. I think she heard the quaver in my voice.

"We're bringing her back to Yachats for the memorial service at the community hall on Sunday," I continued.

"I'll pass along the word to my brothers and sisters," she said, "and we'll bring the food for the memorial."

I hung up the phone, grateful for her empathy and support and relieved not to have to make more calls.

I rode in the white station wagon with Dad and Gram as we followed the hearse to the central Oregon coast. Dad was returning Mom to the Yachats River Valley, where she'd grown up and where they'd become sweethearts. My brother Bill and his wife drove from Okanogan, and Tony came from Seattle. Mom's brothers and sisters traveled to Yachats from up and down the West Coast.

At the memorial, there were a lot of tears and hugs. When I was alone, Aunt Eva came to me and gently asked, "What happened?"

I thought about the times Aunt Eva had come to the ranch to support Mom. She deserved to know the truth. "Mom shot herself in the forehead," I said.

She gasped. "Was it suicide?" she whispered.

"Yes, probably," I said, tears welling up.

"Oh, my dear." She took me in her arms and held me as I sobbed.

We buried Mom at Carson Cemetery next to the graves of her father, mother, and grandparents. Sited on a peaceful hill amid tall evergreens and budding rhododendrons, the small graveyard overlooked the Yachats River and the farmstead where she was raised. Mom had wanted to be buried here, and I'm sure she would have been happy to have this place of honor beside the parents she loved.

In 1936, when Mom was twenty, she celebrated her childhood home in a poem. Someone brought a copy to her memorial service.

YACHATS BOUND
Zelma Carson Lockwood

Oh, my heart is really happy,
    For I am Yachats bound,
And I'm goin' to make the music
    Go round and round and round.

Yes, I'm going back to Yachats,
    The village by the sea,
And I hope the same old welcome
    Is waiting there for me.

The city has done its justice
    And now I long to roam
Amid the valleys and the hills
    Of my dear childhood home.

I'm goin' to roam the woodlands,
    Hear birds sing sweet and clear.
I'm goin' to get close to Nature
    In God's great open air.

Where deer roam over the mountains
    And fish live in the streams.
Yes, I'm going back to Yachats,
    The valley of my dreams.

The first thing she'd do at home, she wrote, is "make the music go round and round." It's a joyful thing, I know, to pump an old player piano and make it play rolls of music, and it soothed me to read her words of happiness and connection to the beautiful valley. Taking her to her childhood home for her final rest gave me a measure of peace.

As Tony drove me back to Seattle after Mom's burial, I couldn't get the questions out of my mind. *Why didn't I tell my own mother I was pregnant? Why didn't I tell her she was about to be a grandmother?* For most of the eight-hour drive, I analyzed myself, trying to understand my motivations. Trying to figure out if I should have acted differently.

———◆———

Almost three years earlier, I'd married Tony and left my ranch home and my parents. We moved to Seattle as newly-weds during the recession of 1969–1970, and Tony was hired as a short-haul truck driver, coming home each evening and bringing in a steady paycheck. With six hundred teachers unemployed across the state, even my graduate degree and new teaching credentials didn't help me get a job, so I settled for a position invoicing book sales for the University of Washington Press. After a year, I landed a slightly better-paying position as a data technician in the UW Department of Medicine. We lived on Tony's salary and saved my $300-a-month take-home pay until we had a thousand dollars to put down on our first home. We moved in, bought a couch, washing machine, and dryer, and saved what I earned during the next year so I could take six months of maternity leave, which would be unpaid after the first six weeks. We were ready at last to have the child we both wanted so much.

Six weeks after going off birth control pills, I was pregnant. Right away, Tony and I called his parents in California to share our wonderful news, and they were thrilled. Then I hesitated. My pregnancy had happened so fast—I needed to slow down. I wanted a week to process the idea of becoming a mother before involving my own mother.

When I learned I'd soon be a parent, I realized all my decisions would have to consider a new little being, a person who would be my responsibility. I wanted to be a loving, supportive mother in all the ways my own mother hadn't, and I'd need to protect my baby, which I knew might call for shielding my child from my mother's illness. While Mom had never lifted a hand to me, her moods had always been unpredictable. There had been times when she'd been very distant, even cold to me, and I'd been deeply hurt by it. Going forward, I wanted to protect my child from that kind of rebuff. Not knowing how I would do that made me resist calling my mother with the wonderful news.

Tony and I had delighted his parents with our call. For days afterward, I looked out to the woods surrounding our house and thought about my mother, trying to envision what kind of grandmother she'd be. During our Thanksgiving visit four months earlier, I'd been rattled by how deeply depressed my mother had become.

Tony and I had driven over the snowy mountains and up the Columbia River to the Okanogan Highlands to spend the holiday with Mom at the ranch. Dad was away on business and grateful we could be with her for the holiday weekend. Mom spent hours cooking a delicious turkey dinner with all the trimmings, the way she'd always done. She served my all-time favorite dessert: her homemade venison mincemeat pie with brown sugary juice bubbling through braided strips of flaky pie crust and, of course, vanilla ice cream melting on top. Tony and I raved about her tasty meal and scrumptious dessert, and in response, she managed a nod, a half-smile, and a barely audible "Thanks." I began to worry about what her lack of reaction meant. Was she in distress?

After dinner, with the dishes done, we moved to the living room, where Mom slumped in her armchair. She stared into the distance and seemed quieter than usual. I knew she wouldn't talk unless I pressed her. I picked up her latest *Reader's Digest* magazine. "Have you read this one?"

"No, I can't seem to concentrate anymore."

"Do you still crochet?"

"No, I don't enjoy that now."

"What do you do to pass the time?"

"I can't get interested in anything."

Her emotions were flat, blunted first by her disease and then by the daily drugs she took from 1962 onward to prevent psychotic episodes. She used to decorate pillowcases with embroidered designs and crocheted lace edges. She used to collect apple recipes to compile a cookbook. Now all her creative projects were put away. Since becoming an empty nester two years earlier, she'd become increasingly depressed. She spoke in a monotone, and I saw no light in her eyes.

"What about the cookbook you were working on?"

"Oh, I've given up on that."

"You seem bored. Isn't there anything you like to do?"

"Not really."

"Mom, do you want to talk about how you're feeling?"

"You wouldn't understand."

With those words, she shut herself off from me, and not for the first time. It was painful seeing her so lost, but I didn't know how to help. The woman who sat before me barely resembled the vibrant, hardworking woman she'd been eighteen years before when we moved to the ranch.

For the next four months, I wrote or phoned nearly every week. She always wrote back, though her letters were brief and perfunctory. Her flat voice on the phone and the lack of emotion in her letters sent sadness through my body.

Then came Dad's call, and she was gone.

CHAPTER THREE

I wasn't always a ranch girl. For my first seven years, I lived the life of a small-town girl in Issaquah, a Seattle suburb. According to a poem my mother wrote in February 1947, when I was six months old, I began life with two doting parents.

OUR BABY GIRL
Zelma Carson Lockwood

When you were just a tiny girl
    You were so very coy.
At times your Daddy said he wished
    You'd been another boy.

But you completely won his heart
    When you began to smile.
He worshipped and adored you too
    In just a little while.

Then you began to crawl and play
    And cut your little teeth,
Wriggle fingers and twist your wrist
    While watching from beneath.

You were so happy-go-lucky,
   Loved being tossed about.
Daddy used to roughhouse you
   To hear you laugh and shout.

You learned to walk and say Da Da,
   Your hair began to curl.
Daddy wouldn't trade you then
   For any boy—or girl.

Dressed in your best blue nylon dress,
   Lace-trimmed, with ribbon ties,
You were the world's sweetest baby
   In Mother's and Daddy's eyes.

In Mom's poem, I was welcomed by both parents with the same joy they'd felt for my brother. In the portraits taken then, I look happy, coy, and fetching in my frilly blue nylon dress. But in 1950, my carefree childhood began to unravel. During the rainy winter, Daddy often took us to the movies at the theater near our home in Issaquah. During the cartoon, he'd let me crawl into his lap. I leaned against his scratchy woolen shirt as his strong arms closed around me and the smell of his Mennen aftershave filled my nose. We laughed together at the antics of Bugs Bunny or Sylvester the Puddy Tat. I felt special in those minutes of closeness. But before long, I began to receive hurtful messages signaling a change.

One January evening at the theater, when I moved from my seat toward Daddy's knee, he raised his hand to block me. "Not this time, Cookie."

I asked, "Why not?"

"You're getting too big to sit in my lap."

Crushed, I crept back to my seat with heat burning up my neck. Being too big made no sense to me. At three and a half years old, I was growing tall and leggy, but at heart, I was still a very little girl. Had I done something wrong? Didn't my daddy love me anymore? My stomach churned, and I couldn't follow the movie. For once, Dean Martin and Jerry Lewis couldn't make me laugh. Finally, I fell asleep in my seat until Mommy roused me, and I clung to her hand as we walked home.

When spring came, Daddy left us for a long time. Mommy said she knew where he was, but to me, he was as far away as the moon that rose over the big mountains. I was scared because my daddy had never been away from the house for more than a few days at a time. I thought he didn't love me enough to come home and play with me.

As Mommy tucked me in each night, I asked, "Where's my daddy? When's he coming home?"

"He'll be home soon, honey."

"I miss my daddy."

In reply, Mommy sang a little song to comfort me: "*Bye, Baby Bunting, Daddy's gone a-hunting / To get a little rabbit skin, to wrap the Baby Bunting in.*"

I didn't want Daddy to skin a rabbit for me, but the idea that he'd gone to search for a bunting of soft fur to keep me warm and cozy helped me slip off to dreamland. He was gone more than a month that first time, and to me, it seemed he was never coming back. When he appeared at the front door, I screamed with joy and danced around. He wrapped Billy and me in one big hug and said, "I really missed you kids." Then he hugged and kissed my smiling mommy. My world was shiny and happy again.

When he left us again the next spring, I wasn't as upset because I knew he'd come back. But just to make sure, I did my best to be extra good all year, both at home and at school.

Dad's business partner had invited him to join him as a crop duster, flying their little planes over wheat fields on the other side of the state and staying in a hotel at night. Before then, he'd come home each night from his work at the nearby airport. But while he was doing the spring wheat spraying, Mom was left by herself with two small children, and she must have worried about him spending so much time in a little plane so high in the sky.

I was never scared about his flying work because I trusted that he was so good at it that he'd always be safe in the air. I was more concerned about Mommy, who never had money to buy the foods I liked or the dresses I needed. As a preschooler, I licked green stamps and pressed them into little books and watched Mommy hand them to the grocer to buy food, including big sacks of dried beans. I suffered through dinner after dinner of beans, sometimes feeling like I'd vomit right there at the table. But I wasn't allowed to leave the table or have dessert until I ate them.

"They're good for you," Mommy said.

Around that age, I began to discover my love of the outdoors. I was happy playing in the woods and along the creek that adjoined our backyard, watching bumble bees, hearing birdsong, picking flowers, making bouquets for Mommy, and braiding grasses or leaves to make wreaths and belts. I wanted to play along the creek, throwing rocks to make splashes or watching the big red fish that sometimes swam up it, but I wasn't allowed near the creek unless Billy was with me. He'd learned to swim and was supposed to make sure I never went too near the water's edge. But Billy was a poor choice of caretaker. In the woods, he'd run at me with a wriggling garter snake or a closed fist that he claimed held a spider. Then he'd pretend to drop the creature down my shirt. I'd run screaming to Mommy, and she'd tell him not to do it again, but he never stopped trying to terrorize me. If I cried, he called me "fraidy cat" or "crybaby." Because of him, I grew up terrified of snakes and spiders.

Despite my efforts to win Daddy's approval, he spent more time with Billy than with me, and the way we played had changed. Daddy would lie on the floor and wrestle with Billy, teaching him the moves. I wanted to join their game, and I tried to, but usually I got hurt and left the game crying. Billy grew more aggressive in their wrestling and made sure he never cried so he could put me down for my tears.

I wanted to learn the things Daddy taught Billy. But I couldn't keep up, and Billy made fun of my efforts until I quit. My only choice was to tag along after them, saying, "Me too." Too often, Daddy's answer was, "No, you're too little."

I was an easy victim of my brother's teasing because I loved animals and sobbed over their injury or loss, like the day Mommy backed the green car away from the house and drove over our beloved cocker spaniel. I cried and whimpered while she caressed him as he died. Then she said, "I'm so sorry, honey, but I didn't mean to. I didn't know Skippy was there." She was quiet and kind, but her eyes didn't get shiny, and no tears fell. Billy didn't cry at all. He stood nearby and didn't speak.

Billy's taunting only grew more hurtful. On a sunny day in 1952, Mommy took me to the park for an Easter egg hunt. She was watching me in the five-and-under group while Billy hunted with older kids. I'd filled my basket with the wrapped taffy that had been scattered in the grass but hadn't found any of the colored eggs I wanted to gather for Mommy.

I heard parents near me telling their children, "Look for the golden egg! No one has found it yet." And then, "Look everywhere, not just on the ground." I looked up, and in the crook of a tree, I spotted the glint of gold foil. I pointed to it, Mommy lifted me up, and I captured the golden egg. With it came the grand prize—the Easter bunny, a real baby bunny! Someone handed me a bunny with red eyes, pink ears, and white fur as soft as a cloud. It was magical! And it was mine!

"Oh, look, Mommy, it's so soft! Can I keep it? Can I, please?"

"I'm not sure we can keep it, honey. We don't have any place to keep a bunny."

"Oh, please, Mommy. We can ask Daddy to make a place for it!"

"Your daddy will have to decide," she said. Once we were home, we put the sweet little animal in a cardboard box in the garage.

When Daddy came home later, I ran to him. "Daddy! Daddy! Come out to the garage to see my prize!" I pulled him by the hand.

As soon as we reached the box, he said, "We can't keep it. We can't afford to buy the food and cage the bunny will need."

Billy said, "I'll help you build the cage, Daddy!"

I said, "I'll feed it and take good care of it!"

Daddy sighed. "Well, it will cost money to feed it, so we can only keep it until it grows big enough to eat."

I heard the part I wanted to hear, that I had a new pet, and pretended I hadn't heard the rest. I named her Bunny.

Daddy and Billy used wood slats and wire mesh to build a cage for Bunny in the garage. Every day, Mom fed her alfalfa pellets, and I brought her grass and carrot tops. I visited her every day, and because I wasn't allowed to take her out of the cage, I reached in to caress her soft ears.

Over the next two months, as Bunny grew larger, Billy often said, "Don't forget, your bunny is being fattened for our dinner table."

I clapped my hands over my ears and ran to Mommy, who shushed him.

One day in early May, Daddy said, "Cookie, I know a way to kill your bunny so it won't suffer."

I looked at him with horror. He meant to kill Bunny *today*. I knew I couldn't stop him because he'd let me keep her only to become food for our dinner table, and I knew he was trying to soften the blow. Scowling, I said, "Only if you promise she won't suffer. And only if you don't make me eat it. I'll never eat my bunny!"

"Okay, Cookie," he said, but he didn't add "promise," the word ensuring that people were telling the truth.

I couldn't save Bunny, but at least I wouldn't eat her. I reached into the cage, stroked Bunny's softness, and cried as I said goodbye to her. Then I ran away to be alone, but not fast enough—I'd gotten only halfway across the backyard when I heard a scuffle and Bunny's horrible shriek as she was being slaughtered. I ran and ran until I reached the big rocks lining the creek bank, then cried and watched the water splashing past. I sat there a long time, and when I went back to the house, Billy laughed at me.

"You crybaby. It was just a silly rabbit."

I let out a shriek like Bunny's and ran to my room. Mommy followed and found me sobbing in bed. She tried to comfort me, but her words meant nothing, and I wouldn't let her hug me. I turned away and curled up, facing the wall.

On a car trip a month later, I was in the back seat with Billy when Mommy handed me a sandwich filled with what looked like dark-meat chicken.

"What is it?" I asked her.

"It's chicken," she said.

The first bite tasted strange, and it didn't smell like chicken. I spat it into my hand, then dawdled over the sandwich, pretending to eat it. It was a hot day, so no one noticed when I rolled my window halfway down. I waited until they were all pointing and looking at something outside the car and then flung the sandwich out the window on the other side.

After a while, Mommy looked back at me and said, "Oh, you've finished. Are you ready for a cookie?"

That's when Billy joyfully blurted out the secret. "Ha! Ha! You just ate your bunny!"

"Did not!" I said. "I threw it out the window when no one was looking."

He kept laughing. My parents said nothing.

I hated them all. They were all in on it: Daddy for hurting Bunny, Mommy for cooking her and keeping the meat in the freezer until she thought I'd forgotten and then lying to me, and Billy, most of all, for trying to make me feel terrible by grinding in the cruelty knowing full well what that beautiful little animal had meant to me. No one was on my side. I vowed I'd never forget they'd all been so horrible to me. How could I ever trust them again?

⬤

As far back as I can remember, I was crazy about horses. When I was four, I heard *clip-clopping* coming from the street outside our house in Issaquah. I raced to the window, leaped onto the couch, and bent the blinds to watch the horse and rider go by. A real horse prancing by, right there on my street! If only that rider could be me!

On Saturday mornings, my brother and I listened to *The Lone Ranger* on the radio. I was thrilled every time I heard the galloping sounds of the horses' hooves and the Lone Ranger's hearty voice calling, "Hi Yo Silver, Awa-a-ay!"

When I was five, I begged to ride the ponies at the town's annual carnival. My parents didn't have extra money, but Mommy bought me a ticket for one pony ride. Then I went to the stall with the sawdust heap where adults had tossed pennies for the children to find. Hot and sweaty, I dug and sorted through the sawdust until I'd found twenty-five pennies for another ride.

When I was six, some friends of Mom and Dad's invited us to their house to watch a championship boxing match on their new television set. When we arrived, I saw a brown horse standing in the pasture next to their yard, so I asked the wife, "Is that your horse?"

"Yes, it is," she said. "She's so gentle you could sit on her. Would you like to do that?"

"Oh, yes!" I cried out.

The lady asked my parents if it was okay, and then she took me into the pasture. Up close, the horse looked massive, twice the size of the pony I'd ridden the year before. She lifted me onto the horse's round back, and there I sat, thrilled to be so high in the air on a big horse for the first time.

"Can I stay here for a while?" I asked.

"I can see you from my kitchen window, so just wave when you want to come in."

It was scary at first, just the big horse and me. I sat with my legs pressed against her sides, feeling her warm, round body under me, and buried my face in her mane, taking in the warm, earthy fragrance that reminded me of the woods I loved. Her pleasant breath wafted up to me, nice and sweet like the green pasture grass she ate. She stood quietly the whole time I was on her back. I talked to her as if she were mine, and she turned her head to look back at me with one big, beautiful, dark eye.

Night fell, and my parents wanted to go home, but no matter how much chocolate Mommy promised me, I refused to come off the horse I now loved. I gripped her mane until my father reached up and pulled me off as I cried. As he carried me to the car, I didn't take my eyes off that beautiful brown horse.

I vowed that someday, somehow, I'd have a horse of my own.

Five months after the glorious evening I'd spent sitting on a horse, my father delivered terrible news. We were leaving Issaquah.

By February 1954, my father's aerial spraying business in eastern Washington was growing. He wanted the family to be near his flying headquarters at the Brewster airport, so he and Mommy decided it was time to leave our little town and move over the mountains. I was in second grade, and I was sure my life was over.

In Brewster, Daddy flew home most nights and landed his plane across from our rented house on the little airfield along the wide river's far shore. When his plane was just a tiny speck in the sky, Mommy would see it and say, "Here he comes." Then she'd start dinner. One evening, when she was on a call with Aunt Eva, Mommy said, "I can see his little plane flying in the sunset. He's coming from the wheat fields to the south, dropping in over the rim of the bluff, and crossing over the Columbia River." I had poor eyesight and couldn't spot the plane, even as I looked where she pointed, but what she described sounded thrilling. In this strange new place, it was comforting to know my daddy was often in the sky right above me.

Life in Brewster was bleak for me, even with Daddy home more often at night. I'd left my best friends and the only home I'd ever known. I entered school during the middle of the year, so I was the new kid. Every other girl already had friends, and there were no girls my age in the homes near ours. My days consisted of shopping with Mommy in Brewster, helping her plant seeds in her garden that spring, planting and watering my own little patch of flowers, tagging along with Billy to collect bottles along the highway for refunds, and reading library books at night.

The one bright spot was that in June, I finally learned to swim across the shallow ends of the enormous water holes that were left after the Columbia River flooded the flat where we lived. But once again, Daddy was about to change our lives.

CHAPTER FOUR

On a sunny Sunday four months after moving to Brewster, our family climbed into Daddy's new cream-colored pickup to go house hunting. Across the truck doors were the words *Sky Ranch Aviation* in big letters, along with our phone number and a flying cowboy logo. Daddy's spring wheat spraying had made good money, and he was ready to move us out of our rental house and into a home of our own.

I looked forward to the change and was happy to leave the hot, dry flat where I had no playmates and where all that loomed ahead was a long, lonely summer. Next month, I'd be eight years old, but there was no one to celebrate my birthday with except my parents and my brother.

Daddy drove up the Okanogan River and turned onto a steep gravel road that led into a widening valley ringed with greening mountains. "This is the Chiliwist Valley," he said. "Mostly cattle ranches up here." He turned off the valley road and drove up a long lane to a small, weathered house, its sides never painted. A red-haired man came out of the house and waved to us. He wore overalls, bulging at the waist, and a white T-shirt. A young black-and-white dog scampered from behind him to our truck, its tail wagging feverishly.

"Hullo," the man said, "I'm Art Hilderbrand. I'll be glad to show you around. Come on inside."

The little house had a living room with a picture window that looked down the grassy lane to the neighbor's barn and past their turning windmill to the broader valley we had driven through.

"There's only one bedroom?" Mommy asked.

Art glanced at my brother and me. "Plenty of room in the basement for the kids now, and you can expand the house later, no problem. Say, I bet these kids would like to have a dog!"

"You mean this one?" Billy asked, patting the eager black-and-white dog waving her white-tipped tail.

"Yep," Art replied. "She's just a pup, about four months old."

"Wow, she's great! Can we have her, please?" Billy pleaded to our parents.

Without hesitation, they both said yes. After Skippy had died so tragically in Issaquah, they'd promised we could have another dog.

"Then she's yours. Her name is Spot," Art said with a toothy grin.

We had a dog again! This place was looking good already.

We headed for our pickup to ride around the farm. Daddy let down the tailgate for Billy and me to climb into the back, and Spot jumped up to join us, her white-tipped tail waving in delight as she tried to lick our faces and hands.

"Now you kids sit down and hold on tight," Art called as he climbed in the cab. "It's going to be rough."

Daddy drove down the lane, splashed the pickup across the shallow creek, and headed it up a bumpy dirt road that curved past an old wooden barn. Art pointed us up another narrow road that was carved into the steep hillside above the barn. On my side of the roaring pickup was a steep drop-off, and I could barely look as we drove way too close to the edge. On the other side loomed a hill so steep it looked like it could topple onto us at any moment. I gripped the side of the pickup bed with both arms.

We climbed and curved and bumped upward, then reached a flat area where a crop was planted. Daddy stopped the truck, and we climbed out to see what looked like green rows of thick grass clumps.

"This is winter wheat," Art said. "There's about thirty acres planted here on these two flats and more on the other side of the hill, a hundred acres that'll be ready for harvest in August." He explained that he'd lived here and farmed the wheat fields for years before he sold it to the current owners, and now he was helping them sell it. "It's a total of 650 acres, about a square mile," he said. It sounded like a lot of space, but it was all abstract to me then.

Daddy took a long time driving up and down the fields as Art talked on and on. I couldn't imagine a life up here at heights from which I could see only one distant ranch. I was tired and bored, but when the pickup stopped beside a huge gray rock bigger than the pickup cab, I was fascinated. That immense rock, resting on the ridge with no others like it around, was a mystery. How did it get there?

Art said, "This here big rock sits at about the center of the farm."

Standing on that ridge, we could see in all directions as Art pointed out the farm's boundaries. "It runs from the creek bottom down there where the house is and up over this here ridge and down the other side."

Billy's eyes grew big. "You mean all of this?" he asked, arms outstretched, turning in a circle.

"Even the corner of that big mountain over there," Art said, pointing to the craggy vertical face of eroding gray rock. "That's Dent Mountain."

We could even own part of a mountain!

We headed home, Billy and me in the cab between our parents, our new dog riding in the pickup bed.

Daddy asked, "Well, what do you think?"

Mommy replied, "The house is too small, but the view down the valley is nice, and we'd have our own little stream. This could be the farm we've always talked about having. Can we afford a place this size?"

"It'll be a lot of work to farm it and make it pay for itself," Daddy said. "I'll need you all to help. What do you think, kids?"

"Let's get it," Billy said.

"I like it too," I said.

My parents started talking about moving after school was out in June. That was the last I heard. I fell asleep with my head in Mommy's lap.

I didn't know it yet, but this move was the start of an entirely new way of life for me, dictated by the land. I was about to enter a vast new territory where I would learn what it meant to wander, explore, defend, and triumph.

———◆———

My eighth birthday arrived as summer began. By then, I'd stopped calling my parents Mommy and Daddy. Now that I was going to live on a huge ranch, those names felt like little girl words. Mom baked my favorite cake, chocolate with chocolate frosting. I blew out the candles, and she served generous slices. The ranch would be ours in ten days. I was so excited about the move I could barely sit still.

On July 1, we moved to our 650-acre farm. When we arrived at the house with our pickup and Dad's work truck piled high, I carried what I could and then helped Mom set up my narrow bed in a corner of the cool basement opposite my brother's corner. We went back into the kitchen, where she busied herself unpacking. I knew I'd be in her way if I hung around, so I asked, "Can I go outside by myself?"

"Yes," she said. "Just stay close enough that you can hear me when I call you."

The house was small and crowded, but the world outside it was huge, open, and enticing. I happily darted out into the grassy yard and went down to the sparkling stream that ran beside the house and along our lane before disappearing under the fence that ran from the neighbor's barn past his creaking windmill and alongside his apple orchard.

Each side of our little valley had its own unique sounds. On one side, frogs croaked from the wet hillside where springs seeped or trickled. On the other, jays, chipmunks, and squirrels chattered from the pines and firs that marched up the dry hillside. I'd been out in my sunny new playground for less than an hour, but already I felt at home in this green wonderland that reminded me of the backyard woods and creek I'd loved in Issaquah.

Spot scampered along with me as I began wandering on my own, exploring the pasture, stalking frogs in the creek and swamps, and watching butterflies float by. This rich world was different from the dry hillsides we'd driven through on our tour with Art. This, to me, was paradise, except for the little garter snakes quickly wriggling into the tall grass when I startled them. I was afraid of them because of how Billy used to taunt me, saying he'd drop them down my blouse. But I knew I was going to have to get used to this wild world, so instead of running to Mom, I gave the snakes a wide berth. I knew they were more afraid of me than I was of them.

Each day, I ventured a little bit farther than the day before. By the third day, I'd wandered to the place where the swamp water drained under our lane and flowed to the creek. Spot left my side and stood in the swampy grass five feet away from me, barking ferociously at a hissing creature. I leaned forward and saw a mottled snake several feet long, then heard an explosive boom. Terrified, I ran to the house. "Dad! Dad!" I yelled. "You have to save Spot!"

He followed me down the lane to where Spot was still barking and lunging at the hissing snake and said, "That's a blow snake, and that loud noise is their defense. They look a lot like rattlesnakes, but they have no rattles and no venom, so they're harmless. Useful, too, because they eat small rodents like shrews, so we want to leave them alone."

When we went back to the house, Mom said, "Are you sure it's safe to let the kids play in the pasture? What about all the snakes?"

"There are plenty of rattlesnakes in this dry country," Dad said, "but they don't like to be around water. You won't find rattlers in the pastures around the house because of the creek and the swampy hillsides."

That day, I learned my first wildlife lesson: whenever possible, don't cross from the damp and green into the dry and dusty.

A week after we moved, Dad's friend Cal Unger drove up to our yard with his wife Jane and her brother Bob. After a few minutes, the three of them headed up the creek and set to work. I went along and watched as they cut down small pine trees, then chopped off the limbs to make long poles, which they used to build a round corral about twice the size of my school classroom, with wings extending outward from the gate. Then Mr. Unger trucked in a flock of sheep to eat our tall pasture grass. Jane and Bob came, too, and stayed to herd the sheep with their dogs.

I thought the sheep were funny-looking creatures with their round, woolly bodies and long, skinny legs, and I thought the herding was the coolest thing I'd ever seen. Each day, Spot and I joined the herders and were assigned to watch a specific area to make sure the sheep didn't leave our property. The ewes were afraid of Spot, who liked to chase them, which was helpful if she was chasing them back onto our land but not if she was chasing them away. She didn't seem to know or care which way was right. I was glad the herders were out beyond the trees and couldn't see my dog making a mess of my work.

The sheep grazed our creek pastures by day and were herded between the pole wings and locked into the corral each night. At dusk, the coyotes howled from the rim above our valley, but they didn't come down to attack the sheep because either Jane or Bob rolled out a sleeping bag near the corral. Coyotes seemed to know that getting too close to people meant a date with the business end of a rifle.

The Chiliwist was cattle country, and its three-strand barbed wire fences were built to hold cattle. But the sheep squeezed under the lowest wire, leaving the barbs padded with tufts of white wool. Dad figured out how to combine a three-foot-high wire mesh panel with one barbed wire along the ground and two along the top. This blocked the sheep from squeezing under the fence and the neighbors' cows from going over. With that fix, our fences held both sheep and cattle.

With the Unger family's help, my parents spent most of the summer building these sheep-proof fences around our creek pastures. Once the sheep were contained, the Ungers headed home, and the sheep spent their nights along the creek where they were safe from coyotes.

I quickly learned that life on a ranch means there's always work to be done. After the sheep were secured, we spent a week putting up the hay crop from the pasture below the barn. I watched as a neighbor used his tractor to mow the long grass and rake it into rows. Then Dad and Mom used pitchforks to fling the loose hay onto a flatbed trailer pulled by the yellow Caterpillar tractor that came with the ranch. When the trailer was full, Dad backed it up to our barn so he and Mom could fork the grassy hay first into the open barn and then into the loft.

Hay pitching in the barn looked like fun. Billy joined in. I wanted to help, too, but I couldn't manage the long-handled pitchforks—they were taller than I was. When I spotted an unused pitchfork with its wooden handle broken off halfway, I asked, "Can I use this one?"

Dad looked over from his pitching and gave his okay.

On my first try, I stuck my pitchfork into the hay with as much force as I could muster. The handle's jagged end bounced back and hit the bone above my right eye. I cried out in pain and felt blood seeping into the hair above my eyebrow.

Dad rushed over to me. "Looks like you'll have a bruise there, but it missed your eye," he said with relief. "You better sit in the corner out of the way while we finish the hay."

I sat in the corner, feeling stupid and clumsy.

That evening after dinner, Dad sawed off the end of the broken handle to flatten it. He said, "I shouldn't have let you use it with that jagged end, Cookie. You could have lost your sight in that eye. Now, show me how you used it."

I took the pitchfork and showed him what had happened.

"From now on," he said, "you want to keep it slanted when you stick it into the hay so it's never aimed at your face."

"Okay, Dad, I will. I promise to be more careful."

It wasn't easy being the smallest family member. I wanted to help, but I wasn't strong enough for many of the chores, like digging post holes in rocky soil, so Dad assigned me easier tasks like fetching tools or unrolling wire. When Dad wasn't around, Billy called me weak and lazy. He also claimed my half of the chores had to be equal to his half. He wanted me to do whatever jobs he did and in equal proportion. I tried my best, but some tasks, like carrying heavy buckets of grain and lifting them over a fence, were easy for him but hard for me, if not impossible.

Billy rarely acted like my big brother. More often, he treated me like an enemy, like when he locked me in the grain bin or left me to finish a chore that was obviously too much for my size or endurance. But I'd occasionally glimpse the kind of brother I wished for, like when he took me up the creek with him to catch little rainbow trout or build roads into a cutbank with his toy trucks and bulldozer. It felt good to be included, but even when we played, he had to be in charge—he made up the rules, and he enforced them. It usually wasn't much better than playing alone.

During that first summer, I realized what a hard worker my mother was. Like Dad, she was full of farming know-how she'd learned growing up. When she wasn't working as part of the crew, building fences or constructing corrals with chutes and platforms for trucks to back up to and load sheep, she was preparing hearty meals for the family and the helpers. On quiet days at the house, while Dad and the others were out working, she fed the chickens, gathered eggs, and mixed up and baked a double batch of bread or an apple pie to go with the casserole she'd prepared for dinner. Then she watered, weeded, or gathered her garden crops and did some canning or salvaged fallen apples to make applesauce. I helped her with garden chores, chicken feeding, and egg gathering, and I was often amazed by all the things she could do. Whenever she told me I was a big help, I was proud to have lightened her load.

By our third month on the ranch, the sheep were the bane of her days. She often had to interrupt a project in the house or garden to chase a sheep that had escaped through our fence and onto the county road. She sometimes had to call Billy and me to help her surround the errant ewe and force her back through the fence or a gate, then prop the fence or block the hole until Dad came in from the upper farm fields or the airport to make a proper repair. Mom often said to Dad, "Those darn sheep are driving me crazy." I was beginning to understand what she meant.

Mom made it her mission to gather the fruits of the land that were free for the taking. As we explored the ranch, we found four or five sites where homes had once stood, each on 160-acre homesteads. Dad said the homesteaders who came here in the early 1900s gave up and left in the dry Depression years after their wheat and corn crops failed. We found their former homesites marked by crumbled stone foundations, collapsed root cellars, and plank-covered well holes. One site had the wooden remains of a windmill, which the homesteaders would have used to pump water from their well, and two gnarled old apple trees with small, wormy apples.

Throughout our years on the ranch, I often lingered at these places, wondering what these early settlers had lived through and hoping they'd had some good years before their wells and crops dried up. They must have hunted grouse and deer and maybe kept a milk cow. They would have used draft horses or oxen to pull their V-shaped plows through the soil, making one furrow at a time. In my imagination, theirs was a magical life, being so connected to the earth, living off the land. But I was also beginning to understand the meaning of hard work and knew that without our modern advantages, their backbreaking labor went from dawn till dusk until too many dry years starved them out. After Mother Nature let them down, where did they go?

Two homesites still had enough groundwater to sustain currant and gooseberry bushes and apple trees, all still bearing fruit. One of the sites also had crab apples, plums, and a tall walnut tree. When the apples were ripe, I helped Mom pick them before they fell and then watched her turn the fruits into pies or jellies or preserves. I loved the sweet things she made from the fruits we gathered. I knew my mother would have been an immensely valuable member of one of those homestead families.

That first summer, my mother took a snapshot to show our relatives our new home. Holding her Kodak folding camera, she stood with her back to the creek and framed the photo. In it, a leggy eight-year-old girl—me—stands in the foreground wearing jeans and looking away from the camera, her dark bobbed hair winging out of side clips. Her hand rests on the black-and-white collie standing beside her, and the dog's tail curves upward. Beyond them, the midsummer meadow grass is high with seeded tops. A dirt lane winds through a meadow dotted with white sheep, passes a tiny wooden shack, and ends in front of our little house, which perches on a dry rise next to the creek. The one-story house has a pitched roof, an exposed cement foundation, and weathered wood sides. Tall pines shade it from the afternoon sun. Beyond the house, the canyon narrows, and its wooded sides rise steeply above the cut of the creek.

Mom's photo beautifully captured our homesite—a small, verdant valley cleft into a hot, dry landscape. When the photos came back from the drugstore, I asked Mom if I could keep this one, and when she said yes, I taped it into my scrapbook.

When school started in September, Billy and I were the only bus riders in the Chiliwist Valley. The "bus" was a four-wheel-drive Willys Jeep station wagon painted yellow with black stripes and lettered *Okanogan School District 105*. It was barely big enough for the driver and one passenger in front and two in the back seat. From our front gate, the bus took us two miles down Chiliwist Road and three miles on the main highway into Malott. I entered the Malott Grade School in third grade, Billy in fifth.

The bus drivers, Paul and Eula Stout, owned a large ranch in the lower part of the valley, where they lived with their son Stanley, who was in high school. They parked the little school bus at their home between trips, and Eula drove in fair weather or when Paul was busy with haying or cattle operations. Paul drove when the road was icy or when the last steep stretch down the canyon to the highway was washed out or blocked by snowdrifts. In the coming years, these folks would be more like family than neighbors.

Paul's brother, Jim Stout, and his wife Gertie owned the ranch next to us. Their Jersey cow gave more milk than the two of them could use, and my daily chore was to collect the milk we bought from them. Each day after school, I carried the empty cans down our lane and across the road to their house, where Gertie exchanged them for one or two cans of chilled milk. I loved the buttery smell of the fresh milk drawn from the cow that very morning. The milk that came in cartons from the grocery store didn't smell rich and fresh like that. When I drank the milk from the Stouts' cows, I could sometimes taste what the animals had eaten, like when Jim turned them out into his lush alfalfa field.

The milk cans had thin wire handles that etched lines into my hands as I carried them home. The reward for my painful efforts came when Gertie invited me in to watch a television show. My family didn't have a television set, and I wanted to see what the kids at school were always chattering and buzzing about in the halls. I arrived at her back door at 4:00 p.m. on school days, just as *The Mickey Mouse Club* was starting and the Mouseketeers were introduced. I looked for my favorite, Annette Funicello, because she had dark hair like mine. I wanted to be pretty and popular like she was.

I was taller than the rest of my classmates, and I didn't like my freckled face and constantly sunburned arms. I was also nearsighted, which meant I'd soon be wearing thick, ugly glasses, and my big nose had a hump in the middle. My eyesight and nose, both inherited from my father, made me stick out when I wanted desperately to fit in. If only I could be more like Annette!

I still missed the friends I'd lived so close to in Issaquah, Patty and Judy, with whom I'd played card games, listened to records, and played with dolls. Now I rode the bus after school to a home at least five miles away from my friends, so the only time I spent with them was during recess or for short stretches before and after school. I longed for more time with them.

In November, Billy and I helped our parents clear out the abandoned two-room house that perched on the steep hill above the creek. Dad said we'd be keeping sixty of Cal Unger's ewes through the winter, so we built a fenced yard around the old house where the flock would be fed and an attached shed against an outside wall to enclose the sheep and keep them warm during the cold winter nights. Dad explained that we'd store hay and grain in the gutted kitchen area and fix up the front room as a maternity ward for the lambs due in February. Baby lambs were coming!

Dad told us that, come spring, forty percent of the lambs would belong to us. We'd have our own starter flock, earned from our labor of caring for Mr. Unger's ewes through the winter. To make the farm profitable, Dad wanted us to raise sheep in addition to growing wheat. Mom often complained about the workload the sheep added to her life when they escaped through fences, became mired in swamps, or suffered from worms or foot rot. I, however, was delighted at the prospect of lambs, and I began looking forward to "the lambing" I'd been hearing about, whatever that meant.

I loved all animals, the young ones best of all. I adored the fluffy little chicks we picked up in a peeping brown box at the post office. I helped water and feed them all summer and watched them grow into little pullets and young roosters. But then their fates separated them into hens that laid eggs and roosters that met the axe and the frying pan. I felt sad for the roosters, but I loved Mom's fried chicken. It wrenched my heart to see Mom pick up a chicken and carry it to the chopping block. It was one thing I refused to do. I helped with plucking them afterward, but I wouldn't be the one to chop off their heads. Hard lessons awaited as I struggled to reconcile my love of animals with the need to not become attached to the ones that earned their keep by giving their lives.

CHAPTER FIVE

The winter of 1955 brought more snow than I'd ever seen. It just kept falling, and it remained one or two feet deep throughout that first winter on the ranch. Mom and Dad slept in the only bedroom, and Billy and I still had our beds set up in opposite corners of the cement-walled basement. In the warm house just before bedtime, my brother and I donned heavy coats over our pajamas and pulled on our snow boots, then crept down the often-icy path to the outside basement door, the only route to our cold beds.

In the center of the basement crouched the monster we had to feed—the sawdust-burning furnace that was topped with a wide, square hopper. Our bedtime task was to fill it to the brim so it could heat the house through the long, cold night. An enclosure in one corner of the basement held a truckload of sawdust from the lumber mill in Omak. We had to fill heavy buckets, lug them to the furnace, and lift them high to dump sawdust into the hopper.

My parents told Billy and me to take turns filling the hopper, which didn't seem fair because I was a head shorter and not as strong as my brother. For me, the lift was higher and harder and so difficult that I had to fill the bucket only halfway and make more trips than he did. When I tipped the sawdust into the hopper, even a slight miscalculation meant sawdust sprinkled down over me. Ragged flakes would stick to my damp skin and flannel pajamas, and I couldn't brush them off, so my neck and arms itched all night. To make it worse, Billy sometimes bullied me into filling the hopper when it wasn't my turn.

On New Year's Eve, Billy and I burrowed into our sleeping bags in the frigid basement. After midnight, I woke to grunts and whimpers coming from Spot's bed on the floor. I turned on my flashlight and saw two tiny wriggling puppies. I yelled to Billy, "Spot's having puppies! Come see!" We hadn't known she was pregnant.

Billy called for Mom to come down, and she watched with us as Spot stretched out on her side and pushed until the third puppy came out. After the birth, Spot rose and licked her baby clean. "She's doing fine without us," Mom said, "but this may take a while, and you two need to get back to sleep." She took us to the living room to sleep on the fold-down davenport. Although we were excited about the newborn pups, we couldn't hear Spot, and the warm room lulled us to sleep. The next morning, we went down to the basement and counted ten little puppies on my bed! Like a good mother, Spot had carried them from her blanket on the cold floor to a warmer place.

Mom and Dad told Billy and me to each choose a puppy to keep. I picked a black-and-white female that looked like Spot, and I named her Gypsy. Billy chose a golden-and-white male and called his pup Tippy. Mom chose two others to give to friends.

Despite our pleadings, Dad said we couldn't afford dog food for any more pups, so we'd have to "dispose" of the extras. He put the six unchosen ones in a burlap gunnysack and carried it toward the pond. Through my tears, I watched him wade into the pond, and then I ran away. I knew we had unpaid bills and no extra money for puppy chow, but for the rest of the winter, I was haunted by imagining those little pups as they drowned. How could my father be so cruel? At eight and a half years old, I had watched him kill sheep for us to eat, shooting them in the head so they died instantly and then butchering them. But why kill newborn puppies in such a horrible, cruel way? Did his own father teach him to be that way on the farm where he grew up? I got past the trauma by making a vow to protect animals whenever I could.

That winter, the coldest weather arrived during the last week of January, with nighttime temperatures falling to zero. That's when the ewes started having their lambs. Three or four times each night, Dad hiked across the creek and up the steep and often icy trail carrying a bright spotlight attached to a heavy battery. He swept the light over all the ewes to check for signs that one was in labor or had a just-born lamb. Once birthed, the wet newborns had to be brought quickly into the maternity pens we had prepared for them in the old house so they wouldn't freeze. There they found their first milk, bonded with their mothers, and fell asleep under a heat lamp.

During the day, it was Mom's turn to go up to the sheep shed every couple of hours to look for ewes with new lambs. When I wasn't in school, I followed along with her. Watching the birthing was fascinating, especially seeing the newborns come to life with their mothers licking them and bleating at them. The drama multiplied if a second or third lamb was coming. Nearly half of the ewes had twins; the rest had triplets or a single lamb.

When we were sure the ewe had "claimed" her lambs by welcoming them to her udder and providing ample milk, we let the new family rejoin the flock. Their pen was then mucked out (a nasty job, shoveling the soiled straw into a wheelbarrow) and refilled with fresh straw for the next arrivals. The air inside the little house always stank with the overpowering odor of manure and urine, and when I asked Mom how she could stand it, she said, "You just have to get used to it, I guess." Over time, I learned to ignore the noxious smell and many others that had to do with raising animals on a farm.

The all-day, all-night routine took a heavy toll on Mom and Dad. After two weeks, Dad called his mother in Oregon and asked her to stay at the ranch for a while to help Mom with the meals and household chores. I hadn't seen my grandmother much, except for once around my fifth birthday when my mother was in the hospital. For three weeks, I'd stayed at Gram's home, which she called the Big House because it was a four-story boarding house on the edge of the state college campus.

One morning during that June 1951 visit, Gram and I stepped out the Big House's back door and down the white-painted wood steps next to a wall of blooms gleaming in the morning sun. Brilliant shades of pink and yellow burst out of the lattice. They were higher than my head and extended past Gram's curly white hair. Their fragrance flooded my nose.

"Oh, Gram," I gushed. "What smells so good?"

"It's the sweet peas," she said.

I'd never seen such flowers before, thrusting their vivid blossoms toward the sun on slender stems, which Gram clipped with her scissors and handed to me. I pointed out the next ones for Gram to cut. Soon I held a riot of color in my hands, and that sweet perfume was right in my nose. I was in heaven! Back inside, we divided the sweet peas into a dozen small bouquets and set them on the long tables in the dining room where the college students would come to eat lunch.

I was dazzled by my kind and pretty grandmother, but I missed my mommy and daddy and didn't know why I was at the Big House. The days seemed long, and I had to play by myself with the coloring books and puzzles Gram gave me when she had other work to do.

Gram had made a little bed for me in her bedroom closet. I didn't like being closed away from her, but each morning when I awoke, I climbed into the big bed with Gram and slipped under the pink satin bedspread that rustled with luxury. Her robe and soft nightie were pink, too, and her matching set of hairbrush, comb, and hand mirror were all decorated with dainty rosebuds. She told me the pretty hairbrush set was a gift from her husband, Perce, my grandfather, who died three weeks before I was born.

Each morning when Gram invited me to join her under the rustling bedspread, I repeated the same questions.

"Where's Mommy and Daddy?"

"Mommy is in the hospital, and Daddy has to work."

"What's wrong with my mommy?"

"She got sick and needed to rest."

"Is Mommy going to be okay?"

"She's getting better, and soon they'll come and take you home."

Although I was young, I wasn't satisfied with Gram's answers. I'd never known Mommy to have been in a hospital or even seriously ill before. Daddy had driven me to Corvallis to stay with Gram, and my aunt Eva and uncle Jimmy were keeping Billy at their home near Olympia, but nobody explained what was wrong with Mommy.

After three weeks with Gram, Daddy came to get me. He had Mommy and Billy with him in the car, and Mommy seemed her usual self, though calmer. I was overjoyed—we were going home together! As much as I liked being around my grandmother, it never made sense to me that I'd been with her for so long without the rest of my family.

Now I was eight, and Gram was coming on the train to stay with us and help Mom. When she first arrived, she seemed like a stranger. I let her hug me but then stood at a distance, staring. Then she opened her suitcase, took out a box of candy, and offered my brother and me Aplets. She laughed when our eyes grew wide as we chewed the nutty, apple-flavored sweetness for the first time. That broke the ice. Billy and I became instantly helpful and nice to her, hoping for more treats from the little pink box.

The next day dawned clear and freezing cold, so we bundled Gram in extra layers of warm clothing before driving her up to see the sheep. Gram had farmed wheat and raised cattle, but she hadn't grown up around lambs, so she'd never seen the way they cavorted in soft, new snow when they were released from a cramped shed into the sunshine.

I can still picture the scene—the high pile of dark manure we'd shoveled out from the shed now white after a fresh snow, rambunctious lambs leaping to the top, butting each other off, and flicking their long tails as they vied to be king of the hill. We watched and laughed, and Gram clapped her thick mittens together with delight. Then Billy and I started a snowball fight with Gram, and she showed us how to make snow angels.

"Come and play in the snow with us," I called to Mom, who had just stepped out of the sheep shed.

"I've got too much work to do," Mom said, frowning. She turned and went back inside the maternity ward.

All the ewes had lambed by early March, ending Mom and Dad's round-the-clock hikes up the hill to check for new births. Now Mom and Dad could sleep again. Each day, they filled the ewes' and lambs' feeders with hay and grain, and then Dad spent time in the basement repairing the farm truck engine while Mom handled the laundry, housework, and cooking with Gram's help. Mom often said, "I'm grateful for your help, Gram." I could tell Mom's workload had eased—instead of the toast, dry cereal, and eggs we'd eaten for breakfast since January, she now made us hot cereal, scrambled eggs, fried bacon, and our favorite cinnamon rolls.

One of Mom's most delightful kitchen creations was her homemade bread, which we ate at every meal. Mom mixed a double batch twice a week. Gram kneaded it down as it rose and then formed it into loaves and baked it. Gram insisted she couldn't mix the bread dough the way Mom did—never measuring but still producing perfect, high-rounded loaves every time. We all called it "Mom's bread," and the only thing better than the yeasty smell of Mom's golden-brown bread fresh from the oven was its flavor. What a treat it was to eat a slice before it cooled, slathered with home-churned butter Mom made from the rich milk of our neighbor's cow. Billy and I vied for the crusty ends and begged Mom to slice them off for us while they were still warm. If guests or a hired man shared our meals, they raved about Mom's wonderful bread, and it made me proud that she was so skilled in the kitchen in addition to all her other abilities.

Mom also made delicious fudge without measuring. She'd learned this skill as a teenager when she and her sisters earned a little money during the holidays by making and selling candy. "Hers was always the best," my aunts later told me. I liked watching her mix a batch of fudge in a saucepan because I wanted to learn how to make it myself. She poured in milk and spooned in sugar, added a Baker's chocolate bar, stirred till it came to a boil, then let it simmer until she could see it was done. Mom never used a thermometer; she knew when the mixture was ready by how it looked bubbling in the pan, and she tested it by taking out a spoonful and beating it in a saucer until it cooled and hardened just right. When it passed the hardening test, the pan came off the burner, and she added a dollop of butter and a dash of vanilla.

The smell of the chocolate, butter, and vanilla made my mouth water, and she let me help her beat the fudge with a spoon once it cooled to the right temperature. It always came out so smooth and creamy that it melted in my mouth. As a teen, I asked her to show me how she made it, but she didn't have a recipe, and she couldn't explain her process. She'd say, "I don't measure. I just know how much to put in. I can tell I have the right amounts when I see how the milk and sugar look in the pan." I watched her mix it many times, but I could never replicate her magic.

Mom made chocolate fudge and peanut butter fudge for our family. She also made fluffy white divinity candy, which she dyed red and green, to send to her relatives for Christmas gifts. On long winter evenings after dinner, our favorite treat was buttered popcorn with several pieces of Mom's creamy, mouthwatering fudge. Despite all the calories they burned doing heavy farm work, both of my parents were overweight, thanks to Mom's delicious creations. In those days, I took Mom's cooking skills for granted, thinking all mothers were gifted cooks. Later, I learned that wasn't true, as my friends' mothers didn't routinely churn out delectable fudge, cakes, cookies, and pies. Taking the time to create such delicious foods was the primary way my mother showed her love for us, and she always roused herself to do it, even in later years when she was lost in depression.

During our first year on the ranch, my mother often astonished me with her energy and seemingly endless cooking and farming skills, but on one freezing cold night, I began to believe she might also have magical powers. From the sixty ewes came eighty lambs that first winter, and only one was a "bummer," an orphan whose mother refused to nurse. Mom found it deserted, cold, and almost dead, so she picked up the little animal and carried it home tucked inside her coat. She ran warm water into our bathtub and showed me how to hold the lamb's head above water as we tried to warm her back to life. I was sure the tiny creature was already dead because of how cold its limp body felt, and watching it lie there in the warm water broke my heart. But as her body began to warm, she opened her eyes, and her little limbs began to twitch. I gasped with joy. Mom helped me lift the lamb from the water and wrap her in a warm towel. As my mother went to the kitchen for a bottle of warm milk, I held the bundled lamb like a baby and felt my heart swell with love. When the lamb began to suck the bottle's nipple, Mom said, "She's going to be all right now." It was the first time I recall feeling two immensely big emotions at the same time: utter gratitude for the little lamb's survival and astonishment that my mother could revive a living creature from the edge of death. I wanted to grow up to be just like her.

The orphaned lamb survived. I named her Frisky and was allowed to make her my pet. Mom showed me how to mix powdered lamb formula and feed Frisky from a curvy green Coca-Cola bottle with a rubber lamb nipple stretched over the mouth. For the next four months, Frisky lived in our yard and came running for her bottle whenever I went out to feed her.

When she was ready to wean, Frisky had to leave the yard and join the rest of the lambs so she could learn to be a sheep. But she remained nearby, just over the backyard fence where we'd built a special grain feeder for the lambs. Whenever she saw me, she came running to beg grain treats from my pocket. She was a joy to me during that first year on the farm, helping to lift my spirits from the drudgery of all the hard work. Eventually, she joined the other ewes and had lambs of her own.

Accepting that Frisky belonged with her flock was one of my early lessons in the separation between humans and wild or farm animals. From my earliest days, I felt deep love for animals, and more than a few times, that love would break my heart. But sometimes, as with the little lamb we brought back from near death, loving animals was magical.

◆◆◆

Dad had no income through that first winter on the ranch, but he kept the promise he'd made to me back in November. Just before the first snowfall, Dad, Billy, and I had been riding in the pickup when Billy pointed to a ponderosa pine silhouetted against the sky above the ridge ahead.

"Hey, Dad, look at the eagle on that branch!"

"What branch?" Dad said.

"What tree?" I asked.

Billy laughed at me, but Dad asked, "Can't you see the tree?"

"I see a couple trees up there, but they're just dark blurs."

"Tell me when you can see branches," Dad said as he drove toward the biggest tree.

"Okay, I see the branches now," I said.

"Too late," Billy said, "the eagle's gone."

That evening after supper, Gram and I did the dishes, and then we all relaxed in the living room. Dad sat in his usual place on the maroon davenport, and I sat in an armchair about six feet away. He chose a comic book from among the magazines on the coffee table, held it up, and asked me, "Cookie, can you read this?"

I knew which magazine it was because of its blue color. "It's my *Tom and Jerry*," I said, "but I can't see the lettering."

"Then come over here and see if you can read this." He pointed to a headline in the newspaper he held up.

I sat next to him and peered at where he pointed. "I can't read that."

"Try it with my glasses. Your eyes can't be as bad as mine."

I held his glasses to my eyes, and suddenly, I could read the headline and even the fine print from two feet away. Amazing! I was used to holding a newspaper within a few inches of my nose to be able to read the fine print.

"I guess you really do need glasses," Dad said.

Until then, he hadn't believed the reports coming home from school. My first-grade teachers had noticed I couldn't see well. They placed me in a front seat, but in second-grade arithmetic, I had to walk up close to the blackboard to copy the homework problems written there. Each year when the school nurse tested me with the eye chart, she sent a note home that I needed to have my vision checked, but my parents didn't do anything about it.

Now convinced, Dad said, "I thought it must be a minor issue because you kept bringing home high marks on your report cards, Cookie." In March 1955, Dad scheduled an appointment with an eye doctor, and we learned that my eyesight was even worse than his, which seemed strange to me because I was only a kid.

A week after the eye exam, Mom drove me to Omak, where I was fitted with glasses. She asked the doctor to show us the least expensive frames that could hold thick lenses. When I tried on the frames with no lenses, I couldn't see what they looked like, so I let Mom choose and hoped for the best.

The drive home was like a miraculous wonderland of sights. I couldn't believe the vividness of the trees and houses we passed and the crisp letters on every road sign. I could see that the chokecherry and serviceberry shrubs lining Chiliwist Road were bursting with new leaves. Instead of seeing the shrubs and trees as blurry clouds of green, I was now able to make out the dainty patterns and precise details of all the different plants, leaves, and branches. For the first time, I saw birds perching in trees and flying in the air.

This wondrous world newly revealed to me was worth having to wear the thick lenses, so I wore my glasses religiously. But that's when I stopped liking how I looked. I thought the glasses distorted my eyes and made them appear smaller. I'd always thought my eyes were my best feature, but no more. I would struggle with this ugly self-image all through my teenage years.

On the first day of April, Dad finished repairing the farm truck and Caterpillar tractor engines just in time for a hired man to plant the spring wheat crop. Two days later, at the Brewster airport, Mom, Billy, and I watched Dad climb into his little two-seater plane. He pulled on his leather helmet, flashed his big grin, and flew away for another session of spraying weeds in the Columbia Basin wheat fields. Dad had been flying away every spring for four years, and I knew it was how he made the money to support us through the year, but this time, his departure left a heavy cloud over the family. It was our first year raising sheep, and Mom, Billy, and I would have to take care of the flock without Dad's help. As we drove back home, Mom was thin-lipped and silent with her brows drawn down. I could see she wasn't happy to be left with the work of the farm and the sheep.

By this time, Gram had been staying with us for two months, and a week after Dad's departure, she received an offer to buy the Big House. She wanted to accept it, so she'd have to get back to Oregon. Two days later, Mom collected Billy and me from school at noon, and we drove Gram to the Wenatchee airport. As she boarded an airliner to Corvallis, I waved goodbye to her with tears in my eyes. The house was going to feel lonelier without Gram.

With one mother leaving, Dad had asked the other for help, and my mother's mother agreed to come from Oregon. We drove Gram Lockwood to Wenatchee to board the airliner in the afternoon and waited there until evening for Grandma Carson to arrive on the Greyhound bus.

"I hate having to ask you for help," Mom said to Grandma Carson as we rode to the ranch.

"I've helped my other children. It's your turn now," Grandma replied.

Mom seemed glad to have her mother's company, and they chatted a lot while working together. Mom did the laundry, and Grandma ironed the clothes and caught up on all the mending. Mom cooked most of our meals, and Grandma washed the dishes. I helped by drying the dishes after supper. Then Grandma played Chinese checkers with me, the game she taught to all her grandchildren. Fiercely competitive, I focused on learning the game's strategies, and I improved until I was good enough to even beat Grandma sometimes.

One night in late April, Mom hung up after a call with Dad and said, "He's sprayed weed killer on five hundred acres of wheat so far. Things are looking better financially, so he'll be moving his base to the Okanogan airport starting in June." Billy and I clapped and cheered at the welcome news. Dad was making money again, and soon he'd be coming home at night. That meant some relief for Mom on both counts.

As May wore on, Mom still looked frayed from the hard winter, but she perked up to plant her spring gardens. She weeded the tulips and daffodils in her flower bed and planted red and yellow primroses along its edges. She also started her big vegetable garden, sowing the lettuce, carrots, and radish seeds, followed by young broccoli and cabbage plants. Grandma and I helped by planting corn and potatoes, Grandma working the hoe to make each hole, and me kneeling to insert corn seeds or a chunk of seed potato "with its little eyes up," as Grandma explained, so the sprouts would grow toward the sunshine.

"Your help makes a big difference," Mom said to us now and then. I could see that getting her garden planted gave her a boost, but in the evenings, she slumped wearily in her chair and said little. As far as I was concerned, Dad couldn't get home soon enough.

CHAPTER SIX

B y the end of April 1955, the snow on the ranch's upper
slopes had melted and given way to green shoots emerging
in the tussocks of native bunchgrass. Soon the sheep could
find good grazing, but Dad hadn't rebuilt the fences to hold
them on our property, so we'd need herders.

The Unger family arrived on a warm spring morning
in early May and brought more sheep with them. I watched
two trucks rumble through our front gate and up the narrow
dirt road that led to our barn. Then came a pickup, and in the
trailer hitched to it, I saw a horse's head bobbing. My parents
got into Dad's pickup, and I climbed in the back with Billy and
Spot. I was so excited about having a horse on our farm that I
jumped up and down to contain my energy. A horse! A horse!

When we arrived at the barn, I stood up in our pickup
bed and watched as the trucks were backed into a steep bank.
One or two at a time, the sheep jumped out and were hazed
and herded through the pasture gate to join the rest of the
flock we'd kept through the winter. Thirsty from being hauled
in the trucks, the new arrivals ran down to the swamps in the
pasture to drink.

We all gathered in the shade of the barn for introductions.
I already knew Cal and Jane Unger and Jane's brother Bob
from the previous fall when they came with some of their

sheep and helped build a corral and fences. Their high-school-aged daughter, Lynn, was with them today. Raising sheep was a family operation for them, and, as Dad had said, we were learning from them as we built our own flock.

I eagerly turned to watch as Lynn and Cal walked back to the trailer, lowered its ramp, and backed out a white horse followed by another with a pretty coat of evenly mixed red and white, an unusual color combination I hadn't seen before. I squealed. I'd always been crazy about horses, and here were *two* of them!

Jane Unger glanced at me as she led the white horse to a fence and tied him there. Then she waved me over and introduced me to him. I petted his neck, and he turned his head and breathed on my hand.

"Smokey's very gentle, and you can pet him, but stay away from the other horse," she said. "She's still being trained, and Lynn is the only one who handles her."

"I'll be careful," I said.

Smokey was tall and loomed above me. "He moves slower because he's an older horse," Jane said as she lifted a saddle onto his back and strapped it on. Lynn's mare was spirited and frisky, and I envied her for being in charge of the young horse. Lynn explained that its color was strawberry roan. I wanted her to be my friend, but when she heard me address her parents as Cal and Jane, she snapped, "You're too young to call them that. You should call them Mr. and Mrs. Unger." Her words stung and embarrassed me, and after that, I kept my distance.

When both horses were saddled and the sheep were finished drinking, Jane and Lynn mounted and rode down into the pasture to gather the sheep and bring them up into the barnyard. Cal unfastened the wire gate that led from the barnyard to the road going up the hill, and the sheep were so desperate to fill their empty bellies they clumped together and pressed against the gate, competing to be the first ones through it, some trying to leapfrog over the ones in front to rush up the road. I delighted at the clamor of two hundred bleating voices and a dozen clanking neck bells.

Once they passed through, I stood at the gate to watch as the ewes quickly spread out on the steep hillside above and below the road. They snatched at the bunchgrass and bit off the tips of the tall bushes that grew along the dry, rocky hillsides. Jane called these bushes bitterbrush, but Paul Stout had said they were also called buckbrush because, in winter, deer survived by eating the evergreen tips that rose above the deepest snow. I marveled at how the tall, woody bushes seemed to grow right out of the rocks on the dry, sandy slopes.

The sheep also gobbled the new sunflower leaves that emerged in clumps during the spring. Even with many of their leaves eaten, the hardy plants lifted bright yellow blossoms into the summer sun to decorate the hillsides. Jane told me that the Native Americans sometimes dug up these plants' deep, fibrous taproots when other foods were scarce. How marvelous that our pretty sunflowers might have been related to the plants the Native Americans dug to survive!

The lead ewes hurried up the hill to reach better grazing on the higher hillsides, calling for their lambs to keep up. When a dozen ewes slowed to grab more bites, Jane and Lynn rode after these stragglers and sent their dogs running to nip at their heels, which propelled the laggards to dash ahead to rejoin the safety of the herd.

On that first day of herding, I watched the whole commotion from the barnyard gate as the horses and dogs pushed the sheep up the road and beyond the adjoining hillsides until they disappeared, leaving behind a thick dust cloud.

When Jane and Lynn came back that evening, I watched them unsaddling the horses. I asked Jane, "Could I go along with you and help with the herding?"

"We could use your help, but you need to make sure it's okay with your mother."

When I asked Mom that night, she said, "You can go with them on days when I don't need your help with anything. Just make sure you check with me at breakfast."

I was going to be a sheep herder! After that, I joined Jane and Lynn on most weekend days and then nearly every day once school was out for the summer.

On my first official day as an apprentice herder, Jane reached down to help me climb up so I could ride double. I sat behind her saddle on Smokey's rump. I was ecstatic to ride a moving horse. That morning, Jane needed Smokey to climb the steep hillside to reach an ewe that was falling behind the herd, and she asked if I wanted to get off or stay on. "It'll be rough," she said.

"I want to stay on," I replied, but as Smokey powered up the steep hillside, it wasn't easy. He scrambled upward, twisting and turning between tall, scratchy bitterbrush bushes. With my legs dangling and my hands gripping the rawhide saddle strings, I felt myself slipping off his rump. "Help!" I called.

"Hang onto my belt," Jane said.

I grabbed her belt, but it wasn't enough. "I'm still slipping!" I yelled.

"Take my arm," she said. Jane was surprisingly strong for a small woman, and with her clasping my arm, I stayed on the horse as he lunged up the hill. Finally, we reached the startled stray and hustled her toward the herd.

After making it through that frightening hill climb, I almost felt like a cowgirl, except I wanted to be sitting in my own saddle with my own hands on the reins. I vowed to make that happen—to become an independent rider, and soon.

When all the ewes had reached the upper bunchgrass pasture and spread out to graze, Jane rode to the place where she wanted me to guard the boundary fence, and I slid off

Smokey. It was a spot where the sheep often squeezed under the cattle fence to eat the neighbor's grass. I stood between the fence and the flock and urged Spot to chase back any sheep that came too close.

"With you guarding the boundary, it's easier for Lynn and me to control the rest of the spread-out flock," Jane said. I once again felt useful, maybe even grown-up. This was an important job, and I was handling it on my own.

By the middle of the day, the woollies had "shaded up" under the scattered pines or in the aspen thickets to escape the heat. They lay there chewing their cud, resting, and digesting the food in their bellies. Jane and I shaded up, too, resting and eating the lunches we'd packed in Jane's saddlebag. Lynn joined us, but she sat apart and napped or read a book.

I unwrapped a peanut butter and jam sandwich, which Mom knew I disliked. She must have run out of tuna. Making a face, I said, "Ugh! Not PB&J."

"Try adding cheese to it," Jane said.

"That sounds gross."

"No, really, it's much better. I have one with cheese today. Here, I'll trade you half of mine for half of yours."

I trusted Jane, so I tried it, and she was right. The peanut butter and jelly with cheddar cheese was delicious. It became "our sandwich," and next to tuna, PB&J with cheese became my favorite. I learned an important lesson: to keep an open mind and try new foods. If Mom had suggested it, I'd have refused to try it. Billy made fun of me eating it, especially at school, but I didn't care what *he* thought. I had a new ally in Jane.

After two hours, the ewes moved out into the field to forage again while we took our stations to contain them for the next four hours, knowing our presence would keep coyotes from attacking them. Before nightfall, we rounded up the sheep and headed them back down the hill to drink at the creek. Then we enclosed them in the area around the sheep shed where they would be safe from the coyotes for another night.

After dinner that night, I went to bed feeling tired but satisfied. We'd kept the sheep on our land and brought them home with full bellies, and now they'd be safe overnight. Best of all, I'd stayed on the horse when the terrain had gotten rough and steep. I felt another step closer to being a cowgirl.

One evening after a day of herding, I begged Jane to let me ride Smokey by myself before she unsaddled him. She smiled as she boosted me into the saddle, then showed me how to get him to walk, stop, and turn. After that first lesson, I practiced every night if Jane had time to wait for me, and before long, I mastered guiding Smokey, who made it easy because he was steady and obedient. I still needed Jane to help me get on and off, and I was determined to correct that.

When Lynn Unger took her pretty horse home to Brewster at the end of June so she could practice with her equestrian drill team, Jane needed another rider to help her herd. The job fell to Mom. Paul Stout loaned us a gentle horse named Red, and Jane gave Mom a worn Mexican saddle. Each day, I rode double with Mom. We followed the flock up the hillside road as Jane and Smokey rode the rough hillside to hurry the stragglers. At day's end, I practiced riding Red myself, and he was as gentle as Smokey.

One day, Mom had to work in the house, so I was allowed to ride Red by myself to help Jane herd the sheep. As that day began, I sat straight and proud in the saddle as Red walked placidly behind the flock. Spot trotted ahead while Jane guided the lead sheep.

When the ewes were spread out browsing the brushy slope, Jane sent me up the road leading to the first wheat field. "You can stay there, and don't let the sheep go up the hill toward that gate. I'll be over there," she said, pointing. Then she rode out of sight.

At my post, I loosened the reins, and Red lowered his nose to eat the bunchgrass. As thrilled as I was to be in charge of my own horse, I'd forgotten I didn't know how to get off him to open a gate and then get back on without a boost from Mom or Jane. I was on my own out there with "my" horse, so like a real cowgirl, I'd just have to figure it out. Red was even taller than Smokey, so I led him next to a big rock and stood on it to climb into his saddle. Success! It felt like my first real victory as an independent cowgirl.

After that, I did the rock trick when I rode solo, and if there was no rock nearby, I led Red to where the hillside sloped steeply, turned him sideways, and stood on his uphill side to climb up. Each time I got back in the saddle, it was a small victory I relished with pride.

At the end of my first day riding solo, I noticed my legs were getting chafed from the saddle. Red made it even worse because he had difficulty going downward on the sloping hill, and his stiff strides jolted me with each step. I squirmed to find a less painful way to sit, but by the time Jane and I corralled the sheep, the insides of my legs had been rubbed raw. My jeans had done little to protect me from the friction, and my every move was painful, even after dismounting to lead Red the rest of the way home. I held back tears because I hated for Jane to know how much I was hurting, but eventually, I couldn't hide my discomfort. She offered to take care of the horses so I could go in the house.

In the bathroom, I gingerly slid down my jeans and was shocked to see my inner legs covered in weeping red sores. I tried not to move or let my legs touch each other as I called, "Mom! Please come! I need help!"

When she saw my flaming rashes, Mom said, "You come and lie down in my bed." She helped me limp into her bedroom, where she turned down the covers.

Lying there with my legs bare, I didn't move, but the fiery pain still raged. "Mom, please bring something to stop the burning," I sobbed.

She brought the Noxzema skin cream she used to heal sunburns, but when she dabbed some on one of my sores, it felt like she'd turned a blowtorch on my skin. "No, no! Stop! That hurts worse!"

Next, she rubbed some of Gram's Ponds cold cream on a sore, but that felt like fiery torture too. I screamed, "Stop! You're hurting me!"

Mom said, "I don't know what else to try."

"What? You must have something that will help me!"

Jane came in from turning out the horses and heard my wailing. She suggested we try fresh cream. We had plenty of cream that Mom had skimmed from the top of the raw milk we bought from Jim and Gertie Stout. That thick cream, cold from the refrigerator, calmed the scorching pain when Mom touched it to the first sore. I tensed, waiting for the fire to follow, but the cream continued to soothe, so I let Mom daub it on all the raw places. I was more grateful to Jane for knowing the solution, but I thanked Mom for applying it, and I soon fell into an exhausted sleep. The next morning, most of the pain was gone, but I had to wait two weeks for my leg sores to heal before I could get back in the saddle again.

That was the first time Mom wasn't very helpful in soothing pain or healing wounds. It wouldn't be the last time she failed when I needed first aid or even a doctor's care, but on that day, when my legs burned in agony, I began to realize I had to learn to take care of myself.

◄━◆━►

Dad returned to the Okanogan airport in early June as he'd planned. When we sat down at the kitchen table for his first supper back home, Mom started unloading, saying things like, "I work so hard, but you never give me enough money to buy decent clothes for the kids or a nice dress now and then. It's because you put all the money back into the spray business, and then you make bad business decisions with it. I could manage our money better than you do."

Dad didn't argue with her. He said, "Zelma, calm down and let us eat our dinner." But she continued to lash out at him until he rose from the table without eating and went into their bedroom. She followed, still yelling, and by then, he was yelling too.

I went to bed scared and tried to block out the sounds of their anger with a pillow. The two people I loved most were fighting, and what really scared me was that Mom seemed to be driving Dad away from us. I knew money was always short, but the way she ranted at him made her sound crazy to me.

Dad stayed away at night after that, eating and sleeping in Okanogan so he could concentrate on his dangerous flying.

At home, Mom was getting worse. I heard Dad tell Grandma Carson that Mom's rants and personal attacks were a sign she was heading for a nervous breakdown, and Grandma agreed that Mom needed medical help. Dad called Mom's sister Eva and her husband Jimmy and asked them to come, hoping they could persuade Mom to accept treatment.

On a day in late June, Eva, Jimmy, and their daughter Kathy, who was a year older than me, came to our ranch from their home near Olympia. After a brief visit, they asked me to show Kathy the sheep. When we returned, it had been decided that Mom would go to Spokane, where she'd receive treatment in a hospital. Billy and I waved as they drove off with Mom between them in the front seat of Jimmy's big Oldsmobile and Kathy in the back seat with Grandma Carson. I was scared and thought back to what had happened four years earlier in 1951 when Mom was in the hospital and I'd stayed with Gram Lockwood at her boarding house. That time, I hadn't known Mom was sick, and no one had told me why she was in the hospital. This time, I'd been exposed to more of her disruptive behavior, and I knew something was wrong. Still, no one told me what was going on or how long she'd be gone. I could only hope she'd get better and come home restored to the mother I knew.

While Mom was away, I was happy to have Dad home each night. Grandma Carson stayed with us to prepare our meals and keep the household running. I missed Mom, but not the angry outbursts that had destroyed the peace and kept Dad away.

As June gave way to July, I rode Red every day to help Jane and Smokey keep the flock on the native grass and away from our ripening wheat crop. By mid-July, our pastures were grazed short and too dry to grow new grass until the fall rains came. Even the long leaves of the sunflower clumps had dried in the heat; they crackled when Red strode through them. It was becoming harder to find places where the sheep could still fill their bellies, and I felt sorry for them as I watched them chew off the tips of the bitterbrush and eat the dried lupine plants.

Dad finished his aerial wheat spraying and turned his attention back to farming, taking Billy as his helper. Their first project was building stock racks for our Willys Jeep pickup and big hay truck so we could haul sheep in them. Once our racks were finished, Cal Unger drove up in his big truck, and we pushed the sheep—about two hundred of them—up the loading chute and into the Ungers' truck and our two rigs, then hauled them into the higher mountains where the grass was still green. In the cooler elevations, they unloaded the sheep and turned them over to Jane and her brother Bob, who would camp with the sheep and move them to fresh, un-grazed areas every week or so. The sheep would stay in the mountains until the fall rains came.

At dinner a few days later, Dad said, "It's time to take Paul Stout's horse back to him. We don't need the horse now that the sheep are gone."

My heart sank.

The next morning, I strapped the little black saddle on Red and rode him down Chiliwist Road to Paul Stout's place. Sad, I patted his neck as I rode and said, "Goodbye, Red. Thanks for being my horse for a while."

Dad had driven ahead, and I fought back tears as I dismounted, pulled off our saddle, and handed Paul the reins. On the way home in the pickup, Dad said, "Sorry, Cookie. I guess you'll miss having a horse."

I could only nod. If I spoke, I would have burst into tears.

I expected the summer ahead would be long and bleak without a horse, but Dad gave me no time to get bored. Instead, he introduced Billy and me to the hardest work on the farm: picking rocks.

After suffering repeated delays and expenses to repair or replace bent and broken plows and seeder blades that had hit rocks in the fields, Dad said we needed to remove the rocks. So on hot July days, while our wheat crop was ripening, Billy and I helped him pick rocks from the fallowed fields that would be seeded in the fall for the next year's crop. We lifted rocks as big as we could carry and trudged across the field to drop them on the old rock piles scattered along the field's edges.

One day, after we'd been carrying heavy rocks out of the field for three hours in the glaring sun, we rested in the shade of an old apple tree. Dad's and Billy's faces were red from exertion, and mine probably was too. I took off my straw Stetson, wiped my dripping forehead on my shirtsleeve, and drank from our shared canvas water bag. Looking across the enormous wheat field, I asked my father, "How in the world did all these rocks get here?"

Seated near me on a cut-off log, Dad replied, "They were left by the glaciers of the last ice age. They were carried here in the moving glacier and then left behind when the ice melted."

"I can't imagine this place was ever covered with ice!" I said.

"How long ago was that?" Billy asked.

"About fifteen thousand years ago," Dad replied.

"It must have looked very different then," I said.

"Yeah, it did. You know how the hills are broken up by flat areas, like the one where I land my plane?"

"Uh-huh," I said, picturing the small sage-covered flat we herded the sheep across and the larger flat above it, which was planted with wheat. Dad's landing strip ran along the edge of the wheat field.

"Those flat areas were made by sediment deposits when they were at the bottom of glacial lakes."

"Wow!" I exclaimed. How incredible to imagine a glacier shaping our dry land, leaving behind big rocks and flat lake bottoms.

After an hour's rest, we resumed picking rocks and adding them to the old piles scattered alongside the field. Those jumbled rocks were havens for rattlesnakes that sunned themselves on the warm rocks and then scrambled back into the safety of the rockpile when we approached. I shouted for Dad when I spotted a snake in the field. He'd come over to kill it, standing within six feet of it and throwing large rocks to crush it. At first, I thought it cruel as I watched the snakes writhe from the blows, but I was terrified of those slithering creatures with their lethal venom. I preferred them dead.

Dad taught us to kill the snakes this way, and he cautioned us to stand at least three feet away to be out of their striking range. On the move, he said, they could travel as fast as a man could walk. When they coiled up, they could launch their venomous fangs forward more than half their length. Big ones could be thirty inches long. The more I learned about those creatures, the scarier I found them.

One day, I startled a big rattler in the open field. The snake quickly slithered into the nearby clumps of tall rye grass that had grown as tall as my shoulders. Dad wasn't close enough to hear me yelling for him to come, and I didn't want Billy to call me a sissy, so I gathered rocks but was afraid to go into the rye patch. My ankles were bare above my low-cut canvas Keds, and I didn't know which clump the snake was hiding in. Later, I told Dad about the big snake that got away because I'd been too scared.

"It's okay, Cookie," he said. "It would have been dangerous to go after it in such cover, even if you had boots on. You were right to let it go."

What a relief. I'd trusted my instincts, and Dad confirmed that my instincts had been right. And I hadn't made a foolish decision just to avoid my brother's belittling. It was a good day.

———◆◆◆———

In early August of 1955, Dad brought Mom home from the hospital. She'd been away for six weeks. I was happy to have her back and relieved that she seemed to be her usual self again, calmly taking up her chores with no more complaints about Dad. Dad told me he'd asked Grandma Carson to stay for another month to lighten Mom's load and make sure she was going to be okay. I wondered if he was nervous that maybe Mom hadn't been "cured."

The wheat crop was ready to harvest, and Dad wanted to make some of it into hay to feed our sheep in the coming winter. He hired Paul Stout to come with his tractor and baling machine to compact the hay into rectangular bales that would each be tied with two strings of baling twine. Three days later, the field was cut to short stubble and strewn with fifty-pound bales made of golden wheat stalks and the heads of grain. It was a beautiful sight, but it spelled more work for all of us.

For the next week, Mom and I helped Dad, Billy, and Chuck, Dad's hired farmhand, gather the bales into our hay truck and unload them into the barn. Wearing wide-brimmed straw hats to shield us from the sun's blaze, we drank often from the canvas water bag we shared with the men, and we all took salt tablets to prevent dehydration and heat stroke. Once again, Mom proved her toughness as she worked long, hot days alongside the men even though she was smaller and not as strong.

My father was so strong he could hold a hay bale between two hay hooks—curved metal prongs with wooden handles— and walk in full stride to the truck, carrying it in front of him. I was nine that summer and could only manage one hay hook stuck into one end of a bale, but with Mom or Billy on the other end, we could drag it to the truck where Dad or Chuck lifted it up and stacked it.

The adults approached each hay bale cautiously, turning it with a booted foot to see if there was a rattler hiding underneath. Several times a day, I heard the shout, "Here's a snake, get the shovel!"

"I'll get it!" I yelled. I raced to the truck to grab the shovel and hurried to hand it to Dad or Chuck. With a well-aimed plunge of the shovel, the snake's venomous head was chopped off and buried to make sure the dogs couldn't get it. I was becoming hardened to watching snakes being killed, and the shovel was mercifully quick compared to rocks. Even so, I was glad I didn't have to do it myself; I hated to inflict pain on other living things, let alone kill them.

After the wheat hay was stored in the barn, Dad hired someone to come with a combine machine to harvest the rest of the wheat fields. The combine separated the grain from the chaff, and when its bin was full, Dad pulled our farm truck alongside it. From the truck's rear window, I watched the harvested seeds stream from the combine's spout like golden water into the truck bed. To me, it was a wondrous sight; to Dad, it was his cash crop. He invited me to ride with him on the haul to the grain elevator in Brewster. I loved joining him on those long, slow drives on the back roads winding past fields dotted with cows and horses and so many interesting old barns and farmhouses.

When the harvesting was done, Dad wanted to buy more sheep, so he took Billy and me to the weekly livestock auction in Okanogan. I was thrilled to go along because everywhere I looked, there were animals.

"Now, thirty, thirty, thirty, yep! Now forty, forty, forty, come forty, now forty, come fifty . . ." The auctioneer at the Okanogan Valley Livestock Market sat at the mic in his white shirt and dark brown cowboy hat, his voice booming in a rapid beat as he worked to raise the bid for each lot of animals.

Billy and I sat high in the wooden bleachers and watched the arena below as batches of sheep, pigs, and cows were herded in and then sold to farmers or slaughterhouses—I couldn't tell which because I didn't know anyone there but Dad. Outside, the August sun cooked the land, and no air circulated in the upper tier where we sat under the arena's peaked tin roof, so the heat was stifling. Everywhere I looked, people fanned themselves with pieces of paper, and sweat dripped from my forehead as I fanned my face with my Stetson.

In the arena below, callers' voices mixed with the animals' frightened mooing, grunting, and bleating as they dashed about and pooped into the sawdust. Cigars, pipes, and cigarettes hazed the air and burned my nose. My bottom ached from sitting on the wooden plank seats with no backs, but horses were next, and that's what I'd been hanging in there for.

Longing for a horse of my own, I pretended Dad was planning to buy me a horse that day and that I'd been brought along to choose the one I wanted.

I leaned forward and held my breath as the first horse being auctioned trotted through the swinging gate. The cowboy reined the stocky brown horse through its moves in the small circular pit, showing how quickly it leaped forward, slid to a stop, and pivoted to his commands. Then the rider hopped down and pulled off the saddle and bridle so buyers could view the horse's sleek, muscular build and watch it walk, trot, and gallop unencumbered. The auctioneer's singsong patter rang out until the bidding slowed then ended abruptly. "Sold! Campbell. One twenty."

The horse trotted out the exit gate to be shooed down the narrow corridors and into a back pen to wait for its new owner. New horses entered—some ridden, others herded in loose—wild-eyed and frightened by the cracking whips. I hated how handlers scared the poor animals by whipping them. I thought it completely unnecessary, and my heart hurt for every horse that looked confused and scared.

Bidders nodded slightly, lifted a finger, or touched the brims of their hats. They seemed to be playing some kind of game, trying to bid without everyone else seeing what they were up to, so Billy and I had made a game out of trying to tell who was bidding. Our eyes were never as sharp as those of the auctioneer and the spotters who stood around the pit watching for bids and cracking their whips to keep the animals moving. When a spotter caught a signal, he pointed his whip into the stands and cried, "Hup!" for the auctioneer to notch up the bid. Interesting as the process was, I kept my eyes fixed on the pit, mesmerized by the horses.

After about six horses had been auctioned, the gate opened, and in leaped a reddish-brown mare with one white hind foot. This horse didn't just walk or trot around the ring—she pranced with her head high, then sprang into the air when someone cracked a whip, tossed her head, and galloped a tight circle around the small pen with her neck and tail arched and her russet mane flying. Dazzled by her spirit, I couldn't take my eyes off her. The auctioneer read from his papers that the mare was a half-Arabian and nine years old. Watching her as the auctioneer began chanting, I couldn't see who was bidding, but I wished it were Dad. He was sitting across from us on the other side of the circular bleachers. I glanced at him, but he was listening to his friend Walt.

I leaned toward Billy and said, "That's the one I'd buy!"

"You're dreaming," Billy shot back. "We're not buying a horse!"

"Fifty now sixty, fifty now sixty, fifty now fifty-five, fifty-five, fifty-five, fifty now fifty-five. Sold, fifty dollars." When the auctioneer couldn't get more than the seller's minimum price of fifty dollars, he banged his gavel. I didn't catch the buyer's name as his voice trailed off.

After watching the half-Arabian, I was barely aware of the other horses that trotted in and were auctioned off. Once the horses were sold, the auctioneers turned to the cows, at which point I wandered off to the tack store and imagined how the various halters, bridles, and saddles would look on that lovely mare.

Billy came to find me, and we found our way to Dad, who said, "Let's go see what we bought."

Dad led the way to the pens and stopped to point at one. What I saw through the boards wasn't white like sheep. I climbed the tall fence to see over it, and in its shadow stood a dark horse. I figured Dad was joking. My pulse started to race, but I didn't want to get my hopes up. I turned to my father. "What did we *really* buy?"

With a cigarette hanging from the corner of his mouth, he grinned wide. "That's it," he said, nodding toward the pen.

I couldn't believe it—he did buy us a horse! Then I climbed the fence again and saw the white sock on her rear leg. I let out a squeal of delight—she was the one I'd picked, the most beautiful horse in the entire auction!

As Dad led her out of the holding pen and up the loading chute, he told me to stay clear because she was still wide-eyed and frightened. She hesitated at the pickup's threshold and then rushed in. Dad tied her halter rope to the front of the rack while she stomped nervously and whinnied.

With her weight shifting and her hooves thudding in the bed of the pickup, we drove the fourteen miles from Okanogan down the Okanogan River, past our grade school in Malott, and then up the dirt road to our home in the Chiliwist Valley. I kept looking through the rear window to make sure she was real. I couldn't wait for Mom to see what we'd bought. We had our own horse at last!

Red Pepper, according to her papers, was a registered half-Arabian mare, color chestnut, with her only marking the white sock on her right rear leg. And when I learned that she was nine years old, the same as me, I knew we had a connection.

Dad had learned the rest of Pepper's story from his friend Walt as they watched the mare in the auction ring.

"I know her owner," Walt had told Dad. "He runs a dude ranch. He's selling her because she's been bucking off the dudes. She'll probably go cheap. And she's got good breeding: half Arab and the rest mostly Thoroughbred. She'll make some good foals for you."

What was Dad thinking that could have made him bid on a horse known for throwing riders? He didn't plan to ride her himself, so that meant Mom, Billy, and I would be the ones using her for herding sheep. Did he want all of us to be bucked off the horse? Mom had grown up around horses and knew how to ride, so maybe Pepper wouldn't buck her off. But Billy and I knew nothing; we were like the others she'd bucked off. I was determined, however. We had a horse, and I was going to become a horsewoman.

At home, I asked Dad, "Could you teach me to ride her?"

"No," he said, "I'm not a horseman."

I guessed he expected us kids to learn from Mom or figure out on our own how to ride Pepper. I'd learned to ride gentle horses like Smokey and Red, but they never bucked. Now we owned a horse I was scared of. I didn't want to be thrown and end up with broken bones or worse. But I was willing to try riding her anyway.

I knew nothing about caring for horses and not much about riding them, but my father had just made my horse dreams come true, so I joyfully committed to learning everything I could from books and from the ranchers around me. I also planned to watch Mom with the new horse and ask for her help, but she didn't seem inclined to ride, and the sheep were still up in the mountains with the herders, so Pepper was left to herself in the pasture near our house.

Right away, the beautiful mare we brought home from the auction drew me like a magnet. I spent hours in the pasture with Pepper, petting her soft neck, brushing her rounded sides, watching her graze, and dreaming of the day I'd be the one riding her fast enough to make that thrilling sound of galloping hooves. Meanwhile, Pepper stood quietly, her tail swishing side to side, warding away biting flies, and allowed me to caress her.

CHAPTER SEVEN

The year 1955 was coming to an end, and our second lambing season loomed ahead. We'd kept the 24 young ewes we'd earned by caring for the Ungers' flock the previous winter, and Dad had bought more at the summer auctions. Our flock, now numbering 140 ewes, were all the sheep shed could contain during the freezing months ahead.

We kept Pepper in the snowy pasture below the hay barn, and I liked to be the one who carried hay out to her. I lingered with her and brushed her thick winter coat.

"It's too dangerous for anyone to ride her in the slippery snow," Mom said, but sometimes she'd tie Pepper to the fence and boost me up so I could sit on her warm back and watch her breathe steamy clouds into the frosty air.

In mid-January, Dad left for one of his business trips. He was buying airplane parts in Seattle or wheat-spraying chemicals in Wenatchee, though I wasn't sure which. Two mornings later, the phone rang. "I'm in the hospital in Wenatchee," he told Mom. "Last night, I stopped to help a man injured in a car accident. It was snowing hard, another car lost control and hit me, and I ended up with a broken leg."

Mom relayed all of this to us in a flat voice, and I heard her tell Dad, "We'll drive down to visit you tomorrow after we finish feeding the sheep." I was confused about what had happened and anxious about Dad being in the hospital, but Mom seemed most concerned about how she was going to fit the four-hour round trip into her busy day. I guessed the situation wasn't very serious, but I was wrong.

In the hospital the next day, I was shocked to see Dad lying with his left leg elevated in a white cast that extended from his mid-thigh to his toes. I'd never seen my strong, capable father laid low, let alone look helpless like this. He held his hand toward me, and I crept nearer and hugged his arm. "Sorry I can't hug you, Cookie," he said. "It hurts too much to move."

The rest of our visit was a blur, and we didn't stay long before heading home over the snowy roads. How could we manage all the work at home with Dad unable to help us? I knew the heavy workload would be hard for Mom, especially when Billy and I were in school. Mom was silent, her hands clenching the wheel as she focused on the slippery country roads.

Dad had phoned Gram, and she took a flight from Corvallis to be with him at the Deaconess Hospital. Sixteen days later, Paul and Eula Stout drove to Wenatchee and brought Dad and Gram home. Dad struggled up the back porch steps on his crutches, grimacing. Then he collapsed on the fold-out sofa.

I worried about Dad but also about Mom. Caring for our sheep now fell on her shoulders, except for the help Billy and I could give. Even with Gram to help prepare meals and care for Dad, I couldn't imagine how Mom would manage the workload with the arriving lambs. What if all the stress caused another of her breakdowns? And if she broke down again, what would happen to the farm animals?

Mom began spending all day up at the sheep shed, distributing food to the flock and caring for the arriving lambs. She also had to go up several times during the night to check on them and bring the wet newborn lambs into the warm maternity ward so they wouldn't freeze.

Ten days passed, and Dad slowly improved, but he had severe headaches and remained bedridden. Meanwhile, Mom looked more and more exhausted. Eventually, Dad phoned Art Hilderbrand, who agreed to come each day to feed the sheep and take the afternoon lambing shift so Mom could rest. He was a husky man, and his strength was a huge help to Mom, who'd been wrangling hay bales and heavy feed sacks by herself every day.

In mid-February, the temperature fell well below zero and stayed there for a week. Our road was closed from snowdrifts built by the gusty winds. After three days, a snowplow went up and down Chiliwist Road and cleared the drifts, and Mom drove to Malott for groceries. Then, over the next three days, twenty inches of new snow fell, and we were snowed in: the pickup stuck, our roads blocked, the school closed, and the phone line out. Each day, Art hiked two miles through the snow to help feed the sheep.

The only benefit to the snow was that it kept us close together. Most evenings after dinner, Mom served hot buttered popcorn and her delicious homemade fudge, and we listened to basketball games on the radio. Those calm evenings tucked in together, safe from the storm, offered a break from our usual frenetic pace. I silently hoped it would help Dad recover and Mom stay calm.

The snowplows worked furiously to clear the county roads, and after three days off, Billy and I went back to school. The sun came out, melting the snow on our roof, and a solid curtain of icicles grew from the house eaves. The longest one measured fifty inches.

"You kids stay away from them," Dad warned. "They're like spears and could really hurt you when they fall."

"We will, Dad," we promised.

─◆─

February 24 was Mom's thirty-ninth birthday. Gram made a frosted angel food cake, and I decorated it with ten candles and twenty-nine chocolate chips to represent her thirty-nine years. The atmosphere in the house was light since Dad was feeling a bit better. Paul Stout brought our week's mail from the post office in Malott, and we all sat around as Mom opened cards and gifts, including a shiny electric mixer with revolving stainless-steel bowls, which her Carson siblings had ordered from Sears Roebuck. Delighted, Mom said, "Now I won't have to blend my cake batters with a spoon!" She added, "Or whip the cream with that old hand-cranked eggbeater!"

"I'm not used to having such a fuss made over me," she said as she ate her birthday cake. "This lovely cake, all the nice cards and gifts—this has been a special birthday."

Little affirmations like that went a long way toward giving me peace. Anytime Mom outwardly expressed contentment, or anytime she wasn't picking a fight with Dad or complaining about exhaustion, I had hope that our home life might continue like normal.

By March 3, the weather warmed to the mid-forties, which launched icicle spears into the snow where they pointed upright, like weapons left outside a tavern by medieval soldiers who'd stopped to refuel.

By the third week of March, Dad's money worries outweighed his need to rest and heal. One morning, his new pilot Ted drove him to the Columbia Basin wheat country to line up customers and prepare for the wheat-spraying season. Three days later, Dad phoned. Mom reported he'd told her, "I've seen the doctor in Wenatchee, and the X-ray showed my leg is healing all right. I now have a much shorter cast." But when he came home, he had *no* cast at all—he'd fooled us! His walk with crutches from the pickup to the house was like a victory lap, with all of us clapping for him. The sight of Dad walking almost normally was as wonderful as the return of spring.

On April Fool's Day, only fifteen months after Spot had had her first litter, she surprised us with ten more puppies. I begged Dad not to drown them this time. "Well, maybe I can find homes for the pups among my friends and the wheat farmers I spray for," Dad said.

Spot was allowed to nurse all ten pups, and I was overjoyed. Six weeks later, when the puppies were weaned, Dad took Spot to the vet and had her spayed. By midsummer, the pups had all been delivered to new homes, and my young female, Gypsy, was also spayed. Our days of being swamped with unexpected puppies were over — what a relief! We needed Spot on the job, herding sheep. In this family, every member had to pull their own weight, even the dogs.

Three weeks later, Dad and Ted took off in the two little spray planes and headed for the Columbia Basin. My heart swelled to see my big, strong father climb into his plane, carefully settle his still-healing leg on the right rudder pedal, pull on his leather helmet, flash us his big grin, and fly away.

Ten days later, Dad called to report good news. "I've finished spraying four hundred acres of spring wheat, and I'm trying to line up more." He was back in the air and making money again. That kind of news was always a relief, but I also felt uneasy. Hovering over life on a ranch was always a sense of *what next?* We'd been rocked with disasters, coming one after another like waves, and we never knew who'd be pulled under next. Last summer, it was Mom's hospitalization, and this winter, Dad's broken leg. I crossed my fingers, wishing for a period of calm.

In early May, Dad and Ted moved their base to the Okanogan airport and started spraying wheat fields from there. Then Gram received a call from her cousin Nell in Corvallis. Nell asked Gram to help with her husband Roy and Gram's sister Clara, both very sick. Gram packed her suitcase, and Dad drove her to Wenatchee early the next morning to catch a plane. Her departure left a hole in our family. Mom missed her help with the meals and household chores, and I missed her soft-spoken, sweet presence and her loving ways.

By this time, we'd been letting the sheep go up the hill to graze on the new spring grass, with Mom riding Pepper and Billy and me herding on foot. Going up the hill, the three of us worked together to urge stragglers to keep up with the main herd and then to keep the flock within our boundaries, grazing on our greening land but not in our planted wheat fields.

Mom seemed to have no problem riding Pepper. The mare did nothing but jog along with Mom riding steady in her saddle. Sometimes, when I got tired hiking up the steep hill and chasing ewes, Mom held out her hand and pulled me up to sit behind her saddle until we got past the steeper parts. It was like riding double on Red but better because this was our own horse.

One day, I asked, "Do you think I could ride Pepper by myself?"

"I don't see why not," Mom said, handing me the reins.

Pepper stood still as I climbed up, and when she walked forward, she was as easy to stop and turn as Smokey and Red had been. On level ground, Pepper shifted into a slow jog, very smooth, and I was delighted to be riding her at last. Maybe she was really going to become my horse!

Billy wasn't interested in sheepherding or horse riding— he liked the machines. At twelve, he had already learned to drive the pickup and was practicing with the Caterpillar tractor. I wasn't interested in those, as I preferred working with the animals, especially our wonderful horse that I loved now more than ever.

In June of 1956, I finished fourth grade and turned ten years old. After school was out for the summer, it became my job to take the sheep up the hill to graze every day. Mounted on Pepper with Spot and her grown daughter Gypsy running alongside us, I felt like a full-fledged cowgirl, and I liked being up on the heights of the ranch with my horse and dogs, watching the sheep. The sheep, however, rarely made things easy for me. They wanted the fresher grass on the neighbor's side of our boundary fence, and time and time again, they found ways to sneak by me. Unfortunately for me, the boundary fence built for cattle couldn't stop them.

One hot afternoon, a ringleader ewe dashed for the three-strand fence and squeezed under the lowest wire. Others swarmed after her, bleating their excitement. Sheep on the wrong side of the fence was going to mean big trouble with Gertie, so I had to hustle to get the woollies back to our side. There wasn't a gate for Pepper, so I tied her to the fence and started running to get around the sheep, who moved faster than I did. My cowboy boots were made for riding, with pointed toes designed for finding a lost stirrup and inch-and-a-half heels for keeping the boot in place. Under the pine trees on the hillside, the smooth leather soles slipped on fallen needles, and as the hillside got steeper, the going got tougher, until I fought for breath and dripped sweat.

My so-called sheepdogs were no help. Spot was half border collie, a Scottish breed used for herding sheep. She had the half that made her eager to chase sheep but not the half that told her to circle around to face them and bring them back. She nipped at their heels and chased them farther away. I had to keep the dogs close to me and scramble as hard as I could across the slippery slope. All the while, I gasped for breath, cried in frustration, and swore at the renegade sheep. They ran ahead, calling to one another as if conspiring against me. As I fell back out of their sight, the leaders slowed, and then the flock spread out to graze on the hilltop.

I figured my only chance to return them to our property was sneaking around the hill below the feeding sheep, popping up on the far side of them, and then letting the dogs loose to chase them back where they belonged. That's what I did, and then, feeling victorious over the rascal ewes, I yelled to the dogs, "Get 'em, Spot! Go get 'em, Gypsy! Take 'em back home!"

As the dogs ran at them, the sheep fled back through the fence to our land. I could only hope Gertie hadn't witnessed any of it from her front window, where she often watched for the telltale white spots moving across her hillside, eating her grass.

The next day, when I visited Gertie's house to pick up the milk, she opened the door and screeched, "I saw your sheep over on our side of the hill again! Was that you up there with them?"

I gulped. "I'm sorry. They got away from me and went through the fence."

"Can't you keep them on your side? We need that grass for our cows!"

"I know, but when they sneak through the fence, I have to tie up my horse and go around them on foot, and it's really hard."

"You shouldn't have sheep up there anyway! The fences are for cows!" she shouted.

Her anger felt harsh, but I knew she was right. It was my fault. All I could think to say was, "I'll try my best to keep them away from the fence from now on."

"Well, you better!" she said, thrusting the gallon cans toward me. "Here's your milk."

I wasn't invited to come in and watch TV with her that day or for some time to come, and the feeling of having damaged a friendship gave me a heavy heart. On the trudge home, the gallon cans' thin wire handles bit into my hands, and our lane seemed longer with each heavy step. Thanks to a bunch of unruly sheep, I'd now lost access to the only fun thing I got to do with a friend, which meant summer was going to feel a lot harder.

It was my dog Gypsy who saved me. Two weeks later, she delighted me by learning to circle to the front of the flock, turn them around, and bring them back. Of all our dogs, Gypsy was the only one to learn this move. I'd chosen Gypsy from Spot's first litter of pups because she looked like Spot. At a quarter border collie, she looked like the real thing in black and white, the way Spot did. She'd been a great choice, and she was proving to be a natural sheepdog.

There was no question she had all the quickness and cleverness of a border collie. From then on, she saved me from chasing the sheep on foot when they escaped under the cattle fence to forage across Gertie's pasture. Thanks to Gypsy, I soon found myself back in Gertie's good graces and was invited to stay and watch TV with her when I picked up the milk.

◄◆►

As July advanced, my sheepherding job became even more difficult. Now, besides having to keep the woollies from crossing the border fence to graze on Jim and Gertie's land, I had to protect our unfenced wheat from those hungry scavengers. Wheat was our most important cash crop, and the sheep craved it at every stage of growth, from succulent green blades in early spring to rising stalks in June to the summer-ripening heads of grain in which the seeds were formed and dried. Forced to graze on the dry hillsides' native vegetation, the ewes tried their mightiest to outwit their herder so they could race into the field to chomp at the delicious wheat.

Earlier that spring, I'd helped Mom with the herding. Working as a team, with her riding Pepper and me on foot with Spot and Gypsy, we kept the sheep away from the wheat. But herding sheep alone was an infinitely more difficult assignment.

One day, I was guarding the edge of the flat wheat field as the grazing flock spread across the dry hillside below me. Watching me, several crafty ewes sprinted into the juicy wheat. Others raced after them. I jogged Pepper over and sicced the dogs on the ewes. We chased them back over the edge, with

Spot and Gypsy barking, dashing at them, and biting at their heels while they scattered down the hillside, bleating.

"Good," I called to the dogs, "that'll take care of them for a while!" Then I saw another gang of cunning marauders dash into the field at the far end. I could practically see our wheat income disappearing before my eyes.

I knew Dad would see the damage the next time he checked the field, which meant I'd hear his disappointment as he asked, "What happened here, Cookie? Can't you keep the sheep out of the wheat?" If it kept happening, he might get angry, and then I'd feel sick about it.

I had no choice but to move down the field as fast as I could to chase out the second group of wheat-eaters. I urged Pepper to trot faster, but she broke into a gallop, and that's when I knew I was in trouble.

─◆─

Earlier that summer, Pepper had thrown me. I was riding her to the lower pasture and came to a dip in the road, which she leaped across just as Spot crossed in front of her. When Pepper arched her back and bucked, I flew off in front of her and landed headfirst on hard-packed earth. The impact knocked the breath out of my lungs, and even with my eyes closed, I saw stars.

Dad had been driving behind me with Billy in the pickup. He braked and came running. Seeing me gasping for breath, he said, "Don't try to move, Cookie. Just lay still."

I couldn't speak. I just lay there drawing shallow breaths, trying to fill my lungs.

After a moment he asked, "Are you okay?"

When I could speak at last, I said, "Yeah, I'm okay." He helped me sit up and wrapped his arms around me. I slowly turned my head right and left and said, "I saw stars."

"Let me see your eyes," he said. Whatever he saw when he looked into my eyes made him say, "I want you to go sit in the shade and rest for a while. Billy and I will start the fence repairs."

Billy came by where I sat under the trees and sniped, "You sure know how to get out of work."

"Leave her alone and come with me," Dad said.

After an hour or so, I walked across the pasture to join them. "I feel better now, Dad."

"I'm glad to hear that, Cookie, but you take it easy the rest of the day."

That was my first time being thrown from a horse, and now, up on the edge of that wheat field, I knew what was coming. When I pulled back on the reins to slow Pepper's gallop, she pinned back her ears and started to buck. In mid-stride, she tucked her nose to her knees, arched her back, leaped with her rear legs, and landed on her stiffened front legs like a pile driver. Rodeo riders call this kind of bucking crow-hopping because it looks like a four-legged version of a crow hopping across a lawn.

Our small Mexican saddle, its leather black with age and half rotted away, offered nothing for me to grab when Pepper started plunging forward and pile-driving. Each stride tossed me forward, then back. First, the seat's high back edge rammed my backside, and then the bare metal horn in front punched my belly. With Pepper's head lowered, there was nothing to stop me as I flew off her, landing face-first.

The force of the thrust was so powerful I thought I might be killed as I slammed into the ground. The impact knocked the air out of my lungs, and now, lying on my chest, I struggled to breathe. I rolled to my side and gently moved my arms and legs; they all still worked. I wanted to lie there until I felt better, but no—I had to get up and get the sheep out. I struggled to my feet, found my glasses, and the broken-off left arm, and looked for Pepper. She'd come to a leisurely stop and was enjoying the tasty wheat herself. The traitor! She'd bucked me off as if she'd wanted me seriously injured. Did she know what she was doing? Pepper started to walk away from me, but I ran to grab her trailing reins. Sobbing from the pain searing through my arms, face, and chest, I wanted to lash her with those reins, but I didn't want to train her to evade me, so I just kicked the dirt and cussed her out. "You stupid horse! I hate you! Why buck me off? I need you to help me, not hurt me!"

I still had to go after the feasting sheep, so I gathered Pepper's reins, pulled her nose up from the wheat, and climbed back on as she pointed her ears back in annoyance. I hoped to keep her to a trot this time. Although I had no confidence she'd do what I wanted, I couldn't quit my herding task. There was only me to run those sheep out of the wheat. I trotted her toward the sheep, then sent the dogs to run them out and keep them away from the wheat field. For the rest of the afternoon, Pepper was her normal, compliant self, but I didn't ask for another gallop.

At the end of the day, I limped into the house. Mom looked at me and said, "What happened?"

I plunked down on a kitchen chair. "Pepper bucked me off," I said. "Look at my elbows." Both elbows were scraped raw.

"Your nose too," Mom said. "We'd better dab Merthiolate on them. Stay put. I'll be right back."

I knew my elbows would burn when Mom painted the scrapes with the red antiseptic, but I held back my tears. I refused to let her paint it on my scraped nose and draw attention to it. Then I realized I'd been holding my glasses in my hand. The fall had flung them from my face and snapped off one of the arms. I held up part of the detached arm and said, "Can you get some tape, please, so I can fix my glasses?"

Mom pulled a roll of adhesive tape from a drawer and handed it to me. I fashioned a bandage of sorts, good enough to let me wear my glasses for now. Great. In addition to being a sore, cut-up mess, now I'd also cost the family for the repair of my frames. At least the thick, expensive lenses hadn't been scratched up.

At dinner, Billy acted exactly as I expected. When I approached the dining room, he looked up, slapped the table, and said, "Ha, ha! Look at your nose! Looks like you ground it in the gravel!" Never a sympathetic word from my brother. Never a nurturing moment nor so much as a look of concern.

I was glad Dad wasn't home that evening because I couldn't take a bashing of my pride along with my bruised body. He would have been kind, but I just couldn't bear for him to think of me as incapable.

The next day, Pepper threw me again. The sheep raced into the wheat at the far end of the field, and when I hurried Pepper to trot faster, she broke into a canter, lowered her head, and catapulted me into a three-point airplane-type landing, the three points being my elbows and my nose. I picked myself up, caught her, and went after the sheep again, this time keeping to the slow trot she preferred. I stayed in the middle of the field for the rest of the day and sent the dogs ahead as I jogged Pepper slowly toward the marauders when they rushed into the wheat once more.

Dad came home for dinner that second night. He took one look at my injured nose and taped glasses, and his eyes grew wide. "What happened to you?"

"Pepper bucked me off yesterday. And again today."

Wrinkling his brow, he asked, "Why, Cookie? Why can't you hang on?"

"There's nothing on that old saddle to get a grip on."

This time, something about seeing me injured again by an unruly horse must have stirred my father's protective instincts. The next evening, he came in the back door and called to me, "Cookie, go take a look at what's in the front yard."

Out in the yard, I wondered if I was dreaming. My nose

filled with the deep, rich aroma of tanned leather. It was a Western saddle that gleamed like amber honey. It had a wide leather seat, a large flat horn, and an equally flat cantle where the back of the seat ended in a rolled edge big enough to make a good handgrip. Everywhere, the leather was tooled with beautiful designs, except for the padded seat covered in soft suede leather. The saddle was brand-new, shining in the sun.

Mom came out to see. "How can we afford a saddle like this?" she asked.

"I bought it on credit at Hand's Store," Dad replied.

The Hand family ran the general store and post office in Malott, selling almost everything the locals needed: gas, groceries, apparel, hunting and fishing licenses, magazines, hardware, tack, and other necessities. I'd found my winter thermal boots and my Stetson hat at Hand's. They extended credit to Dad through the winter when he had no income, and we bought our groceries from them, running up a big tab. Dad made sure to pay off their account each summer after he collected from the farmers for spraying their spring wheat. I'd always looked longingly at the new Western saddles in the back near the post office boxes, and now we had one!

Mom showed me how to lift the new saddle onto Pepper's back and fasten the two cinches. She took a turn down the lane in it and said, "It really is more comfortable."

I knew riding that saddle was going to make me feel like a real cowgirl. The problem was that I could barely lift it. At ten years old, I was almost five feet tall but only weighed eighty-four pounds, and the thirty pounds of leather were too much for me to lift higher than my head and onto the horse's back. Every morning, I had to ask Mom or the hired man to help me lift the saddle onto Pepper before I could mount and ride off to herd the sheep.

By the end of summer, I'd grown tired of asking for help, so one day, I lugged the awkward thirty-pound saddle out of the shed toward Pepper. I stopped to hook the far side stirrup onto the saddle horn to keep it from folding under as I heaved the heavy saddle up, up—but the stirrup came off the horn, landing between the saddle and Pepper's back, so I had to let the saddle drop to the ground and start over. This time, the stirrup stayed attached, and at last, I had the saddle perched on her back with the front fork fitted over the high point of her shoulders. I'd done it! I took a second to shift and adjust the beautiful saddle on Pepper's back as if I were straightening a fine painting on a wall. Exhausted but relieved, I stepped around to her other side and lifted down the stirrup and the two long girths. Crossing back again, I pulled the girths under Pepper's belly and fastened them. I'd just saddled my own horse by myself! This felt like a victory. Then I stepped in the stirrup, climbed up onto my horse's back, settled into the saddle, and let out a whoop of joy.

I tied a half-knot in the reins and tucked them around the saddle horn so Pepper couldn't get her head down to buck. She flattened her ears and shook her head to show me what she thought of it, but I said, "Too bad—you earned this." From that day on, any time she caught me without the knot secured and arched her body to start bucking, I reached behind myself, grabbed the lip of the cantle, and hung on to keep from being pitched forward.

I was no rodeo rider. Those daredevils earned prizes by riding a bucker for eight seconds with one hand waving in the air. They were all about the show, while I was holding on for my life. But I kept at it, kept urging Pepper into a gallop, and kept holding on when she bucked.

The first time I was able to keep my seat for three or four crow-hops, Pepper gave up and leveled out into a gallop. Elated, I laughed, leaned forward, and let her run. After that day, Pepper tried to unseat me a couple more times but soon learned I could stay on when she bucked, so she stopped trying to unseat me, and I gave her free rein to let her race the length of Dad's airplane runway on the first flat field. She needed no urging to run, and I leaned into the onrushing wind, pretending we were the lead horse and jockey at the kind of racetrack her Thoroughbred father might have competed on. We both loved it!

What a summer. At only ten years old, I'd graduated from being just another dude rider Pepper bucked off to being a rider who'd worked to saddle and eventually manage the horse of my dreams. The thunder of Pepper's gallop became my favorite sound in the world, and I could tell she was meant to run, so I let her go all out. But thrilling as that was, I would soon learn what it could mean to ride a horse into danger.

CHAPTER EIGHT

As the summer of 1956 rolled into fall, I realized that Mom had seemed fine for more than a year. She'd made it through a hard winter without another psychotic episode, and we'd just finished a summer that had me taking over the sheepherding from her, at least until school started. As autumn began, I'd step outside on many clear nights, look up to the stars, and thank the heavens that Dad's business was fine, our ranch was thriving, and my mother was healthy. Maybe her mysterious breakdowns were behind us.

One September evening, when Dad came home from his work at the airport, he called out, "Who wants to go up the hill with me and check on the wheat?"

"Not me," Billy said. "I have homework."

I said, "*I* do." I was glad Billy declined so I could be with my father, just the two of us.

Dad and I climbed into the pickup, drove past the barnyard, and went up the hillside road. As the truck labored up the steep incline to the big field, the open windows mixed dust from the road with smoke from the Pall Mall cigarette hanging from the corner of Dad's mouth. We made it to the top of the big wheat field and hopped out of the truck. I followed him into the furrowed field.

As we walked, my canvas Keds and Dad's leather boots sank into the billowy dust. Dad stopped and kneeled between two of the parallel furrows that ran about twelve inches apart. With one hand, Dad dug in the bottom of the furrow, moving the dry, powdery earth to one side, going deeper with each slow swipe of his hand.

"See, Cookie?" He pointed to the hole he was scraping. "I set the seeder to plant the seeds below this layer of dust into the moist ground beneath it. If I got the right depth, then the seed will absorb the moisture until it swells up and sprouts and comes up through the dust."

"I don't see anything but dust," I said.

"I'm already down ten inches, so there should be moisture showing. Yes, there it is," he said, sweeping the dust away in the trench he'd made.

"Yes, I see. The soil is darker down there."

"Now I need to find some wheat seeds and see what they're doing."

He dug into the dark brown soil and carefully sifted it through his fingers. "There's one!" he said. "Look. It was in the moisture, and it sprouted." He lifted a swollen wheat seed with a tiny white tail extending out of one end. It resembled the corn kernels I'd helped Mom plant. They, too, had sprouted white tails and then grown into cornstalks that towered above me.

Pointing to the tail, Dad said, "That's the sprout that will grow upward toward the sunshine while the seed sends roots down into the moisture."

"It'll grow up through all that dust?"

"Yes, isn't that something? And the thick layer of dust acts like insulation to keep the sun from drying out the moisture below, so the plant will have enough water to keep growing until the fall rains come."

"Wow, that's amazing!"

"Nature is wonderful, isn't it? Looks like I got the depth right, and we may have a crop. We'll come back in a week and see how it's doing."

The promise of a return outing made my heart swell.

We repeated our foray each week to find the sprouts lengthening until thin green stalks poked up in the furrows like needles pushed through a quilt. Week by week, the needles widened into stems that branched into blades and stretched toward the sun. Eventually, the fall rains turned the fluffy dust into firm, dark earth around the roots, and the wheat field turned into a sea of green. *How beautiful!*

Dad was a good teacher, and I loved when he took the time to show me how things worked as he built or repaired them or asked me along for an evening drive to check on the crops and fences. Our time together helped heal the wound I'd suffered back when I was three and a half years old and he'd turned me out of his lap while saying I was too big.

—◆—

The next summer, Mom was glad to turn the daily herding chore over to me once school was out. Every morning after breakfast, I saddled Pepper and rode up to the barnyard to start another long day with the flock. The ewes were hungry in the mornings, so the leaders dashed up to the better pastures as soon as they were released.

I was eleven that summer and comfortable riding Pepper bareback. Some days I herded the sheep that way—proof of my skill as a rider. Dad and the hired helpers were slowly completing new sheep-proof boundary fences. They were also adding these fences around the wheat fields, which made the herding a lot easier for me. Pepper and I were getting along beautifully. She was no longer bucking, but she wasn't done threatening my life yet.

One evening, after heading the sheep toward home, I wanted to let Pepper run on Dad's airstrip. When I pointed her down the runway and let out the reins, she broke into a run. I could tell Pepper was feeling good that day, and she was really pickin' 'em up and layin' 'em down, as the cowboys described a fast-running horse. When we neared the end of the flat, I turned her, and she ran the length of the airstrip back to where we'd started. When we neared that end, I turned her, and she ran the length of it again. I clamped down my hat with one hand, and the wind in my face was glorious.

After the second round trip, she'd run nearly a mile and was breathing heavily. I decided we'd had enough. I pulled on the reins and called, "Whoa, Pepper," but she resisted. I couldn't pull harder because I was riding bareback with no stirrups to brace my feet for leverage. She refused to slow or even turn. Instead, she galloped over the rounded end of the flat and down a rough shortcut to the road that wound down the hillside to the barnyard. I had to loosen the reins and hang on to her mane with both hands as she galloped faster and faster.

Pepper careened down the narrow road while I bounced toward one side of her and then the other. At one time, I was hanging off her with the road rushing by beneath me, but thanks to Pepper's thick mane, I managed to pull myself back upright and hang on for dear life, aware that falling at that speed would hurl me onto the rock-hard road or over the edge into the boulders that lined the shoulder. Or I could be impaled by broken-off branches from the pine trees that flanked the road.

We came to the switchback in the road, and I braced myself, expecting to be thrown off at the first downward curve. But Pepper was going too fast to make the sharp turn, so she leaped up the banked roadside and galloped across the hillside. Then the slope flattened, and she slowed at last. I turned her head toward the hill to stop her and then slid off, clutching the reins. Her chest heaved, my heart pounded, and hot sweat foamed on her neck and legs. The experience was almost worse than all the times she'd bucked me off because my terror lasted not for seconds but for minutes, *long* minutes. Either I was undeservedly lucky, or I had a powerful guardian angel who intervened to protect me. After giving myself several minutes to recover, I mounted my lathered horse and walked her slowly the rest of the way home.

I learned my lesson and never again let Pepper run with me on her bare back, but she managed one last runaway that summer. Saddled up, we raced an imaginary competitor the length of the airstrip toward the canyon drop-off where Dad's plane would rise into the air. She'd always been willing to turn here, but this time she sprinted toward the edge, resisting my tugging reins.

When she finally relented, she had too much momentum to stop, so over the edge she went, loping down the steep hillside dotted with stiff clumps of woody bitterbrush that stood taller than a horse. She extended her rear legs beneath her and slid on them down the sandy slope, then pushed off in another leap while twisting to dodge the bush ahead. It was a terrifying ride. With each downward stride, I bounced to one side of the saddle and then the other while gripping the horn to pull myself back on as Pepper alternately slid and zigzagged between the clumps.

After that heart-stopping ordeal, she turned across the hillside and halted just after I'd bounced to the right side, which left me hanging down on her right side, my left foot hooked over the saddle, and my left hand clutching the horn. Awkwardly clinging there, looking at the sky, I realized I couldn't haul myself back into the saddle, so I let go. I landed on my back with a *thump*.

Sprawled on my back under her belly and between her front and back legs, I begged. "Whoa, Pepper, whoa! Don't move. Wait till I get out. Whoa, girl!"

She stood there trembling, her sides heaving. If she had moved in any direction, she would have stepped on me. But she turned her head and looked at me with one eye, probably wondering, *What are you doing under there?* She stood perfectly still as if to show she didn't want to hurt me. She'd simply wanted to run, and while running, she lost all concern for safety—hers and mine.

When Pepper wasn't racing the wind, she was gentle and tolerated me. I could pass under her belly or stand on her bare back, balancing with my arms outstretched while she stood still. She let me spend hours trying to swing onto her back from the ground. We began on a hillside as I stood on her uphill side and swung my leg over her body to lever myself up. Mastering that bareback mount took three years of practicing in the pasture when Pepper wasn't saddled for work. She didn't like it, but she remained patient as I clambered onto her back. By the age of thirteen, with longer legs and a stronger spring, I could stand beside her on flat ground and swing myself up to sit on her back in one smooth move, just like my favorite movie cowboy, Audie Murphy, did all the time.

❖

Every year, we went to the Okanogan County Fair during the first weekend in September. Billy and I had exhibited garden produce and then moved up to chickens, ducks, and sheep, but I'd seen horses being shown, too, and I wanted to show Pepper. In 1957, I begged and wheedled Mom and Dad to help me take Pepper to the fair, and when they agreed, I knew it was no small gesture. Before he could start his workday on the ranch, Dad had to haul Pepper fifteen miles to the fairgrounds, where she'd be lodged in a stall for three nights. He also had to drop me off each morning and then pick me up at the end of his day's work. Mom had to borrow Paul Stout's horse again so she could do the sheepherding while I hung around the fair all day feeding, watering, grooming, and exercising Pepper and keeping her stall spotless. I didn't take their efforts for granted and dedicated myself to winning a blue ribbon.

The horse judging was on Friday, and when Pepper was to be judged for conformation, I led her around the judge in a circle along with five other mares and their owners, all the while copying what the other horse owners did. As the judge directed, I walked Pepper away from him and back toward him, then trotted her away and back. He jotted notes, then lined us up and called out the awards. All entries were given blue, red, or white ribbons based on merit. He awarded Pepper a red second-place ribbon, and I felt my beautiful half-Arabian mare had been slighted.

The judge came by to explain his scoring. I didn't understand the language of a horse's conformation. Something about "short in the croup" was all I remembered.

Though I was untutored in the details of what made one horse more valuable than another, I knew what I liked, and when three Arabian stallions were brought out for judging, I fell in love. They were the most beautiful creatures I'd ever seen.

The most beautiful of the three was the fiery black one named Zay Mir. He snorted and cavorted when he was supposed to trot for the judge. I could have easily been convinced the horse had danced right out of the pages of *The Black Stallion* books I always begged for at Christmas and then devoured when they materialized. I couldn't take my eyes off him as he tossed his delicate head, whipping his thick mane above his arched neck. He pranced proudly, and his body floated as gracefully as his high-arched tail. I'd gotten myself so wound up with admiration for the spectacular animal that when he took the blue ribbon, it felt like my victory too.

When Dad came to pick me up, I was jumping with excitement. "Dad! Dad! You've got to see this one black stallion! He won a blue ribbon, and he's just gorgeous!" I grabbed Dad's hand and pulled him down the barn aisle to the stall where Zay Mir stood.

Dad said, "Yep, he *is* a nice one." The next thing I knew, the owner was bringing out the black wonder so Dad could see him in action.

After that, Dad and the stallion's owner fell into conversation. I didn't hear what they discussed, but when the fair ended on Sunday, Pepper didn't come home with us. We loaded her in our pickup, hauled her a few miles north, and unloaded her to the welcoming screams of the black stallion. She stayed there a week, and then the stallion's owner called to say Pepper was pregnant.

After paying the stallion's owner fifty dollars, Dad brought Pepper home to us. She went back to work on the ranch, and as far as I could tell, nothing about her had changed. She was still both as tolerant and spirited as ever. I calculated her due date and began what felt like an impossible test of patience—waiting eleven months for the birth of her foal, due the following August.

CHAPTER NINE

At the end of September 1957, Gram Lockwood returned to the ranch. I hadn't seen her in a year and a half, since she'd gone back to Corvallis to help sick relatives. Shortly after her arrival there, she had a heart attack. She'd spent five and a half weeks in the hospital and then rested for another year with help from friends. Now she was back to stay with us through the winter, and the minute she stepped into our house, I threw my arms around her.

A few days after Gram's return, my brother started feeling achy enough to stay home from school. His joints began to hurt, and his temperature rose to 101, so the next day, Dad took him to a doctor, who detected a heart murmur and admitted my brother directly to the hospital. They ran tests, and the resulting news wasn't good. Billy had rheumatic fever.

When Dad came home from the hospital, he sounded very serious. "The doctor said the illness sometimes develops in young people after strep throat infections. It can damage their heart valves."

I'd wished many times for a different brother, but I'd never wished Billy ill. And I didn't understand how something so serious could happen so suddenly and with no warning. Apparently, Billy'd had strep throat for several months, and he'd complained of stomach pains several times, but Mom hadn't taken him to the doctor. That it became an emergency so quickly was what shook me most.

After four days in the hospital, Billy was sent home with a prescription for penicillin and strict instructions for complete bed rest.

Riding the little yellow school bus up and down the Chiliwist as its only passenger was strange and lonely. Even though my brother often teased me or was mean, I missed his company. He was my only sibling, and I admired him for all the things he could do that I couldn't, like drive the rigs, play bugle and cornet, and tie a nonslip knot.

Dad had recently landed an additional two months of profitable flying work. In September, he'd begun spraying apple orchards with a hormone that would keep ripening apples from falling off the trees before they were ready to be picked. With the new income, Dad hired a carpenter and began work to expand the house and add two bedrooms. Finally, a bedroom of my own! For a while, I'd share the room with Gram, but it would be mine. And it would be warm!

As I looked ahead to Christmas, I felt sorry for Billy, who had to stay in bed and miss all the holiday activities. Gram read to him, but he was bored and complained about his food not being cooked the way he preferred. I thought, *Stuck in bed for months—no wonder he's cranky. What can I do to cheer him up?*

Every day when I crossed the creek and climbed the steep path to the sheep shed, I passed a small fir tree about halfway up the hill. The sheep had gnawed off the limbs on the lower half, along with some of its bark, and I wondered how long it could survive like that. One day, I noticed the still-living treetop had formed a perfect Christmas tree about eighteen inches tall, so I decided I'd cut off the top to make Billy a tiny Christmas tree.

On the last day of November, I sawed off the treetop and stood it in a coffee can that I filled with rocks to hold the little trunk upright, then added water to keep it fresh. I asked Mom for the Christmas decorations box and chose the smallest multicolored lights and bulbs and the silvery tinsel to decorate the tree. Finished, I stood back and looked at my holiday creation, so cheery and festive. I couldn't wait to present it to my brother.

When Billy awoke, I carried the tree to his bedside. "Surprise!" I exclaimed.

"Well, what's this?" he said.

"It's your very own Christmas tree!"

"Who made it?"

"*I* did!"

He asked me to place it on the table near his head so he could look at the bright, tiny tree for the whole month of December. Smiling, he said, "It's nice to have my own tree."

Giving him something he could enjoy while bedbound and seeing his smile delighted me. It was reward enough for now, though I hoped he might remember my kindness and bully me less when he got better.

<hr />

As my brother began easing back into normal life, two things about his months of illness stuck out for me: from then on, he insisted on being called Bill, and he refused to do any of the chores that had shifted to Mom and me during his illness. It seemed as if he'd grown up and started taking unfair control of what he would or would not do. That's when an even greater divide emerged between my brother and me. He started spending most of his time helping Dad on the farm, learning to drive and fly. I resented that he was given greater freedoms and fun activities, like building and flying model airplanes, while I was kept busy helping Mom with the animals.

Despite Bill's protests, my parents and his teachers decided he needed to repeat eighth grade. After that, he and I went through junior high, high school, and college one grade level apart instead of two. That threw us into even more direct competition and turned him into even more of a bully. Probably because he thought the grade change made him look dumb, he decided I should be the target of his bitterness.

Seventh grade marked my first year of transferring to the big yellow bus at the grade school in Malott and then riding another nine miles upriver to the Okanogan Junior/Senior High School. I liked my new homeroom teacher and even had a little crush on him. Mr. Levenson taught math, social studies, and English. One of his routines was to have us exchange our math homework, mark someone else's paper as he called out the answers, and then announce the score on the paper we graded. I was used to hearing "one hundred" when Mr. Levenson called my name. One day, I heard "forty-five."

"What?" I blurted. Did Mark make a mistake in his scoring? Or was he making a joke? Wasn't he my friend?

Mr. Levenson looked up from his grade book. Mark repeated the score.

My cheeks flamed. "Let me see that!"

Mark handed back my paper. The sheet had twenty problems on it, and more than half of them were marked with an *X*.

I couldn't believe it. I'd understood the lesson and solved the problems correctly. What on earth was happening?

I bent my head over my homework paper in shame and confusion. Then the answers on the page came into focus. "Wait!" I protested. "These aren't my answers!"

Mr. Levenson asked, "Is that your paper?"

"It's my paper, but these aren't my answers. Someone has changed them!"

He said, "If that's your paper, that's your score. Let's move on now." He called out the next name.

I slumped in my seat. Then I thought back to what had happened on the school bus that morning.

My brother had taunted, "I bet you don't have your homework done."

I had tried to ignore his teasing, but my pride got the best of me, as he knew it would. I pulled out my homework sheet and waved it to show it was filled out.

"Let me check it. It's probably all wrong," Bill said.

He was seated two rows in front of me, and I passed the sheet to him. He faced forward and made a show of looking it over.

"Maybe I won't give it back and you'll get a zero on it." He had everyone's attention now.

"Give it back," I pleaded.

"I think it would be good for you to get a zero on your homework," he said. All the guys around him laughed.

"You give that back to me right now!" My face was hot. Now everyone on the bus was watching.

"Stop this, Bill, or I'll tell the bus driver!"

His friends laughed and hooted, "You'd better give it back, or she'll tell on you!"

"Well, if you insist," he drawled.

Hands passed it back, and I tucked the paper safely into my notebook. I felt the humiliation flushing my neck and face, so I turned to look out the bus window. Beyond the reflection of my angry red face, trees streamed by laden with apples of the same hue.

In class, I looked again at my corrected paper. Every answer marked with an X had been changed. Bill must have quickly erased and changed the answers while he pretended to check my paper. I'd fallen right into his trap. But how could my brother set me up and betray me like that? How could I ever trust him again?

When the bell rang, I marched up to Mr. Levenson to tell him my brother had changed my answers.

"Don't worry," he said. "This one assignment won't count much in the final grade."

I couldn't believe he was going to leave it like that. And to think I'd had a crush on him!

Mr. Levenson was right. I got an A for the class, but that low score in the grade book stood out from the others, like the guilty traitor in a lineup, and I felt branded by the undeserved blemish. Worst of all, my own brother had embarrassed me in front of the other kids, first on the bus and again in my classroom. I dreamed of taking revenge on him, but I knew it would trigger greater retribution. I'd lost my ability to count on him that day. More than ever, I felt that I was on my own.

CHAPTER TEN

As the summer of 1958 began, Pepper's rounding belly made clear she was pregnant. We didn't know much about the care of pregnant mares or that we shouldn't have worked her as hard as we did. Through the spring and early summer, Pepper trudged up the hill behind the sheep each day carrying Mom or me and then moved around the grazing sheep as we directed her. She grabbed hungrily at the bunchgrass whenever we stopped and let her lower her head to eat. She spent the night in the creek pasture above the house, where the moist grass was greener but, as I later learned, not as nourishing as the native bunchgrass on the dry upper slopes.

Our good friends William and Eleanor Harms, who sold Mom their peaches, apricots, and pears, offered to lend us their son's unneeded horse and saddle to relieve Pepper from sheepherding as her time drew near. On a day in mid-July, Mom drove me to their home in the Okanogan Valley. We thanked them, and then I mounted Blaze for the ride home. The young red-brown gelding with black mane and tail, a color called a bay, was pastured with Pepper.

In our side yard, between the horse pasture and the creek, we had a rabbit pen. Its fencing enclosed a large rectangle of tall, green grass for the bunnies to nibble. I knew the rabbits were being raised for sale or eating, so I didn't get too attached to them.

One bright August morning, I went out to feed the rabbits and found Pepper standing in the rabbit pen, hungrily munching the grass. Finding her there was surprising, and even more amazing was the baby deer beside her. No, wait . . . not a deer—a new foal on long, wobbly legs! Thunderstruck, I ran back into the house. "Mom! Mom! Pepper's had her baby and she's in the rabbit pen!"

Mom hurried out to see the new foal, calling as she ran, "Get some grain for Pepper. She'll need it to make milk for her baby."

I brought Pepper some grain in a pan. She gobbled it ravenously, so I ran off and came back with more. Only then did we see how thin she was. We hadn't noticed before because her expanding belly had made her appear fat. Now her belly was thin, and her ribs showed.

Then I saw where the rabbit pen fence was crumpled between two posts. "Mom, look at the fence," I said, pointing.

"That must be how she got into the pen," Mom said. Lifting herself over a four-foot fence wasn't something Pepper would ordinarily do, at least not for greener grass. Suddenly, Pepper flattened her ears and charged at the curious gelding hanging around on the other side of the fence.

"Look, Mom, she's protecting her foal from the other horse."

"That explains it," Mom said. "When she went into labor, her instinct told her to get away from the gelding to a safer place."

I always knew Dad was Pepper's owner, but he'd agreed to my plea for her firstborn foal to be mine in exchange for my help with the sheep. I was twelve years old, and this delightful little filly was my very own. I intended to raise her from birth as my friend, and she'd be the fulfillment of my new dream to raise spirited Arabian horses like her father, Zay Mir. I named her Lucky Babe and sent in the paperwork to register her as three-quarters Arabian.

At first, Lucky was afraid of me and stayed on the far side of her mother to avoid me. But I was determined to make her understand I could be trusted. When she was nursing, I sneaked up from behind and caught her in my arms. She tried to escape at first, but I held her and spoke gently until she calmed and let me run my hands over her coat. After a week of my daily catching and petting, she let me approach without trying to run away. After two weeks, she came to me and let me groom her with a soft brush. When she sprawled on her side to sleep in the sun, I sat beside her to stroke her neck and brush away the flies that tried to bite and made her shudder. I marveled at the exquisite softness of her tan coat and fluffed her short black mane; it felt as soft and fine as a human baby's hair. She was colored like a buckskin horse with a dun coat and a black stripe running down her back between her black mane and tail.

When Lucky was three days old, Mom took a photo of us. In it, Lucky stands next to Pepper, the two of them broadside to the camera. My hand is on Pepper's neck as she nuzzles her foal's forehead. We're squeezed into the frame, and the crown of my straw Stetson, the tip of Pepper's ears, part of her tail, and all our feet are cut off. Lucky and I both have long legs, out of proportion to our short, slender torsos. Her ribs show, and mine would have if not for the camouflaging stripes on my knit shirt. My tight shirt reveals the beginnings of breasts; I'd soon need a bra. My worn jeans hang down my beanpole legs, stretch out at the faded knees, and end well above my ankles, where the sides of my cowboy boots rise. This photo of two scrawny young things will always remind me of the pride I felt for Pepper and her foal at the remarkable beginning of my long and wonderful friendship with Lucky.

Lucky's buckskin coat didn't last. Within a month, she shed her birth coat and revealed her permanent coat of mahogany bay, a beautiful color blending her sire's black and

Pepper's chestnut red. Her mane and the hair on her legs grew out pure black, with white socks on both rear legs.

Before Lucky was born, I plotted to join 4-H so I could make raising her my 4-H project. Two years before, my brother had joined the all-boys Malott Bearcats 4-H Club. When Mom took Bill to the monthly meetings, I tagged along because I was too young to stay home by myself. Bill always insisted on "no girls allowed" and made me leave the room when the meeting started. I left but often eavesdropped on the meetings, especially if one of the boys was giving a demonstration of what he'd learned in his project. I envied the boys' animal projects, which culminated with fitting and showing their prize sheep or fat steers at the Okanogan County Fair in early September, and I wanted nothing more than to learn to properly prepare and show my young horse at the fair.

In the spring of 1958, I began asking Mom, "Why can't I be in 4-H too?"

She said another set of monthly meetings would be hard to fit into her day, but she took me to a meeting of the girls' 4-H Club in Malott anyway. At the meeting, the girls talked about sewing, cooking, and raising garden produce for the fair. This was definitely not the club for me. I wanted to do animal projects. I even wanted to become a veterinarian someday. Above all, I wanted to learn all there was to know about horses—conformation, diet, training, and showing.

I asked to join the boys club. "No girls allowed!" Bill repeated.

The club parents all had sons. None had daughters of our age, let alone a girl who wanted to do livestock projects. Mom was assistant leader of the Bearcats that year, and I urged her, "Mom, Jim Hamilton is the leader. Would you please ask him if there's any rule against girls joining?"

She did, and at the next monthly meeting in June, Jim reported, "I've checked with the 4-H organization. There's no rule against admitting girls."

At their July meeting, the boys took up the topic. Someone said, "I move that we admit Linda to the club."

The president said, "The motion is open for discussion."

I listened, red-faced from being the object of discussion.

My brother said, "It's an all-boys club now, and making an exception for Linda could start a new trend."

Someone said, "I don't see why we should mind, provided she does animal projects."

The boy serving as recorder said, "Maybe she'd be willing to keep the meeting minutes so the rest of us wouldn't have to."

I nodded and heard a murmur of agreement.

The president said, "All in favor say 'Aye.'" There was a chorus of "aye" votes.

Next, he said, "All opposed say 'No.'" No one spoke, but everyone looked at Bill.

"My vote is 'abstain,'" Bill said.

Someone asked, "What does that mean?"

"That means I don't vote either for or against admitting her," he said.

"Okay," the president said. "The ayes have it."

Despite my own brother's lack of support, I was in!

Learning to raise Lucky properly would be my 4-H project. During the first year, I researched the proper diet to feed her, wrote up my results, and reported them at a club meeting. For my second year's project, I demonstrated to the Bearcats that I'd learned to wash, trim, and polish Lucky for the show ring.

My hard work and study paid off. When Lucky was one year old, she earned a blue ribbon at the fair. I'd done all the hard work, and as I tied the blue ribbon on her halter, I felt like a proud parent.

In my mind, something happened to me that year. With my own horse, membership in a previously all-boys club, and a blue ribbon in the most important competition of my life, I no longer felt like a child.

CHAPTER ELEVEN

In June 1959, another of my long days as a shepherd was ending. I didn't have a wristwatch, so I glanced west to gauge the time remaining before the sun sank behind the mountains. Only another hour of sunshine. Time to go home.

All day I'd been waiting and watching while our flock grazed over the big field and Pepper munched grass around me. I'd perched on a large rock and read *Little Women*. Hanging out with my brother was always on his terms, so I avoided him and ended up spending quite a lot of time alone.

I was glad for the peaceful day, the meadowlarks singing from fence to fence, the low clumps of yellow sunflowers spreading through the native bunchgrass, the wide sky edged with mountains, and the home awaiting me by the creek below. I wasn't glad to be spending every summer day up here with no one to share the joy of it. I left my rock with a sigh, mounted Pepper, and urged her toward the scattered ewes that lingered to grab a few last bites.

I sang a tune they recognized: "*Let's go ho-ome, sheepies! Let's go ho-ome!*" They lifted their heads and called to their lambs, then headed down the slope to catch up with the others. Spot and Gypsy ran ahead to nip at their heels as I urged Pepper to trot after the stragglers.

Just then, my eyes were drawn to a swirl of dust rising from the lower flat. I couldn't see the cause of the disturbance, but I could hear panicked bleating, and my heart began to thunder in my chest. I pressed Pepper from her slow jog to a faster trot, afraid to go too fast because of the badger holes she might step into and fall. Where the ground leveled a bit and the holes were more visible, I urged her into a careful gallop, all the while shouting, "Hey, what's going on down there? I'm coming!"

When we crested the lower hills and I could see the flat field below, I saw the flock milling in a circle. In the center of their commotion was one still white form. My heart sank. I knew what had happened, and it had happened on my watch.

I looked for the coyotes, but they had already disappeared into the hillside sagebrush. I rode up to the fallen ewe, sprawled on her belly in the spot where her legs had given out as she had run for her poor little vulnerable life. She was dead, probably from a slash to her jugular. I was sickened that I hadn't arrived in time to save her from the terrifying slaughter.

The stragglers caught up to the rest of the flock, and the ewes calmed down when they had their rider and dogs to protect and guide them to the edge of the flat and down the hill to their barnyard sanctuary. The coyotes never bothered them there, and I felt less agonized knowing that for tonight at least, these sheep would be safe.

That evening at dinner, I told my parents, Gram, and Bill about the attack. "I couldn't get down there in time," I lamented. "The coyotes were gone by the time I got there, and the ewe was dead."

"Pretty bold, sneaking up like that when you were just up the hill out of sight," Dad said. "Guess that makes about a half dozen we've lost to the coyotes so far."

"I saw that killer coyote up on the hill last fall, but I didn't have a gun to shoot at him," Mom said.

Dad shook his head. "Last winter, I asked the game warden what he could do about it."

"Much talk and nothing done," Gram said.

"Well, I think it's time to call Boyd," Dad said.

Boyd Hilderbrand specialized in hunting and trapping predators like coyotes. The state no longer offered bounties on coyotes, but farmers paid Boyd when they lost livestock.

He came to examine the ground around the dead ewe and quickly identified the unique tracks of the largest coyote in the pack. Boyd named him "Three Toes" because the tracks revealed a missing toe on one of his front feet.

Boyd's theory that the coyote leader had lost his toe in a trap was soon borne out. When Boyd set steel traps around a bait of meat, Three Toes would approach the area, sniff out the hidden traps, and scratch dirt onto the traps to spring them. He was a clever one, and Boyd never did trap or kill him.

—◆—

One sunny morning in July, the flock had reached the hillside pasture and spread out to graze. The hungry ewes and lambs called to one another as they rushed across the hillside to their next bites of brush, grass, lupines, and sunflowers. As I walked Pepper up the nearby road, she stepped over a series of S curves etched into the puffy road dust that showed where a snake had bellied its way across. I could tell from the clarity of the undisturbed tracks that they had probably been made within the hour.

From across the hillside, Spot barked her furious alarm. *Snake!* I hurried Pepper toward the urgent barking. The air filled with a high-pitched buzzing as Spot's black-and-white form lunged in and out of a woody bush. In the bush was the coiled body of a big rattlesnake, probably well over two feet long, its head repeatedly striking at Spot in defense against her frenzied attack.

"Spot! *No!* Come here!" I screamed.

Spot's next bark was a pained *Yip!* as she jerked back with the snake's head attached to her face. Then the snake fell away and coiled its extended body, ready to strike again. Oh, my precious Spot! The snake had just injected its venom into her muzzle! I leaped off my horse and grabbed Spot's collar to pull her away and prevent her from starting another attack on the snake.

Only thirteen, I wasn't yet allowed to carry a saddle gun, so I tied Pepper to a nearby pine tree and cracked off a thick branch to jab at the snake in the bush. It struck at the stick, but its fangs glanced off. Then it scrambled away from its sheltering bush, and I sprinted after it, grateful for the protection of my thick leather cowboy boots but wishing the stick were longer. Whacking at the slithering snake, I finally broke its back, so it lost coordination and flailed helplessly. Then I bashed its flailing head until the creature stopped writhing.

When I was sure the snake was dead, I turned to where Spot stood a few feet away and knelt to cradle her head in my hands. On her muzzle, between her nose and left eye, were two round red punctures. She wagged and whimpered as I stroked her head. *Now what?* I couldn't leave the sheep to invade our wheat crop and destroy it, and they wouldn't willingly go back to the barnyard until they had a chance to fill their empty stomachs. But what would happen if I didn't get Spot help immediately? I chose to let the sheep eat for a short time. I made Spot lie in the shade, and I offered her canteen water poured into my cupped hand. She lapped gratefully.

Two hours later, I decided Spot shouldn't wait any longer. Pepper, Gypsy, and I rounded up the sheep before they were done grazing and pushed them down the hillside road toward home. Spot followed along, but her tail drooped, her muzzle was swollen, her tongue lolled out, and she panted. I didn't know much about rattlesnake bites, and I started thinking the venom was working its way into her body and would soon kill her.

With the sheep locked in the barnyard, I rode Pepper to the creek. Spot gulped the cool water, dragged her belly through it, and submerged herself in a deep spot, where she stayed until her panting slowed. I waited with her for ten minutes, and then she dripped slowly up the lane to the house and disappeared into the dark crawl space where the ground was cool.

I rushed into the house, calling, "Mom! Spot got bit on the nose by a big rattler and her face is swelling up!"

"Where is she?" Mom asked.

"She's lying under the house now. How can we help her?"

"I don't know," Mom said.

"Then we've got to call the vet. We can't let her die!"

Mom grabbed the phone and called our veterinarian, then held the receiver so I could listen. He said not to bring Spot in because there wasn't much he could do. "Better to just keep her cool and quiet with plenty of water to drink."

"What about anti-venom shots?" Mom asked.

"We don't use those for dogs because the supply is limited and expensive."

"Ask him what will happen to her," I said, my voice trembling.

The vet heard me and said, "Her head and neck will swell up from the bite on her nose, but if it doesn't kill her in the next day or so, eventually the swelling will go down and she'll be okay."

"What are her chances?" I asked.

"Hard to know. About fifty-fifty, I'd say."

He had no further advice, and Mom hung up.

We could only wait and hope Spot could fight the venom. My parents, both raised on farms, knew the kind of patience required when life and death were in the balance, but it was a new lesson for me. That night, I thought about how my poor dog must be suffering under the house and how much I'd miss caressing her fluffy ears if she died. I didn't know if I believed in God, but I pleaded with him anyway. "Please let Spot live."

The next morning, Spot didn't come out when I called, and I feared the worst. I crawled under the house and found her in one of the cool depressions she'd dug long ago to help her cope with hot days. But now the heat was inside her. I dragged in her water and food bowls and set them beside her, but she only thumped her tail, unable to lift her swollen, heavy head.

"I'm sorry, girl," I said as I stroked her back. "You're so brave. Don't die on me. You're the *best* sheepdog. Please, Spot, you *have* to get well."

An hour later, new hope showed up in the form of Art Hilderbrand. He had inherited this ranch and farmed it until he got too old to manage it alone. After he sold the place, Art was hired to help us get started. I suspected Art, a bachelor, was also coming back for the hot meals and Mom's homemade bread. When he drove up our lane, I ran to meet his car. "Art, you should see Spot!" I said breathlessly. "She got bit by a rattler, and it was a big one! Her head swelled up like a basketball!"

"Where is she?"

"Under the house. She won't come out and can't eat or drink anything. Do you think she's going to die?"

"Well, now, I've had dogs get bit before, and they didn't die, but they get fevered, and you need to keep her cool. She has all that hair, and she'll get dehydrated panting to cool off. You get some gunnysacks and soak them in the creek. We'll wrap them around her neck to help her cool down."

I ran to get the empty burlap feed sacks in the chicken house. Art helped me wet them in the creek, and we carried them, heavy and dripping, to the house. I called Spot to come until she staggered out to me. We wrapped a burlap sack around her neck, and Art used baling twine to hold it in place.

Spot looked funny and sad but also cooler. She wobbled back into the dimness under the house, and I crawled in and covered her with another wet sack.

"You keep soaking those gunnysacks with fresh, cold water," Art advised. "Her tongue and neck are so swollen that she won't be able to eat or drink now, but in a few days when the swelling starts to go down a bit, you give her some canned milk to drink. That will get some nutrition in her."

Art seemed to know a lot, so I asked, "Do you think she'll make it?"

Smiling, he said, "If she's strong enough, she'll pull through in time. And if she survives it the first time, she'll never die from a snakebite. The second time will be easier; she'll only swell up half as much."

What a relief to have people like Art around. Sometimes my fear came from simply not knowing what was going on. Now that Art had given me direction, I was relieved that I'd taken action to ease my dog's suffering and maybe even save her life.

Three days later, Spot was still under the house. Each morning I'd crawled in to place fresh water beside her and rewet the gunnysacks, but she hadn't tried the PET Milk I'd offered. On the third evening, when I called her to come, she wobbled out on trembling legs, lowered her head stiffly to the dog bowl, and tried to lap the evaporated milk with her swollen tongue.

"Mom, come look! She's taking the milk!"

Mom came out with a dish towel over her shoulder, and we both watched as Spot smeared at the milk with her awkward tongue, spilled some and swallowed some, and worked at it until the bowl was emptied. Mom and I clapped our hands for Spot's victory, and I squealed, "Hooray! Good girl!"

Mom smiled. "Looks like she's going to make it." Then she turned and headed back to the kitchen.

Spot lapped more milk each day, and the swelling around her neck began to go down. A week later, she started to eat moistened dog chow and slowly recovered her energy. It had been a touch-and-go situation, and throughout that week, I'd prayed for Spot to make it. My prayers and her will to live were rewarded, and I started to believe more that a presence was watching over me.

Back in the fields with the sheep, Spot still attacked any snakes she found. Her canine instincts were stronger than her sense of caution, but now she barked and whimpered when she engaged in a face-off with a rattler. Two years later she was struck again on the muzzle, but that time, as Art had predicted, she swelled up only half as much and got over it within a few days. And her immunity kept building; the third time she was struck, the snake's venom had little effect.

Rattlesnakes are common in the arid lands of north central Washington, and their numbers increased on our high desert ranch because we grew wheat. Field mice fattened on the grain and multiplied rapidly; rattlers hunted the mice and found safe lodging in the rock piles. I wore cowboy boots to keep my feet in the stirrups during hard riding and for protection from snakes when I was on the ground. I knew I was likely to get bit by a rattlesnake only if I was attacking it. Dad had explained that rattlesnakes prey on mice and fear people. When rattlers sense danger, they slither away to gain cover or stay perfectly still to avoid discovery, but if the danger comes too near, the snake coils up and buzzes its warning. Dad expected me to kill rattlers to reduce their numbers, as all ranchers did in those days.

I sometimes heard a quiet stirring as I rode, like the sound of papers rustling or seeds shifting in dried weed pods moved by a breeze. I froze to listen, then jumped off my horse to locate the snake and kill it with whatever I could find—a stick or a hefty rock—anything that would do the job without having to get too close.

My father had given me a snakebite kit supplied by the feed store in town. "Always carry it with you when riding alone on the ranch," he said. I pocketed the kit every time I donned my worn black cowboy boots and rumpled Stetson and left the house to bring my horse from the pasture and saddle up. I hoped I'd never have to use the kit, but I needed to know how just in case.

Sometimes, when the sheep were grazing and I hadn't brought a book, I'd dig the snakebite kit out of my pocket to review the instructions. The kit's rose-colored rubber tube had a corrugated surface and rounded ends, and it was about the size of a man's thumb. The tube came apart in the center, and each end could be used as a suction cup to draw out the blood and venom. I practiced squeezing one cup and placing it against my arm. It adhered, and when I released the suction, the cup left a round reddish mark on my skin.

From the other cup, I extracted a folded white paper rolled around a long, braided string meant to serve as a tourniquet. I also took out the tiny razor that had a sharp blade on one end and a flat handle on the other. I unfolded the paper and read the steps: tie the tourniquet on the arm or leg well above the bite, cut an *X* with the knife just above the bite, and suck out the venom with the suction cups. Little diagrams depicted these actions.

On a finger bite, the cup wouldn't attach, so I knew in that instance I'd have to suck with my mouth and spit out the blood and venom. I'd been told this, and later I saw it done by John Wayne in *True Grit*. I believed that with luck or protection from that higher power, I'd never have to do any of it.

Dad had also explained that if I should be bitten, I'd need to get to a hospital for anti-venom, administered intravenously. He'd said it was best to keep calm to slow the movement of the venom in the bloodstream, but I never understood how I was supposed to do that when my heart would be booming in my chest from pain and terror. If I shouted for help, no one would hear me. I'd have to open the snakebite kit and use it on myself. Then Pepper would carry me a mile back down the steep and winding dirt road to our house and phone, and Mom would drive me in our truck for twelve miles to the nearest hospital in Brewster—a long, slow journey.

I couldn't decide whether carrying that snakebite kit made me feel safer or just served as a frightening reminder—probably both.

We all had snake stories. Mom once rode down the hill on top of a load of wheat hay while Bill and I rode in the cab with Dad. When the truck stopped at the barnyard gate, she heard a rattler buzzing from somewhere in the hay. She yelled, "There's a snake up here!" as she grabbed a pitchfork, spotted the snake coiling up not six feet from where she'd sat, and used the fork to pitch the snake to the ground, where Dad chopped off its head with a shovel. She "got the shakes" afterward, she said, realizing she'd ridden all the way down the hill next to a rattlesnake.

Late one evening in our third summer, we'd stacked the last truckload of wheat bales in the barn. With everyone tuckered out and darkness falling, Dad said to Bill and me, "Let's get one more pickup load while Mom starts dinner, and then we'll quit for the day." He drove back up the road and pulled the flatbed pickup into the wheat field, locating the hay bales in the headlights. Bill and I, at ages twelve and ten, were dead tired and slow to get out. "Let's go!" Dad said as he opened his door and stepped out toward the nearest bale.

To his right, a snake started to buzz. Jumping backward, Dad heard a second rattler buzz behind him and a third on the other side. He leaped for the open door, yelling, "Get back in the pickup!" Fortunately, my brother and I hadn't gotten out yet. Dad hopped back in with us and fingered his holstered pistol on the dashboard. "Yipe!" he said. "I guess we're not getting any more hay tonight!" That was the fastest I ever saw my father move. It was the only time he didn't kill a snake he encountered.

I never lost my fear of rattlesnakes. For the rest of my ranching days, my whole body went on instant alert when I heard their warning sound, every nerve on edge, every hair on end. The sound of the rattle jolted me into action to kill the snake. Today my reaction to meeting a snake in the wild would be different. I'd back away and leave it alone, knowing it's part of the natural balance of snakes and mice.

While I grew confident in what to expect from animals, my mother's emotional inconsistency taught me that people were more complex. In the summer of 1959, my family experienced another scene that told me we were headed for a new round of upheaval.

One night, as we took our first bites of dinner, Mom started snapping at Dad. "I just don't see why I never have money for nice clothes, Al. You just sold the wheat crop and had a good spray season. But when the money comes in, you just buy more planes, and I never see any of it."

Dad said, "I'm plowing it back so we'll have more income in the future, Zelma."

"You don't even know how to run a business. We're always running up debt, even for the food we eat." Her voice got louder.

"Now, calm down, Zelma, and let us eat our dinner."

"I don't want to calm down, and I'm tired of not having a say around here. You don't make good business decisions, and you don't discuss them with me."

Dad's voice grew firmer. "Let's talk about this later. You need to stop this. You're upsetting the kids."

Bill leaned back in his chair and said, "Yeah, Mom."

"No, I'm going to have my say for once!" Mom screeched.

"Dammit!" Bill said, scraping back his chair. He stomped to his bedroom and slammed the door.

I stared at the uneaten food on Bill's plate while trying to chew my last bite, but I couldn't swallow it past the lump in my throat. I didn't know if Mom's complaints were unreasonable or fair, but my parents didn't usually discuss such things in front of Bill and me.

"Zelma, you're not making sense. Come into the bedroom with me and let the kids eat their dinner."

"No! I'm tired of not having any say around here," Mom shouted. "I'm just as smart or smarter than you are, and you should include me in your decisions."

I shrank back against the wall and tried to be invisible.

"If you won't let me eat dinner, I'm going to bed. I have to get up at daylight to fly."

"Oh, yes, your needs are always more important than mine."

Dad rose, and Mom did too. That's when I escaped around them, fled to my bedroom, and flung myself onto my bed. Their angry words escalated into a shouting match, and I pulled my pillow around my head, trying to muffle the sounds of my troubled family.

Finally, the noise stopped. Dad stayed in the bedroom, but Mom went to the kitchen and finished her dinner. The rest of us went to bed hungry.

The next morning, Dad was gone, and Mom served breakfast as usual to Bill and me. She didn't say a word about what had happened the night before, and neither did we.

That night, when Dad came home for dinner, it repeated again as if on a loop. After two nights of this, Dad stayed away. A week later, I was with him at the Okanogan airport, tagging along as he tied down one spray plane and checked on another parked in a hangar. There was a single bed against the inside wall.

"Is that your bed?" I asked.

"Yes," he said. "That's where I sleep when I need to fly the next morning." I knew it was also where he slept when he didn't want to come home for dinner with Mom. I missed him at home, but I was glad he'd found a place where he could get the rest he needed to be safe in the air.

For the next two months, Dad worked at the airport, ate dinner in restaurants, and avoided Mom. At home, dinners were peaceful as long as my parents weren't both there. In November, Dad came home to stay for the winter. For no reason I could see, Mom stopped attacking him, but many nights passed before I trusted that the calm was something I could count on. The winter and spring of 1960 went by without any major upsets from Mom, and that let me keep my attention where I liked it: at school as much as necessary and out with Lucky.

———◆◆———

The next summer, my goal was to train Lucky to ride. To familiarize her with wearing a saddle, I first let her sniff it so she could breathe the smell of Pepper's sweaty back. For the next three days, I strapped the saddle on her and had her wear it as she grazed in the pasture. She showed no reaction even when the stirrups flapped against her sides as she trotted. She was ready for a rider, and I wanted to be the one, but I worried about what Lucky might do when I got on her back. I thought she might buck like Pepper. I asked Dad, "Will you be there the first time I ride her?"

"Sure, I'll be there for you, Cookie," he said.

On the big day in late June, Mom, Bill, and Gram came out to watch. I put a bitless bridle, called a hackamore, on Lucky's head and asked Dad to hold the rope I looped around her neck. Then I asked Bill, "Would you give me a leg up?" When he clasped his hands together, I stepped on them and swung my other leg over Lucky's bare back.

When my weight settled onto her back, she spread her legs

to keep her balance. She pointed her ears back at me once or twice and shifted uneasily beneath me, then she bent her head around and sniffed my leg. "Yes, Babe, it's me," I assured her.

Dad led her around for five minutes, and she didn't try to buck or act up, so he took off the rope and left Lucky under my control. This was it. Just me and my horse. I urged with my voice and legs to make her go forward, but she stood without moving.

I thought a moment then pointed to Pepper, who was grazing nearby. I said, "Bill, would you get Pepper and lead her toward the house?"

"Okay," he said. When he did, Lucky started to follow her mother.

As Lucky walked up the lane, I stopped and started her by tightening the reins to apply pressure on her nose while saying, "Whoa, Lucky." Then I let her start after Pepper again by loosening the reins, nudging her with my heels, and saying, "C'mon, let's go." After several trips up and down the lane, I could easily start her, stop her, and turn her left or right. She was a quick learner.

Still apprehensive, I gave her one last test. On the final trip up the lane, I urged Lucky to speed up, and she shifted willingly to a trot. What a relief that she didn't buck. And how delightful to trot on my own horse for the first time!

Dad, Mom, and Gram stood by the chicken house watching my maiden voyage with Lucky, so I trotted her over to them, stopped there, pivoted my leg over her rump, and slipped to the ground. She stood quietly, and when I took the hackamore off and freed her, she stayed to be scratched between the ears.

Dad said, "It takes a lot of nerve to crawl up on a horse the first time like that, doesn't it, Cookie?"

"It sure does!" I responded, grinning widely. But my grin masked how scared I'd been. I'd gripped Lucky's bare sides so tightly with my legs that my muscles ached.

Mom had been filming the whole event with the movie camera. "I was hoping to catch some action," she joked. I was grateful to hear Mom joke and even more grateful my horse hadn't provided anything exciting to film. All my time building trust with Lucky had paid off.

I began riding Lucky while herding sheep, and she was so cooperative that she made the chore fun. Coming home, she pranced eagerly and pressed to run, so I let her gallop fast where the terrain was level, and then we slowed to a lope through the sloped bunchgrass to the first flat. Galloping downhill in rough terrain would have been dangerous with most horses, but Lucky already seemed like a mature, wise animal since she picked her way carefully and stopped whenever I asked.

With Pepper no longer bucking and Lucky already a calm, trustworthy companion, I felt secure and confident whenever I was on a horse's back. Unfortunately, my judgment sometimes got both horse and rider in trouble.

CHAPTER TWELVE

S ky Ranch Aviation was the name of my father's flying busi-ness, and over the years, we began to call our farm the Sky Ranch. It deserved that name for its wide-open vistas, and its highest corner reached the summit of Dent Mountain with an elevation of 3,110 feet.

While I herded the sheep in the wheat fields five hundred feet below, I often gazed up at the near-vertical face of Dent Mountain, its crumbling granite making it useless for farming or grazing but not for the native creatures. A pair of golden eagles raised nestlings in a pile of brown sticks on a ledge halfway up the sheer gray cliff. As I relaxed in the saddle of my grazing horse, the young eaglets' demanding chatter alerted me to look up and see one of their parents winging in with food in its talons. For me, sights like this were among the greatest joys of ranch life.

Of course wild creatures are unpredictable, and on one hot July day in 1960, I learned that sometimes the smartest decision is to trust what one animal tries to tell me about another.

It was past noon when I turned Pepper off the county road to enter the narrow canyon that snaked around the eastern base of Dent Mountain. After five years of riding the ranch, this dark canyon was the only part of our acreage I hadn't explored. Now I wanted to claim it as part of my dominion.

A few steps into the canyon, Pepper halted and whirled back toward the road, but I forced her to turn around, keeping her head pointed to the trail and pressing her forward with my legs. I couldn't understand why she was resisting me. She wasn't usually skittish and would go wherever I asked, but today she refused to take the trail the cows used to traverse the narrow, steeply walled canyon.

I urged Pepper forward as the cattle trail dove under a thicket of young pines. Tree limbs closed over the path as if to block my way. Cows ran low enough to pass under the limbs, but the stiff branches scratched at me and threatened to sweep me out of the saddle. I couldn't control Pepper while bending flat to avoid the branches, but refusing to give up, I slid off to lead her on foot. She planted her front feet and balked, but I insisted, tugging on the reins. As she came along haltingly, the saddle horn scraped through the tree limbs.

I pressed ahead, leading Pepper along the narrow trail as it climbed the outer side of the canyon to skirt a jumble of jagged boulders that had fallen from the mountain's eroding granite face. The roller coaster–like path climbed up and down over embedded rocks and around big old ponderosa pine trees, and the farther into the canyon we went, the more Pepper pulled back on the reins.

As we advanced, the trees thinned and I could see both sides of the canyon, which was about two hundred feet wide. To my right, the mountain's sheer face jutted up seven hundred feet above the jumbled rocks. To my left, the canyon slope, dotted with bitterbrush and bunchgrass, rose to intersect the level plain of our largest wheat field.

I remounted Pepper and pressed her forward on the trail. When we came to a sunlit clearing where the hot midday air vibrated with the sawing of grasshopper wings as they crackled from perch to perch, Pepper trembled, turning her ears to test in all directions as she stepped cautiously, taking in and blowing out big breaths of air. There was no doubt something was spooking her, and the more she fretted, the more unsettled I felt. The atmosphere started feeling downright eerie, and I wondered if I'd gotten us into a bad situation.

We kept stalking down the cattle trail, but before we reached the boundary fence marking the southern edge of our property, I decided to stop fighting Pepper. As soon as she understood I was no longer pushing her forward, she wheeled around and broke into an urgent trot. Back at the clearing, the air seemed to vibrate with the presence of something other than grasshoppers, and I kept looking over my shoulder.

At the same moment, Pepper and I both spotted the diagonal hillside trail cattle and deer used to climb out of the canyon to the wheat field above, and Pepper leaped up the steep, narrow path as I gripped her thick mane with both hands to stay with her. I didn't know what she was afraid of, but now I was scared too. Between spooky thick pines, the canyon's throbbing eeriness, and Pepper's increasing agitation, I wanted away from there as much as she did.

That night at the supper table, I said, "I rode Pepper down the Cougar Canyon trail today, but she didn't want to go in there."

"You did *what*?" Dad dropped his fork, which clanked against his plate. "You made the horse go in?"

"Yeah, she kind of fought me. She didn't want to go, and then she acted pretty spooked when we got into the canyon."

"Don't you know that you shouldn't go in there alone? The horse knew better. You shouldn't have made her go against her will."

I couldn't understand what he was so riled up about. He'd once told me not to go in there, but not why.

"What's in there?" I asked.

"It's called Cougar Canyon for a reason. Back in the twenties, a boy was killed by a cougar in there."

I knew mountain lions were to be avoided, but I'd never seen one. "But there aren't cougars in there today, are there?"

"Maybe not, but you never know. You should use as much sense as the horse did. I don't want you to go in there alone. Not ever again. You hear me?"

"Okay, yes, I hear you."

Dad's tone of voice and his stern order got my attention. When I was nine, I'd learned not to oppose my father. Bill and I had disobeyed a safety rule by starting a trash fire too close to the house, and Dad punished us with a willow switch on our bare legs. After that painful experience, I obeyed his orders, did my chores, and helped my mother with anything she asked of me.

My parents weren't overprotective, especially Dad. He expected me to be self-sufficient and learn to take care of myself. His previous direction to avoid the canyon had come without explanation, and my curiosity had led me to explore. Now I knew better.

Later that summer, Mom once again began attacking Dad, challenging and berating him as she'd done the summer before. But this time, Dad didn't have to sleep at the airport or eat in restaurants. He'd expanded the business by buying out an aerial applicator who'd managed the Tonasket airport and built a hangar big enough to hold two or three airplanes plus equipment and tools. Dad moved his whole business operation there in June, and during the summer and fall of 1960, he lived in the small two-bedroom home attached to the hangar. He asked Gram to come and cook for him, Bill, and one or two other helpers. This was a major change in my family's living arrangements. On most summer days, I was the only one at the ranch with Mom.

LINDA M. LOCKWOOD ✦ 133

She kept up her tirades against Dad through the fall, as she had the year before, and he stayed at the Tonasket airport until the orchard spraying ended. In November, Dad closed the Tonasket airport for the winter and came home. After a few weeks, Mom's manic attacks diminished, and my parents seemed to get along with each other for the rest of the winter.

⬥

One January day in 1961, Boyd Hilderbrand stopped by to report to Dad on his efforts to reduce the number of coyotes in the Chiliwist, and Mom invited him to stay for dinner. As we enjoyed Mom's applesauce raisin loaf cake, Dad asked Boyd, "Can you tell us what happened to that boy in Cougar Canyon?"

"Sure," Boyd said, shaking his head at the memory. "That was Jimmie Fehlhaber back in 1924. It was just before Christmas and freezing cold when Bob Nash sent Jimmie to borrow the neighbor's team of mules to pull out a car stranded in the snow and ice. When Jimmie didn't return, Nash hiked to the neighbor's house. The neighbor said Jimmie had never arrived. Nash figured he'd taken the shortcut through the canyon that he'd been warned against using."

"That's the trail on our place that goes around the base of Dent Mountain?" Dad asked.

"That's right," Boyd said. "So Nash and the neighbor searched the canyon trail with flashlights and found the boy's cap and gloves. They went back for a gun and a dog, and three hours later, they found the half-eaten body. They came back in daylight to follow the tracks and found the cougar's lair in the nearby rocks. They also found the place where the tracks showed the cougar had leaped on the boy from ten feet behind. Then they called the sheriff to report a cougar had killed Jimmie."

He paused and shook his head again. "I was there that morning when the sheriff came to take away the body. I've never forgotten that grisly scene."

"Cougars don't usually attack people, do they?" Mom asked.

"It had never happened before," Boyd said. "But word spread like wildfire through the whole county, and all the parents in the Chiliwist kept their kids from walking to school until the cougar was killed."

"How long did that take?" Bill asked.

"Three weeks. A cougar tracker from Canada came down with his dog, and he, the game warden, and I kept up the search until someone shot a cougar over in Winthrop that we agreed was probably the killer."

Boyd took a deep breath and a sip of coffee. "You know, Jimmie was so young, almost fourteen, and I've always wanted to put up a permanent marker on that spot where he died."

"That would be a good thing to do," Dad agreed, clapping Boyd on the back as he saw him out the door.

As I listened to Boyd's terrifying story, I felt deeply spooked all over again. I couldn't shake the thought that a cougar might have been watching us when Pepper and I were in the canyon. That could have been the source of Pepper's agitation and eventually mine. She could smell cougar all along the trail. Just thinking about it made me shiver, and I vowed never to go in there by myself again.

CHAPTER THIRTEEN

In the winter of 1961, light snowfalls and near-zero temperatures offered the wrong road conditions for our customary 4-H club sledding parties. We usually waited for a Saturday when fresh snow on the rural roads, packed and smoothed by the snowplow, would make for good, fast runs. That year, the ideal weather never came.

On a bright February day, Bill invited two of his buddies to the ranch to look for a good sled run, and I wanted to go with them. They were sixteen. I was fourteen and had no other playmates to sled with.

"You're not welcome," Bill had said when he realized I'd overheard him planning the event. But I'd kept asking to be included, and that February morning, he'd said, "You can come as long as you take care of yourself and don't make any fuss."

I always thought sledding was great fun, but I'd never had a good long sled like the boys used. I'd always used our old short one, which had to be ridden sitting up. But this year, Bill had gotten a new sled for Christmas and gave me his old one. Though I was a bit rusty at sledding, I was eager to try it out.

The four of us pulled our four-foot-long sleds up the steep road above the barn. The road's surface was so slick with ice that even my deep-treaded rubber boots slipped, so I walked gingerly on the crusty snow near the road's edge. When we reached the first flat where the road surface leveled, the four of us turned to look down the road. Bright ice glared back.

"Looks pretty fast, doesn't it?" Bill observed.

"It's so steep! We'll get up a lot of speed," Gary replied.

Before us was a short run, then an easy inside turn to the right followed by a steep straightaway. The road then disappeared around a steeply angled left turn. The road was flat at that last corner, and the edge had no barrier—nothing to keep us on the road if we lost our steering on the ice. We all knew what was over the edge at that corner. On our way up the road, we'd stood at the edge looking down. The drop-off fell away for a hundred yards, and large brush and scattered rocks stuck out of the snow here and there. Then it leveled out for another hundred yards with more big rocks and woody brush.

Bruce looked more hesitant than my brother and Gary. "I don't know if we can make that last turn," he said. "How would we be able to slow down?"

"Well, you wanted a good run," Bill said. "This is it!"

Standing at the top of the sled run and staring down the ice-glazed road, I thought Bruce had a very good point and that Bill shouldn't be so dismissive. In fact, I questioned the whole crazy idea. This didn't look like fun.

"Are you guys chicken?" Bill asked.

"We can try it once, I guess," Bruce said.

"We all have to do it then," my brother declared. "Nobody chickens out."

He glanced at his friends as they shook their heads, confirming that they weren't going to be the guy who didn't have the guts to take the run.

"Okay," said Bill, "who goes first?"

"I'll go," Bruce said. "Then I can watch as the rest of you try not to wipe out or fly off the edge!"

Bill turned to me. "You have to go second. If you're last, you'll probably chicken out." They all looked at me.

"No, I won't!" I was determined to prove I was as brave as they were.

Bruce faced down the road, holding his sled against his right side. Then he took a few careful steps, set the sled on the sparkling snow, lowered his chest onto the wooden slats, and grabbed the front handles to steer the metal runners down the road. From that headfirst takeoff, he gathered speed quickly, whisked through the first turn, and then shot down the steep slope to where the road disappeared at the last sharp turn. He dragged his leather-booted toes all the way, attempting to slow his ever-increasing speed, but he still went faster and faster. Before I could determine whether he was in control or speeding toward disaster, he rocketed around the turn and out of sight.

"Looks like he made it around the turn!" Bill exclaimed.

I was next. I swallowed hard and launched my sled the same way Bruce had. I steered around the first easy turn, but on the long, steep slope, the sled flew faster on the glaring ice. I knew I wouldn't make that last turn if I didn't slow down, so I tried to drag the toes of my rubber thermal boots on the ice the way Bruce had—anything to reduce the speed of this death rocket that was propelling me faster and faster toward the turn—but my rubber toes bounced off the ice with no effect. I was a torpedo on runners.

Nearing the turn, I wrenched the sled handles hard left and leaned my weight into the turn, but the sled went into a slide, the right runner leading, and headed straight for the edge.

The road was turning, but I wasn't. I was going to speed straight ahead and over the edge of a cliff.

I tried to center myself on the sled, to keep more of the sled between me and whatever I was going to smash into when I careened over the edge. Then the right runner collapsed inward, rolling my body off the sled toward the curve's outside edge.

I gripped the handles and hung on as if my life depended on it. Somehow, the collapsed sled and I scraped around the curve with me sliding along on my right side, inches from the edge with the steep drop beyond it. My hip bone struck a buried rock that rounded up from the frozen surface, and that collision deflected me from the edge and slowed my pell-mell slide until the sled and I ground to a halt.

I'd made it!

As I lifted my head to see Bruce pulling his sled back up the road toward me, I heard the swish and clatter of another sled barreling down the hill.

If I didn't get out of the way, I might get sliced open, but my banged hip wouldn't let me move. I twisted to look over my shoulder just as Gary shot off the corner and launched into the air on his sled, flying like a missile toward the brush and snow. I struggled to sit up just as Bill flew around the corner, fighting his sled to make the turn. His runners tracked over the edge, and he plowed down the hillside. I crawled to the edge and looked down. Bill and Gary had disappeared.

Peering over the edge, I waited, holding my breath until two snow-crusted figures emerged from the bushes far below. They climbed back up through the rocks and snow to stand on the roadway, both of them looking sheepish but triumphant.

"Bruce, how'd you make that turn? You were the only one," Bill said.

"Yeah, I watched Gary fly off that corner," Bruce said. "He must have been airborne for fifty feet! You okay, Gary?"

"Yeah, just lucky, I guess. What happened to you down there, Bill?"

"I thought I was going to ram into those rocks at the bottom, so I rolled off my sled and ended up in the bushes, which was a lot better. Close call."

They were standing near me, but no one asked why I wasn't getting up. I struggled to my feet, noticing my hip was numb.

Bill pointed. "Look at her sled. She ruined it. The runners are completely collapsed."

"I hit something coming around the turn," I said, trying not to cry. "My hip really hurts."

Bruce and Gary looked at me like they were concerned, but my own brother said, "Aw, don't be a sissy. You're all right." The other two said nothing.

The feeling was returning in my right hip, and with it came pain. With every step I took toward my sled, a hot, sharp pain shot through my hip. I wanted to pull down my pants and ask them to check my hip for any serious injuries. If they saw whatever was causing these shooting, stabbing, and now throbbing pains, maybe then they'd believe me. Or maybe they'd be able to reassure me that it wasn't as bad as it felt. But I couldn't. My face reddened at the thought of baring my skin to these older boys.

Bill turned to head down the road, and the other two followed him, pulling their sleds behind them.

"Hey, you guys, I'm really hurt. Feels like I may have broken something. Would you take my sled back for me?"

"Nothing doing," Bill called over his shoulder. "You wanted to come along, and you're all right. You're just a cry-baby. Carry your own sled back."

They kept walking, and I held back my tears as I pleaded once more. "Please, I need help. I'm not sure I can walk back. At least take my sled."

Bruce and Gary hesitated. They looked to Bill, but he shook his head, continuing down the road, and the others trooped after him. At the barnyard gate, they took the short-cut through the unbroken snow to the sheep shed, then down the steep hill to the creek bottom, and eventually to the house. They left me standing alone in the bitter cold.

Hunched over and beginning to shiver, I limped a little of the way home, dragging my damaged sled behind me, then stopped, sat in the snow, and gave way to my tears. Why was my brother so awful to me? A good brother would have believed me and helped me back to the house. But I didn't have a good brother.

After five minutes of useless sobbing, which made me feel even more alone, I stood and hobbled down the road, trying to step in the guys' tracks as I trudged in agony through the foot-deep snow to the sheep shed. From the crest of the hill, I peered down at the light-filled windows of the warm house below. The boys would be inside by now, probably drinking hot chocolate and warming up while they told exaggerated, heroic versions of their big sledding adventure.

I sat down on the sloping path. The snow had soaked my flannel-lined jeans and coveralls, and the cold wetness reached my skin. Inching feet first down the slanted path of ice, I braked against the crunchy snow at the trail's edges and managed to pull the wrecked sled behind me for two hundred feet down to the creek. I was responsible for the sled, and I knew we couldn't afford a new one, so I was determined not to leave it where the sheep and cows might trample it and damage it further.

I made it to the bottom of the hill, where the rushing creek was lined with icy snow. The footbridge was a single plank of wood twelve inches wide, caked with crusty snow and icy footprints. I wouldn't be able to carry the sled across with my bum hip, so I abandoned it on the edge of the creek and crept across the snow-covered board with my boots turned sideways and arms extended, fearing I might slip into the freezing water at any second. I made it, heaved a sigh of relief, and then limped another twenty yards up the creek bank, into the yard, up the back steps, and through the kitchen door.

Sure enough, Mom was serving hot cocoa and fresh-baked cookies to the boys who relaxed around the kitchen table, their wet jackets and boots already stripped off and laid out to dry in the warmth of the well-stocked Franklin stove. The room smelled of woodsmoke, cinnamon, vanilla, and cocoa. When my mother saw my tear-soaked face, she knitted her brows and said with concern, "What's wrong? They said you were all right, just slow coming back."

"I'm not all right," I mumbled with disgust, not looking at the guys. Then I shucked my coat and boots at the kitchen entry and limped toward my bedroom. "Mom," I called, with frustration, after I realized she wasn't right behind me. "Come help me, *please*."

Mom came through my door, looking bothered, and asked, "What's the matter?"

"Shut the door," I said. I peeled off my coveralls, unzipped my jeans, and slipped them slowly down over my right hip, afraid of what I'd find. Blood oozed from a two-inch gash across my hip bone where the collision with the unmoving rock had ripped open my flesh.

"Oh, dear," Mom said when she saw the wound. "That doesn't look too bad. It just needs some Merthiolate and Band-Aids. I'll get them."

Tears fought their way out as Mom painted on the stinging red liquid. I cried because it hurt and because now, in the privacy and safety of my room, I no longer needed to be brave.

She applied two large Band-Aids to cover the oozing wound. "Mom," I whimpered. "Do you think I should see the doctor?"

Without pausing, she said firmly, "Let's wait and see how it looks in the morning."

"It hurts bad. Can I have some aspirin?"

She brought me two aspirin along with milk and cookies. I ate them and then fell asleep, exhausted from the ordeal. The pain woke me several times when I rolled onto my bruised hip, and I worried how bad the injury was beneath the torn skin where the deeper hurt throbbed.

When I woke the next morning, I could hardly move my leg without severe pain. I sat up, put my feet in my slippers, stood on my left leg, and lurched toward the bathroom, holding onto the walls and doorways. Every time I put weight on my right leg, the hip screamed with pain. Frightened, I asked Mom again, "Shouldn't I go to the doctor and have him look at it?"

"It's Sunday. The doctor won't be in his office until Monday," she said.

I took more aspirin and stayed off my feet for the rest of the day to avoid the pain, bored and anxious for the next day to come so I could see the doctor.

I didn't want to go to school in the morning because it still hurt to walk with my wounded hip. To relieve my fears, I wanted the doctor to examine me as soon as possible. I assumed my mother would rush me straight to our family physician, but she insisted I go to school so she could do chores and call for an appointment with the doctor.

"It won't hurt for me to skip school today. I can easily make it up," I said.

Mom shook her head, saying, "No, you go to school, and I'll pick you up there."

"At least drive me down the lane so I don't have to walk to the bus," I said.

"I guess I can do that," she responded.

I walked into school limping badly and trying not to grimace from the pain.

Friends who saw me in the hall or entering our classroom asked, "What's wrong?" and I had to explain over and over, "I had a sledding accident, and my hip struck a rock, but I'll be okay."

I couldn't walk without limping, and even kids who barely knew me stopped in the hallway and asked, "What happened?" Each break between classes brought the cascade of embarrassment I'd hoped to avoid. If only Mom had let me stay home.

When my brother saw me in the hallway, he hooted and said, "You're such a pantywaist!" I wanted to become invisible. During afternoon study hall, a class I shared with Bill, I hid in the adjoining library to avoid his taunts. Pretending to browse the stacks, I grieved that I had a brother who was such a jerk and a mother who wasn't concerned about my pain. Even students I barely knew showed more concern and sympathy.

School was nearly over when Mom picked me up and took me to the doctor's office. We were ushered into an exam room, where I undressed and put on a gown. We waited silently for fifteen long minutes while I worried about what the doctor would find. At last, he came in.

Mom said to him, "She had a sledding accident."

"I struck a rock, and my hip is bruised and torn. It's painful to walk on," I said.

"Let's see it," he said. I lay on my back on the exam table and pulled up the gown, baring my right hip.

He pulled off the Band-Aids and saw a swollen purple bruise around my hip bone. There was a two-inch gash across it, still weeping blood. He felt around the bone with soft fingers. Straightening up, he said, "Nothing is broken. It's just a bad bruise."

"That's all?" I said, my relief mixing with disbelief.

"I need to treat that cut, though. I would have stitched it up if you'd come in sooner so you wouldn't have a scar, but it's too late. I can't do it now." He pulled the wound's gaping edges together with butterfly bandages and said, "There. Now it will heal up just fine, but you'll have a scar."

I looked at my mother, who'd been responsible for the two-day delay, but she said nothing. She was probably just worried about what this treatment would cost.

The doctor was right on both counts. I limped for the rest of the week, and a month passed before the bruised bone and ripped flesh healed, leaving a narrow two-inch-long scar. But the painful hip was nothing compared to my wounded pride. I hadn't pretended the pain to get sympathy. I was injured, frightened, and needed help at the scene, but I had to struggle home alone. I needed sympathy and comfort from my mother, but she showed little concern. I longed for Gram's loving care, but she was with friends in Portland as she recovered from gallbladder surgery. I wanted to boast with the boys about our brave exploit. I wanted to tell how I made it around the turn and stayed on the road like Bruce did. I should have had greater bragging rights because I was wounded, but my brother killed all chance of that. Instead, I was awarded a limp and a scar and was branded a sissy.

My brother had no protective instincts, and not having a brother I could turn to for help or care left me stranded and demeaned. In his world, girls were less—a nuisance, a bother to be tolerated.

After that day on the icy hill, I never again asked to tag along with the boys. I was already isolated, and my decision to be excluded from my brother's activities left me feeling even more alone. Although I occasionally spent time with other girls, I mostly turned to Lucky for companionship. My beautiful, spirited horse became my very best friend, the one friend I could always trust. I'd need to rely on myself. I'd have to teach myself, entertain myself, and protect myself.

❖

On a cold day in early April, I was out riding Pepper in the big wheat field on the south side of the ranch when I saw a pickup drive across the field to the rim of Cougar Canyon. People started packing loads of something from the pickup down the steep trail into the canyon. Bill was there, plowing the wheat field with the Cat. At dinner that night, he explained it had been his Boy Scout troop from Malott with Louie Larsen, their scoutmaster. Bill said Louie was a friend of Boyd Hilderbrand's, and what I'd seen that afternoon was Boyd taking the scoutmaster and his scouts into the canyon to the spot where Jimmie was killed.

Larsen and the boys spent the afternoon packing cement and water into the canyon to build a concrete monument in the shape of a pyramid set on a square base. They also carried a bronze plaque that they embedded on one side of the pyramid.

The next day, our local newspaper carried a photo of the scouts' monument along with Boyd's story of what had happened to Jimmie. That's when I learned the plaque had been engraved JIMMMIE FEHLHABER, 13 YEARS OLD, KILLED BY COUGAR ON THIS SPOT, DECEMBER 17, 1924. On April 6, 1961, Larsen and his scouts had helped Boyd fulfill his dream of honoring Jimmie.

Later that spring, Dad said it would be safe for Mom and me to go into the canyon if we were together, so we hiked down from the wheat field to see the monument. The canyon still seemed wild and eerie, but knowing people had been there tamed it for me, so I was no longer afraid. Jimmie's story became real to me as I stood before the pyramid, reading the words on the memorial plaque. I blinked back tears as I thought about the horrific death he had suffered as a young boy, terrified and all alone.

CHAPTER FOURTEEN

After the wheat harvest in August 1961, the now-familiar pattern of Mom's belligerent summer attacks on Dad returned and worsened, with Mom extending her attacks to include my brother and grandmother. From then on, Gram avoided Mom by renting an apartment in Okanogan when the airport was closed during the winter. In the summer, Bill lived and worked at Dad's airport headquarters, but he lived at the ranch during the school year, unable to avoid Mom's attacks.

By December, life at home had become unbearable as Mom kept attacking Dad. Again and again, he tried to get her to see a psychiatrist in Spokane or to be admitted to the hospital for treatment, but she continued to say there was nothing wrong with her.

As her attacks continued, I was afraid Mom was driving Dad away—from her, from us, from me. They needed to get away from each other, but thinking about a separation that might end in divorce terrified me. If Dad left, who'd get Mom into the hospital and pay for her treatments? But the word *divorce* was never uttered in my presence, so I pushed away the unthinkable idea.

The final crisis came in February 1962.

Mom woke us up on a Monday morning and served our usual breakfast of hot cereal, scrambled eggs, bacon, and toast with jam. Then my brother and I headed off to school. We boarded the little Jeep school bus and greeted our driver, Eula Stout. Bill was a junior, and I was a sophomore.

After school, we got off the big school bus at the highway intersection, where the yellow Jeep waited for us. We hopped in, and Eula drove us up Chiliwist Road, stopping at our front gate. She turned to face us with a frown.

"I'm sorry to tell you this," she began, "but no one will be home when you get to the house. Your father asked me to tell you what's happened. This morning, your mother came to my door, very upset and frantic. She told me she knew that something terrible had happened to Al, and she was beside herself. She wanted me to help find Al, so I suggested we call the sheriff's office and ask them to locate him. The sheriff came to my house and talked with Zelma, and then he took her into custody to keep her safe. They found Al, and he's in Okanogan now, working with the sheriff."

"Is she okay?" I asked.

"She's not herself right now, but they're getting her some help."

Mom had seemed fine that morning—maybe a bit quieter than usual—but otherwise normal. What could have changed so quickly? Eula's call had brought the county sheriff, who knew Dad well and knew about Mom's condition. *She's not herself, and she's in the hands of the sheriff? What does all this mean?*

Eula asked gently, "Will you two be all right by yourselves? You can come have dinner with us if you want."

"We'll be okay," Bill said.

I chimed in. "We have chores and homework to do."

At dinnertime, Eula drove up our lane and delivered a hot homemade casserole, bless her kind heart. We ate the cheese-topped hamburger and macaroni in silence, except for an occasional "This is really good."

Dad came home later that night. "Your mom is not in good shape," he explained. "I'm trying to get her some help. The sheriff has her in the county jail in Okanogan, where she can't hurt herself."

Thinking of my mother spending the night in jail left me frightened and ashamed for her. She'd always avoided having meltdowns in public.

The next morning, with no idea what was going on with our mother, Bill and I boarded the bus for school. When Eula dropped us back at home that afternoon, Dad was waiting for us.

"Your mom is safe," he said. "I'm leaving now to pick her up from the sheriff, and I'll be taking her to the hospital in Medical Lake. Stan Stout will go along with me. We'll keep her between us so she can't try to grab the wheel or leap out of the pickup. We'll be very late getting home, but you don't need to worry. We'll be all right." When I heard this, I heaved a sigh of relief that Mom would be cared for, but I was also rattled by the idea that my mother was at risk for grabbing a steering wheel or jumping from a moving truck.

At midnight, I heard Dad come into the house. "Everything go okay?" I called from my bedroom as he passed by.

"Yes, just fine."

With Mom away, our home life was peaceful again. Each day, Bill and I helped Dad load hay bales from the barn into the pickup, then broke and scattered them in the pasture for the cows and horses. We also threw hay into the feeders for the fifty ewes in the sheep shed area with their new lambs. Bill filled the wood box for the Franklin stove, Dad helped me with the cooking, and I also did the dishes and laundry. Life at home felt pretty good again. We spoke little about Mom, though her absence weighed on my heart.

Six days later, our phone rang, and when I answered it, Mom's voice surprised me. "Hey, it's Mom!" I called out to Dad and Bill, and we handed the phone around. "You sound really good," I told her, delighted by how normal she sounded. But after that one phone call, almost four more weeks dragged by before Dad received word from her doctor that she was ready for release. He drove to Eastern State Hospital near Spokane, where she'd been committed, and brought her home on March 17.

Mom walked into the house and said, "It's good to be home." The next day, she rose to build the fire and cook breakfast, as she'd always done, and the house soon filled with the yeasty aroma of her fabulous homemade bread.

I was glad to have my mother home and to see her back to her old self. She brought me a gift of two white pillowcases she'd embroidered with happy bluebirds and edged with crocheted lace, proof she'd been thinking of me in the hospital. Delighted, I put them on my pillows right away.

A month later, Mom was pacing around the house, walking stiffly. I asked, "What's wrong? Does your back hurt?"

"No, but it seems very stiff, and I can't hardly get to sleep at night."

She grew agitated over the next month; she couldn't sit still and couldn't sleep. Dad took her to her local physician, who gave her some pills, but she grew worse. Her condition must have been frightening for her because, in early June, Dad drove Mom back to the state mental hospital, where she voluntarily signed herself in.

When she returned home five weeks later, she seemed fine to me. She even started a writing project and spent hours typing away at the dining room table. After watching her for two weeks, I asked, "Mom, what have you been writing?"

"I guess you can read it," she said, handing me the typewritten pages. I sat in a chair in the living room and began to read.

It was a story about a woman being admitted to a mental hospital. I'd never heard Mom talk about what went on during her times in the psychiatric hospitals other than saying to her relatives, "I just needed a rest and to get away from Al." Reading her story left me completely floored.

ADMITTANCE—THREE FLIGHTS UP

Have you ever wondered what goes on behind the locked doors and padlocked gates of a mental hospital, how patients are screened and released or assigned to various wards for further treatment? This screening took place on the third floor. Here is my experience.

My doctor prescribed a rest and a screening test and advised my husband to take me to the Eastern State Hospital at Medical Lake, where mental patients and wards of the state are screened and housed.

The journey by car was made in mute silence on my part as I listened to the conversation on various subjects between my husband and Stan, the neighbor who was asked to go along.

. . . There were tense moments—when passing another car with a radio, etc. One never knows whether a passing car contains a communist bent on some mission of destruction or is tailing another car or if the passing car contains a Secret Service officer of the FBI. Maybe that car on the side of the road did just have a flat tire, and then maybe a scene is being set for another front-page accident. In these days, "no one knows who's tailing who."

. . . When a lighted match could disclose the occupants to a passing car, I reached over and removed the unlighted cigarette from the neighbor's mouth. Another time, when passing another car with radio static, I tensed up so much that my husband reached

over and turned the radio off. The radio was left off during the rest of the trip.

. . . Finally we arrived at the sprawling buildings of ESH. The Falcon pickup with its three passengers pulled up to the building marked "Entrance." A guard stepped out, and my husband identified himself. Then Stan helped me from the car. The guard said, "Come with me," and the car pulled away, heading homeward. . . . It was a relief to have arrived after the long trip and be out of the fog and darkness.

I was led through the hallway to the elevator, which took us up to the third floor, then down the long corridor flanked by numerous office doors, until a windowed door marked "C-1" blocked our passage. A nurse came and unlocked the door. This was the ward where all patients were admitted and classified for treatment. The guard led me into a small office at the far end of C-1 and said, "Wait here. A doctor will be here shortly for an interview."

. . . Most of the patients were drugged so they would relax and rest for the first week or so. I was no exception and spent most of the first week in restful sleep, going to meals down in the ladies dining room on the ground floor along with the rest of the ladies from C-1.

. . . The blonde nurse with the dark-rimmed glasses was named Pat. She proved to be the life of the attendants, encouraging the ladies to watch their weight, putting up their hair, keeping their spirits high and their muscles limbered by exercises. After three weeks, when Pat asked why I was mute at first, she got my answer—"There is nothing to talk about—I came here mainly for rest and to avert a nervous breakdown."

. . . After two weeks I was assigned to work in the dining room, serving meals, drying dishes, etc. This helped the time to pass more quickly. Each afternoon we were taken to recreation classes where one could play volleyball, pool, or shuffleboard, learn crafts, etc. And we were allowed to see the weekly show and attend church in the main auditorium.

As I looked forward to going home after six weeks, I could see that many of the more mentally ill patients had little to look forward to and that some of them might spend many years here behind closed and locked doors. I was thrilled to be going home.

When I finished reading and got over my surprise at what she'd revealed, I said, "Mom, this is very good. I'm sure you could get it published."

"Oh, I couldn't do that. I wouldn't want anyone to know it was me."

"You could write it in the third person and not use your real name."

"Oh, I don't know. I don't think so."

A day later, she said, "I can't publish that story, but I'm going to send it to my doctor at ESH. I liked him, and he encouraged me to write. It's a way of thanking him."

She sent a copy to the psychiatrist she'd liked, then tucked her story away.

Mom continued taking the Mellaril and Artane she'd been prescribed, but she occasionally tried to stop. Dad said it was important she continued taking her medication and asked me to make sure of it. I'd been doing adult work for five years since Mom turned over the sheepherding to me when I was eleven. Now I was being asked to see that she took her pills. I didn't like that—it felt like spying—but apparently, it was now one of my jobs.

I read the directions on her pill bottles: *to be taken in the morning on a full stomach.* One morning she took out the pills and stood with her back to me while appearing to swallow them, but after a few minutes, she slid open the lid on the garbage pail beside the sink. I waited an hour, then asked, "Mom, are you taking your pills?"

"Yes, I took them this morning."

I suspected she was lying. When I hid around the corner the next morning, I saw her lean into the wood box, make a scrabbling noise as if she was gathering some kindling, and spit out the pills she'd been holding in her mouth.

"Mom's not taking her pills," I reported to Dad, feeling like a traitor. "She pretends to swallow them, but this morning I saw her spit them out."

"Thanks, Cookie. I'll talk to her," he said. And after that, she'd start taking them again. For a while.

——◆——

In the summer of 1962, we pastured our small flock of fifty ewes and their lambs in the fenced fields around the house and below the barn when Mom or I weren't available to herd them up the hill. After she came home from the mental hospital, Dad didn't want Mom herding them anymore to reduce her stress level.

Whenever the sheep were in the pasture above the house, one of my daily chores involved hiking up the creek and looping through the pasture to check the swampy areas where springs emerged from the hillside. I patrolled those places to make sure a sheep hadn't gotten stuck in any of the soft, wet spots. As they sank to their bellies, their sharp hooves churned the watery earth with no purchase until they gave up the struggle. If I didn't find them in time, they would die there.

One hot day in early August, I came across a woolly ewe trapped in the reed grass swamp. I waded in, my feet disappearing into the wet mire until I'd sunk to my knees. I lifted and turned the sheep's rump to point her head toward the dry land, then raised her rear legs and pushed. Her wool coat had absorbed swamp water like a sponge, so she was too heavy for me to manage on my own. I could see she'd already worn herself out, so I sprinted down to the house, where Mom was working in the kitchen.

"Mom," I gasped, "there's another ewe stuck. I need you to help me get her out."

"Not again," Mom replied. "Those darn sheep!" She turned off the stove, and together, we huffed up the hillside.

With Mom lifting and pulling the ewe's front legs while I raised and pushed the rear legs, we managed to push the sheep only a foot toward the edge of the swamp. The sun felt hotter each time we stopped to catch our breath, and we were both tiring, but after about fifteen minutes, we wrestled the animal out of the muck and onto dry land. She lay with her legs splayed until we pushed her upright and folded her legs beneath her.

"She'll be okay now," Mom said, wiping sweat from her forehead.

"Thanks for your help, Mom," I said. "I'll stay with her until she can get up."

Mom went back to her cooking, and I watched the ewe as she rested and gradually began to nibble grass. The poor thing must have been ravenous because she clambered to her feet and snatched and chomped bites of grass as water streamed and dripped from her soaked wool. Watching her eat, I knew she'd be all right.

I skipped joyfully down to the house, knowing I'd just saved that ewe's life. For the next two weeks, I made daily forays through the pasture and rescued several mired sheep. Unfortunately, the swamp wasn't the only threat to the helpless creatures.

One day I headed up the creek with my dogs, checking the fence along the way. I expected to loop back through the swampy areas to make sure no sheep were stuck. However, as we reached the far corner of the pasture, the dogs scooted under the boundary fence, disappeared into the thick underbrush of the neighbor's land, and started growling and barking. Where they'd gone under, the fence was twisted and stretched upward to make a passageway. I studied the mangled fence and wondered what could have done that kind of damage. Then I crawled through the gap and followed the dogs. I found them sniffing the ground and circling an ewe carcass. Something had eaten parts of her abdomen and shoulder, and the stench told me she'd been dead for a week or more. But a dead sheep or even a stinking carcass wouldn't upset the dogs. Something else was causing them to sniff and growl. What was it?

The damaged fence told me something had killed the ewe on our property then dragged her under the fence and through about ten yards of dense growth. When I thought about how big an animal would have to be to manage that, a jolt of dread shot through me. I crawled back under the fence, called the dogs, and fast-stepped across the creek on rocks to continue my patrol of the swamps. I found all the sheep were grazing or resting on dry ground.

When I jogged back to the house and up the steps into the kitchen, I was glad to see Bill, who'd come in for lunch.

"Bill!" I said, trying to catch my breath. "The dogs found a dead ewe that something killed and dragged through the fence up at the creek corner. It must have taken something big to do that!"

"I'll be right back," Bill said, then left with the dogs trailing behind him.

When he came back, he said, "I think the killer was a bear."

"Wow," I said. "Remember when the hired man said he'd seen a black bear in the wheat field on the first flat, and it ran for cover in the brush?"

"Yeah, and that's pretty much where the dead ewe is."

It was the first time anything other than a coyote had killed one of our sheep, and the idea of it being a bear scared me.

"If it was a bear, now it has a taste for mutton," Bill said.

From that day on, I never checked the pasture without bringing the dogs. I couldn't avoid the corner where the ewe was killed, but I certainly didn't have to linger there. As soon as I finished checking that area, I'd carefully step across the creek on its slippery stones and speed away as fast as my Keds would take me.

Two months after I found the dead ewe, I was eating breakfast with Mom and Bill when we heard fierce barking from up the creek. Bill went to see what was upsetting the dogs and spotted a lone sheep lying on the ground about two hundred feet from the house. He found a buck lamb still alive but with a large patch of flesh eaten from its back. On the ground nearby were bear tracks. Bill came back to the house, grabbed Dad's hunting rifle, and told me to take Spot into the house and stay there with Mom.

I watched him set out with his dog, Tippy, and heard the shot that finished off the mortally wounded sheep. Soon after that, I heard Tippy's fierce barking and then several more shots followed by a single blast. Within minutes, my brother had found the bear on the wooded hillside and killed it. I shuddered over how close to the house it had all happened.

That afternoon, our friend and local news reporter, Mabel Gavin, arrived and interviewed my brother. Her article "Boy Kills Bear with Aid of Dog" ran the next day on the front page of the *Wenatchee Daily World*. Mabel had let Bill tell the story:

> *I hadn't gone far up the creek when I heard*
> *fierce barking and hurried toward the sound. Soon*
> *the sound indicated the bear, followed by the dog,*
> *was climbing up the hillside to a little flat above*

the creek. I followed. When I got to the rim of the flat where I could look over, I put my scope on the scene and saw the bear coming right toward me. His eyes, his nose, and even his ears looked terribly big to me. Tippy tried to help by nipping the bear's hind legs, but the bear turned on him and began trying to slap him.

I leveled my gun to fire, but the bear and Tippy were going around and around. I didn't dare fire for fear I'd kill the dog. Finally, they got behind the brush, and I maneuvered around until I found an open space between two trees. I got ready, for I felt certain that the bear would come across that opening.

Mabel finished the story, writing, "The bear did appear, Bill fired two or three times, and the animal dropped and rolled down the hill. Bill approached the bear and finished its life with a bullet in the neck."

The day before, after I'd heard Bill yell, "I got him! He's dead," I walked across the creek to see the dead bear. It was huge, with shaggy brownish-black hair and long, ugly claws on its powerful arms and legs.

Bill called our neighbor, and Stan Stout came to help Bill dress and skin the bear. They agreed the male bear was old because of its badly worn teeth. Bill stretched the bear's hide on the outside wall of the former chicken house, which I'd converted into my tack room. I passed by it every time I went to saddle my horse, and the hide served as a stark reminder that for many years, a very big bear had lived not far beyond our door.

My brother shot that old bear on the same hillside where I'd cut a Christmas tree five years earlier. I shivered to think how long it had probably lived in the dense trees and bushes bordering our pasture, how many times I'd entered its hunting territory, and how boldly it came near our house to kill a second sheep. I went on patrolling the ranch, protecting my animals, and watching out for rattlesnakes, coyotes, and cougars. And now I had to watch out for bears too—a thought that never stopped giving me chills.

CHAPTER FIFTEEN

All through high school, I felt like an outsider. I didn't know how to engage in small talk, and I had limited time to chat with my schoolmates during school hours. Ten minutes after the closing bell, I had to catch the only bus home and do my chores. I was afraid my classmates mistook my shyness for being stuck-up and arrogant, but I just didn't know how to connect with them, especially when they were chatting in a group. If I seemed aloof, it was because I carried the pain and shame of growing up with a parent who had a mental illness and was hospitalized for it about every five years. In my classes and in the hallways, I was alone with my secret.

Throughout adolescence, I nurtured a close relationship with Judy, a girlfriend I trusted enough to confide in about what was going on with my mother's episodes and hospitalizations. Judy made me feel safe by telling me about her domineering father forcing strict church standards and beliefs on her and her mother. Her trust gave me the kind of comfort I felt with my horses when they performed their mutual grooming and let me participate. Unfortunately, Judy and I didn't have much time to connect at school, and there was no privacy at home for talking on the phone, so we sometimes met at the city park for an hour on Saturdays while Mom shopped for groceries in Okanogan. I slept over at Judy's house a time or two, but she wasn't allowed to go to anyone else's home where her father or mother wouldn't be able to supervise her.

With so few social connections, I was always watching my words and actions during school. I tried to detect any negative comments or gossip about me and then hide my reaction to cover up my sensitive feelings. I feared being seen, and I also feared failing, which prevented me from being spontaneous. I was constantly thinking back over something I'd said or done, trying to judge whether it had been a poor choice. I was sure I was constantly doing things that would make other kids laugh at me behind my back.

Then, in the spring of 1963, someone came to my rescue in an unlikely way. Mrs. Irmal Jones taught English, speech, and drama to the juniors and seniors. She was usually perched on a stool behind the lectern that faced rows of seats in her auditorium-style classroom. Her black hair, flecked with gray, was always rolled into a bun on top of her head, and stabbed into the bun was a yellow pencil. As she taught, her dark eyes studied us from behind black-rimmed glasses. "Anyone caught sleeping in my class will get a rude awakening," she announced at the beginning of each year.

She was a strict and severe teacher. She had large bosoms and sometimes paused her lecture to lift the padded shoulders of her flowered jersey dress and adjust her biting bra straps while saying, "My back hurts. It's because of the weight of the years—and other things." Her joke cracked us up, but we laughed respectfully.

One winter day during lunch, a classmate called out to me. "Mrs. Jones is looking for you!"

I whirled to face the girl. Having a teacher look for you was never good. "Why?"

"She wants to see you in her classroom."

I visited the restroom to tuck in my blouse and check my hair. I knew I was in trouble. But why? Could it have been my last composition? I knocked on Mrs. Jones's classroom door and walked in.

"Hello, Linda. I'm over here," she called from her desk in a dark corner of the room. When I stood before her, she let her reading glasses fall, suspended by the neck strap she wore to hold them, and stuck the trademark yellow pencil into her bun. "I'm casting for the all-school play in March. It's a comedy of mix-ups, and I'd like you to be in it."

"Oh!" I gasped. Wouldn't that be great! But I knew it was impossible. I didn't even ask what the part would be. I said, "I'd love to, but I'm afraid I can't."

"And why is that?"

"I can't stay after school for rehearsals. It's a long way home, and I don't have a car, so I need to ride home on the school bus."

"Your brother was in the senior play last fall."

"He has a car."

"And if he's also in the play this time, then you'd have a ride home."

"I guess so, yes."

"Then I'll see to it. Go and have your lunch."

On my way to the cafeteria, I thought about watching Bill in the senior play that fall, *The Teahouse of the August Moon*, the story of the American military occupation of Okinawa following World War II. In the play, army officers try to teach the native islanders about all things American, including building construction, democracy, and capitalism. When things go awry, the young captains start to see the beauty of the islanders' way of life. Bill had played a supporting role as Captain McLean, and he'd looked so handsome in his dress uniform under the lights. I wished I could perform onstage and feel as confident as he looked. Was Mrs. Jones actually going to make it possible for me to be in the all-school spring play?

At home that evening, Bill said, "Mrs. Jones asked if I want to be in the all-school play. She said you want to be in it too."

"Yeah, I do," I said, realizing what Mrs. Jones was doing. "And if you're in it, you can drive us home afterward."

"What if I don't want to be in the play with you and a bunch of juniors?" Bill said as if he were holding a toy away from a child.

"Oh, please. Didn't you have fun doing the teahouse play?"

"Sure, but that was my senior class play, and all my friends were in it."

"You'll have fun in this one too. She said it's a comedy."

"Maybe I'll do it if you'll feed my steer on the weekends so I can sleep in."

"Okay, but only for as long as the rehearsals last."

He'd named his price, and we were in the play.

⊷◆⊶

Mrs. Jones handed out the scripts for *Harvey*, had us underline our parts in red ink, and told us to start memorizing them. The play featured a courtly gentleman named Elwood P. Dowd, often accompanied by his best friend, a six-foot-tall invisible white rabbit named Harvey. Much of the story's action took place in a sanatorium for mental patients. I was cast as young Nurse Kelly, and Bill had the role of the newly arrived psychiatrist, Dr. Sanderson. When we learned our characters would move from conflict to romance, Bill objected, but Mrs. Jones assured him— and me—we wouldn't have to touch or kiss on stage.

We worked on our lines at home and practiced stage movements at rehearsals. The world of theater was entirely foreign to me, but I loved learning what was involved. With my shy personality and general isolation, I didn't know how to portray another person, but Mrs. Jones coached me on how to deliver my lines and carry myself as if I were Nurse Kelly. She told me, "Nurse Kelly is beautiful, Linda, and you will be, too, in your stage makeup and without your glasses."

For two weeks, I memorized my lines, but when I read into Act Three, I saw that I *was* going to be kissed onstage—by old Mr. Dowd. And the role of Elwood Dowd was being played by Robert Marshall, one of the most popular guys in my class. I thought he was one of the nicer guys at my school, and I secretly liked him, but he was going steady with one of the popular girls. At sixteen, I hadn't had a date, let alone been kissed. I was the "brain" with the highest grades and no social standing.

Two weeks before the performance, we were onstage in the auditorium doing our first walkthrough of the scene where Elwood Dowd kisses Nurse Kelly. Mrs. Jones was demonstrating our movements across the stage. Robert broke in to say, "I'm not going to practice the kiss in rehearsals."

"Why not?" Mrs. Jones asked.

"Because my friends have been ribbing me about it."

"It's a key part of the scene, and I want to make sure we get it right," Mrs. Jones said.

"I'll do the kiss, but only once, in the performance," Robert declared. "I know how to kiss, and I don't need to practice."

"Well, I guess we can skip the kiss until the dress rehearsal," Mrs. Jones said. And that's how it was left.

I felt relieved we didn't have to practice sooner, but what if we didn't do the kiss in front of the audience the way Mrs. Jones wanted it done?

For the next two weeks, we cast members worked together five days a week on lines, blocking, and emotional delivery while the crew learned lighting, sound, and stage makeup. Then, it was the day before the dress rehearsal when we'd have our first "practice" kiss. I wavered between terrified and embarrassed but then decided to play it cool.

A classmate's mother, a real nurse, offered her white uniform, shoes, and nurse's cap to dress me as Ruth Kelly, RN. The uniform had a sheath skirt and it fitted me snugly in the waist, hips, and bust, which embarrassed me at first. The full, gathered skirts and blouses I usually wore to school didn't reveal my figure like this did. But Mrs. Jones said I looked authentic in the nurse uniform, and during rehearsal, the other girls said I looked pretty in the slim dress, so I began to like my costume.

To me, the best part of becoming Ruth Kelly was that I wasn't allowed to wear my glasses. I couldn't see the audience or even the other players' expressions, but for once, I thought I looked pretty. That, plus knowing exactly what I was supposed to say and do, gave me a miraculous feeling of freedom and confidence.

On the day of the dress rehearsal, Robert still refused to do the kiss. "Not until the actual performance," he said as Mrs. Jones glared at him. But what could she do? The show was going on the next night. That meant that one day from now, I was going to be kissed by a boy for the first time ever, and it was going to be in front of a crowd that included parents.

The next evening, as the auditorium filled with the cast members' families and friends and guests from the community, we paced backstage, trying to lock in our stage directions and lines. Then the play began. Nurse Kelly didn't appear in the first scene, so I watched from behind the side curtain, where Mrs. Jones listened for hesitations and used a stage whisper to project lines into the gaps.

When the curtain rose for Act Two, I sat at a desk onstage as Nurse Kelly and interviewed Mrs. Veta Simmons, who wished to admit her brother Elwood to the sanitorium for treatment. The new psychiatrist, Dr. Sanderson, joined us, and Veta explained that she was tired of Elwood having his best friend Harvey living at their house and going out in public with him. She was embarrassed because Harvey was an invisible white rabbit who chose to be seen only by specific people, like Elwood, who talked to the rabbit in public. When Veta confided that she herself had seen the rabbit a time or two, the doctor concluded it was Veta who needed treatment and ordered her to be admitted. Gales of laughter came from the audience.

In Act Three, the nurse and the young doctor discovered that they liked each other. Meanwhile, Dowd grew fond of the pretty young nurse who treated him kindly. Then it was time for the big onstage kiss. Robert leaned toward me and, there in the lights of center stage, pressed a loud *smack!* right on my lips while the audience clapped and whistled. I blinked and raised my hand to my cheek, turning my head to watch Robert exit upstage. He'd done it! The shock I portrayed as Nurse Kelly was authentic. My heart was thundering. It had been my first kiss, and as it turned out, it had been in front of an audience of 250 people. To make it more dramatic, the kiss had been delivered by a popular guy I secretly liked. I silently prayed the heavy stage makeup hid my flushed face, which I knew was bright red.

After the final curtain and the final bows, I went backstage and transformed back into myself, glasses and all. On my way to the auditorium, I passed friends who told me they'd overheard people asking, "Who played the nurse? She was good." My makeover into an attractive nurse had been successful and convincing! People also thought I'd done a good job of my acting. I felt a kind of euphoria I'd never experienced before.

I entered the auditorium and looked across the thinning crowd for my parents, eventually spotting my mother in the bleachers.

Bursting with the exhilaration of my performance, I stepped up to join her, but she had a flat expression on her face. "What did you think? Did you like it?" I asked.

"It was okay," was all she said.

Her uninspired response completely deflated me. This was my big night. Couldn't she even fake enthusiasm? Didn't she understand how much being in the play meant to me?

"Where's Dad?" I asked.

"He didn't make it," she said. I was even more crestfallen. Dad hadn't seen the performance I'd worked so hard to get right. With Dad a no-show and Bill out with friends, I'd be riding home alone with Mom, which would mean sitting in a tense car filled with still energy. Why wasn't my mother excited for me?

Then I had a jolting thought. *Of course.* My mother had just sat through a play about mental illness, a comedy full of laughs about a family's embarrassment because of their eccentric brother. It made light of mental health issues and their psychiatric treatments. *Oh my,* I thought. *Of course that would make Mom uncomfortable.*

Sitting in the quiet car as we rode home, I prayed the play hadn't been painful for her, that maybe her medication had kept her from reading too much into the show. Maybe that was it. Maybe drugs had caused her flat reaction.

After a while, I turned toward the window, watched stars sparkle in the deep, dark sky, and let the magic of the evening slip back into my thoughts. Being part of the play had been so exhilarating that my body began to hum and buzz again right there in the car as I thought back to the show's key moments. Everything had gone beautifully: remembering my lines, the audience's laughter and applause, even the kiss. That night, people in my school and community had seen me differently. More than two hundred people had seen me as a theater girl, convincing in the role of an attractive nurse. The transformation felt like the stuff of magic, and my head swam with the delicious wonder of it. Thanks to Mrs. Jones, for one evening I went from ugly duckling to swan.

CHAPTER SIXTEEN

B ill started attending Central Washington State College in September 1963 as I began my senior year of high school. By the time he left for college, he'd begun acting brotherly, taking me along with him to music hall dances over the summer.

Winter came early that year, with a foot of snow dumped on the ranch by mid-November. When Bill came home for Christmas break, he took Mom and me to our local ski area, and I tried downhill skiing for the first time. Mom watched from the lodge as I repeatedly fell off the rope tow. After struggling all the way to the top, I tried to ski down, only to crash because I hadn't learned how to slow down or stop. I gave up early and came in exhausted, embarrassed that she'd witnessed my ineptness. But it was wonderful to see her laughing.

Mom had been staying on her meds, so life at home was pretty steady. She was even writing poems again, which gave me a sense of peace. If she felt like writing creatively, I knew she was returning to her old self. That January, Mom wrote a poem describing the winter's magical scenes and the difficulties the snow created.

OKANOGAN WINTER
Zelma Carson Lockwood

Three-foot icicles fringe the housetop,
    The snow is twenty-one inches deep.
Firewood "picnics" were interrupted,
    The nine-inch storm bluffed out the new Jeep.

Our green trees droop from each new snowfall,
    The fence posts resemble ice cream cones.
Some of us are watching our diets,
    Holiday treats still surround our bones.

Bill and Linda are learning to ski,
    Now they are all equipped at last.
To the Loop they go each time they can,
    Where the tow goes up and snow is fast.

Dad was forced to ask a neighbor for help,
    To plow the snow from our own driveways.
The Jeep required chains on all four wheels
    To feed the stock on "one of those days."

More days than not the sun does shine through,
    And the moon and stars sparkle so bright.
Sometimes the fog freezes on the trees,
    When near-zero weather comes at night.

Bookkeeper's figuring up the tax
    Al can now fix up his planes to spray.
Now that we are ready for winter
    Spring cannot be too far away.

She sent copies of her poem to our relatives, and I also saved one for myself. I loved how she captured the magic of the winter scenes—and how she omitted the embarrassing details of my first skiing attempt.

The first few months of 1964 had been viciously cold, but as I stood in the yard one balmy day in mid-March, I heard the *drip, drip, drip* of snow and ice melting all around me. I hoped this meant the deep snow on the ranch's northern slope would melt enough to let me ride between the remaining drifts to the top of the ridge and over to the far south side, where the snow had melted earlier from direct sun.

During lunch with Mom, I said, "I want to see if I can ride up through the snow on this side. If I can get to the top, the fields will be bare on the south side, and I can see how the wheat fields there have made it through the winter."

"Really?" Mom said. "The snow on this side is still pretty deep, and the road's not open."

"I know, but I want to see how far the horse can go. If I can't make it, I'll turn around and come back."

"Okay, but don't be gone too long."

"I won't. I'll get back well before dark for sure," I said as I headed for the former chicken house to get a halter.

Three years earlier, Pepper had given birth to another foal sired by the same black stallion who fathered Lucky. He was Bill's, and my brother named him Prince. Bill didn't handle Prince enough to make him calm and gentle, so we were left with a distrustful, skittish young gelding. I'd started riding Prince the previous summer, and he threw me off twice, but then I knotted the reins around the saddle horn as I had with Pepper, remounted, and galloped him until he stopped trying to thrust his nose down. He'd stopped bucking but still needed more riding to settle him. I caught and saddled him and headed him up the hill to see if we could get through to the ridgetop.

Bill's dog Tippy trotted ahead on the road, his white-tipped tail waving, and Smokey, Dad's Weimaraner, ran joyful circles above me on the steep, brushy hillside. The soft spring breeze carried the promise of swelling buds, green spikes in the bunchgrass, and the subtle fragrance of new blossoms.

I scanned the bare patches of ground under the pine trees where the snow was first to melt. Nestled among the fallen needles were clusters of spring beauties with their white faces of five petals. Mom said the pioneers ate these wildflowers in sandwiches because they had few other sources of vitamin C in early spring. I'd tried them in a sandwich once. They were edible but mildly bitter, so I instead chose to feast on them with my eyes when their blossoms popped up from beneath their brown blanket of pine needles.

We had to trudge through foot-deep patches of snow along the upward route. Prince found it tough going as the crust broke from his weight and scraped his ankles. He tried to turn back toward home, but I urged him forward, saying, "We're almost there, Prince!" When we topped the ridge, he was blowing hard and lathered with sweat, and he broke into a run when he reached the bare ground. I let him gallop a hundred yards as a reward, then forced him to slow to a walk so he could rest and relax. After burning so much energy, he began to settle down.

A hundred feet ahead, the bunchgrass exploded around Smokey and Tippy when they flushed a covey of sharp-tailed grouse. A dozen birds rocketed in different directions. Prince bolted in fright and almost unseated me before I battled him to a stop, calmed him with my voice and hand, and coaxed him forward along the ridge.

We headed for the eighteen-acre field on the south slope to see if the wheat crop we'd sown last fall had survived the snowy winter. Dad would be glad to have my report. Then, sudden angry barking erupted ahead where the dogs had gone out of sight over a hill. I'd never heard them sound so ferocious, and Prince was clearly rattled by their outburst. He whirled then danced up and down, refusing to go forward. Using both my legs and the reins, I pressed him toward the commotion.

As we approached, we saw in the swale below us the two dogs snarling and snapping as they attacked a deer standing in the greening wheat field. I was baffled. *A deer? How could they have caught a deer?* But when I rode closer, I saw the doe's useless front leg dangling from a shoulder wound red with blood. It leaped on its other legs and bleated in terror as the dogs charged and bit with a savagery I'd never seen from them.

The scene made no sense until my eyes caught movement on a nearby hillock. A stranger slinked away, looking back at me as he headed toward the lower gate. He carried his rifle low, as if he was trying to hide it from me. All I could think of was how I'd left my saddle gun at home, not expecting to need it and not wanting its lump in the scabbard tied under my right thigh. I was flooded with adrenaline, and for a moment, I sat frozen, unable to think. Then the violation sank in. *Who the hell does this guy think he is?* The defenseless deer's high, thin cries made me stop, and the gunman stopped too. We stared at each other, then he turned and hurried away.

Prince was jigging up and down, wanting to flee the blood, the crazed dogs, the stranger, and probably my tenseness. Holding him in place with tight reins, I yelled at the man with the rifle. "Hey, you! Come back here! You can't leave it like that— it's suffering! Come back and shoot it! Kill the poor thing!"

The man started back, unsure of me and wary of the dogs still attacking the deer. "I'll hit your dogs!" he shouted. "I don't want to shoot your dogs."

"I'll hold them off, but for God's sake, put a bullet in its head."

He came forward as I dismounted, keeping a tight grip on the reins. The dogs were lunging at the stumbling deer, and I screamed, "Tippy! Smokey! Here! No! Tippy, no! Stop! No!"

Smokey came to me, but Tippy kept attacking. I managed to grip his collar and pull him away while he leaped and snapped his foaming jaws. I held Tippy's collar in one hand and wide-eyed Prince's reins in the other. Both animals pulled hard, trying to break free of my hold.

"Okay. Shoot it!"

So close now he couldn't miss, the man fired his gun, and the disabled deer fell on her side. Then, as if still trying to run, her legs flailed against the moist earth until her breathing stopped, and she was still.

I let the dogs go to see the dead deer, controlled my terrified horse, and turned to face the trespasser, now standing ten feet away with his rifle lowered. "Why'd you do it? What're you doing here?"

"Look, miss, I'm sorry. I've got a family, and I'm out of work. The kids are hungry. I wanted to get them some deer meat."

"This is private property. It's posted. And we both know it's not deer season."

"Miss, I told you. I'm out of a job. My kids need to eat."

He moved closer. His bright blue eyes, furtive under the bill of his greasy cap, appraised my boots and my thigh. They were still moving up when it struck me: *Oh, God, not that too.* He almost smiled in the creepy way people with bad teeth do.

"Didn't think anyone would be up here," he said. "Where'd you come from, anyway?"

"It's my ranch. I live here."

For the first time, I noticed a white station wagon parked at the lower edge of the field. Two men stood next to it. "Those your friends down there?"

"Yeah."

"Well, it's done now. You might as well take the meat. No sense wasting it." If his story was true, at least his starving kids would have some food.

I'd caught him in the act, but I couldn't turn him in without knowing who he was. The car waiting down at the field gate was too far away for me to read the license plate, but if I could get a bit closer, I could memorize it. After that, Dad would know what to do.

"Let's go down and get your friends, and you can take the meat home."

"Okay." He shrugged and started walking, and I mounted Prince to follow. Just then, the two men got in the car and drove away.

"Looks like your friends aren't waiting around," I said, catching up with him.

"Guess they don't want to meet up with you, miss."

The retreating car stopped on the last rise before the county road dipped out of sight into the next valley. The men got out of the car and looked back at us.

"All right," I said to him. "I'll leave now, but you should at least take the meat."

"I'll come back for it later on."

I let Prince whirl toward home, both of us trembling. He tried to break into a run, but I kept him to a jigging walk while I agonized over the young deer's slaughter.

A week later, I rode Prince back to the place where the trespasser had killed the doe, expecting that she'd been taken by the men or eaten by hungry coyotes. But her body remained untouched. It sickened me that she'd been wasted that way, that her death had served no purpose, even to feed some hungry kids. I knew critters would eat her eventually, but looking at the senselessly fallen creature, I could feel only grief.

A chill wind ruffled the long hairs of her stiff brown body and stirred my tears. I wept for the beautiful, gentle creature. She'd simply been foraging on the spring slopes where she belonged. It was the hunter who had trespassed. I knew that ordering her death had been the only merciful thing to do, but she was the only deer I would ever want to see killed.

I became more vigilant as a steward of our land to preserve its deer and our livestock from invading hunters, but every death that followed brought pain and guilt. Once, I discovered a cut in our fence where a valuable young steer we were fattening for sale had been shot, dragged through to the county road, and hauled away—an outright theft. I felt cheated and sorry for the poor steer. But the worst trespass was still to come.

CHAPTER SEVENTEEN

In May 1964, I graduated from Okanogan High School. As the salutatorian, I was expected to write a speech, memorize it, and then recite it for the audience assembled in the gymnasium. It meant revealing myself in my own words, not acting a role on stage. The whole process was torture. I wallowed in fear that I'd speak a few sentences into the microphone and then forget what came next. And sure enough, I went blank twice. Mrs. Jones, my speech and English teacher, had to whisper the next line, just as she'd done in the play, and I went on, red with embarrassment.

After that dreadful experience, I was released to enjoy my summer on the ranch before entering college in the fall. I had cattle to manage, fences to check, and another young horse to train.

One July day I hiked up to the highest point of Dent Mountain. The stiff upwind at the cliff's edge forced me to clamp down my rumpled Stetson to enjoy the view. Spread out below me was a sprawling panorama of the glorious ranch I loved, and I stood there for several minutes, taking it in. How lucky I'd been to be raised here. What a magical and adventurous girlhood I'd had thanks to this wild country that had taught me so much and given me so much.

My gaze followed the middle ridge that ran east and west, topping the north- and south-facing slopes like a horse saddle. We called the ridge "the top of the ranch" because it was the highest part we cultivated. Our dirt road wound up the hill from our house to the barnyard, cut up the steep hillside to access the flats and fields Dad farmed, gained the summit of the ridge, and continued down through more fields on what we called "the back side." The view from atop Dent Mountain included the whole of the Chiliwist Valley to the north and the next valley to the south, Davis Canyon. Looking out over those tributary valleys, I caught glimpses of the Okanogan River winding through its carved-out valley with apple orchards and small towns nestled along its banks. "It's all so beautiful!" I called to the mountain. "Thank you for the gift of this gorgeous view!"

When we moved to the ranch, fulfilling my childhood dream of riding horses and my parents' dream of farming, I didn't know how this vast new territory would both stretch and sustain me or how it would harden me and forge in me an unrelenting work ethic, much like what I saw in my father. I witnessed the same kind of work ethic in my mother during those first years before her mental illness, whatever it was, began taking its toll and sporadically after her dark moods rendered her unable to keep up her former pace as a hard-working ranchwoman.

From the age of ten, I spent weekends and summers riding with my horse and dogs, managing the sheep and, later, the cattle. Through the years, through all the seasons, I explored every incline, field, and hollow of Sky Ranch. I herded sheep in all weather, sorted and moved cows, mended fences, observed wild creatures, killed rattlesnakes, and got myself into scrapes that handed me both bloody defeats and exhilarating victories.

Riding alone in the wild and boundless terrain, I often imagined a presence looking down from above and protecting me as I took risks to protect our crops and animals. Quite often, I was the only one out there, and I had to do what the situation called for despite my fears. Making it through my rough childhood without any broken bones or permanent injuries only made me more of a believer.

◆•◆

In a month I'd be leaving the ranch and my beloved horses to start college in Ellensburg, Washington, three hours from home by car and six by bus. Despite being rattled by the idea of life away from the ranch, I turned my attention to college. I had no idea where I should focus my studies or where I might want to live after graduation. Other than my high school teachers, I had no role models to help me imagine the life I might create for myself off the ranch, but I was excited to get started and to see where it would lead. I expected to attend parties and school functions and make new friends. I also decided college was going to mark a brand-new era of social life and wider learning.

I'd never given much thought to my wardrobe in high school, but now clothes were on my mind. What kind of clothes did college women wear to classes and social events? I owned mostly worn-out ranch wear, and I had no idea what I might need in college. To make the situation worse, I had no money for new clothes except my savings from babysitting jobs, and that didn't even total twenty dollars.

One day in August, Dad dropped me off at the Brewster clinic for my pre-college checkup while he went looking for farmers who hadn't paid for their wheat-spraying. The receptionist said Doc Lamberton had an emergency at the hospital, so I had more than an hour's wait. I walked the few blocks to the town center to see if I could find some new clothes that said "college woman."

I wandered into a small clothing shop and looked for my size on a rack that shouted *Sale!* My fingers touched something soft and satiny, like Lucky's coat after I'd given her a soapy bath and rinsed her clean. The deep royal-blue color of the dress also caught my eye, and I pulled it off the rack. I was charmed by the short-skirted sheath with cap sleeves, then stunned at the price: five dollars. That much, I could afford. If it looked good on me, I could wear it for dress-up events in college.

I found a cramped dressing room at the end of a corridor and pulled shut the cloth curtain. I shucked off my Keds, unbuttoned my plaid cotton blouse, and dropped my worn turquoise Lady Lee jeans to the floor, stepping out of them in once-white panties now gray from many launderings and a bra yellowed from sweat.

I stepped out of the dressing room wrapped in the startling blue of the acetate satin dress and faced my image in the full-length mirror. I'd never had a sophisticated dress like this, only a couple of cheap prom dresses, very demure with full skirts. This dress clung to my body from neck to knees, following every curve of my slender figure, outlining my waist, rounding out over my hips, and narrowing as it slid down my long thighs. Somehow the fashionable garment transformed me into a glamorous lady, except for the dark little eyes peering through thick lenses in white plastic cat-eye frames. The mirror reflected my homely face but also the figure in the dress, which was undeniably good-looking. In the mirror at home, my naked body looked tall and awkward, with muscle bulges but no feminine curves. This mirror showed a different body—slender, curvaceous, glamorous, and even sexy.

I decided the dress was my ticket to beautiful, and I simply had to have it. I would bring Dad here after my doctor's visit and ask him to lend me the five dollars until we got home, at which point I'd pay him right back. With no car of my own, there was no telling how or when I might get back here with my money. By then the dress would be gone.

Still picturing myself looking great in the blue dress, I walked back to the clinic for my appointment. Afterward, Dad drove up, and I climbed in his pickup.

"Dad, I found something I need to show you."

"What is it?"

"It's over at the dress shop on Main Street. Can we just drop by there so I can show you? It's on sale, really cheap, and it's something I'll need for college this year."

"We need to be getting on home now."

"Oh, please, Dad, it won't take very long, I promise."

"Well, all right, but make it fast."

Back in the dressing room, I slipped the blue dress over my head and worked it down my body. With its snug fit, I had to wriggle its narrow parts past my wider ones. It bunched above my wide hip bones, and I had to grab the hem to pull it down over my hips and thighs.

I stepped out of the dressing room, blushing because I was wearing such a formfitting dress in front of my father. His reaction made me blush even more.

"Yipe!" is all he said, but he clamped harder at the unlit Raleigh's cigar he sucked on. He stared and rocked back on his feet.

"Dad, it's on sale, only five dollars. It's a really good price. Would you get it for me?"

"Nope," he said, shaking his head. I saw his face redden a shade. I felt mine flaming.

"Why not? At college, I'll need a dress like this for parties, dances, and things. I don't have anything in style."

"Nope."

"Can't you afford it?"

"That's not it."

"I have money saved. Dad, I'll pay you back when we get home. I can pay you back."

Another shake.

"Please, Dad! This is the nicest dress I could ever afford. It's a good sale price!"

"Get your clothes back on. I'll be waiting in the pickup." He walked away toward the front of the store, leaving me confused, embarrassed, and deflated.

I'd worn a dress like this once before, as Nurse Kelly in my high school play. When Dad hadn't come that night, I'd felt a rush of disappointment. I'd wanted him to see me transformed into a grown-up woman, slender and beautiful, but he'd missed the performance.

Returning to the mirror, I saw a plain farm girl looking awkward in a show-off floozy dress, her bespectacled face red with shame. *Maybe Dad was right.* Maybe the dress made me look like a loose woman. He didn't say it, but he was thinking it.

My cheeks burned as I pulled off the dress. It stuck to my sweaty skin, but it rolled upward over itself and then over my head. My throat ached as I whispered farewell to the innocent dress hanging empty on the hanger.

The shiny blue satin still held the curves of my body.

The previous summer, I'd adopted a three-year-old mare that had been badly frightened during some rough cowboy's attempt to break her. The gray mare was three-quarters Arabian and pretty despite the scars on her head. Her mistreatment left her with a fear of ropes and any sudden movements. She was gentle enough, but when I rode her, she was very skittish and shied at even a rag on the fence or a weed blowing in the wind. She'd always be an unpleasant and unsafe riding horse, but with her bloodlines, I thought she might be a good broodmare. I named her Marica because it meant "sissy," according to my high school Spanish-English dictionary, and the name fit her well.

I'd found a white Arabian stallion with a good pedigree and a stud fee of fifty dollars, which Dad was willing to pay, and I hauled Marica to him for breeding. Then eleven months passed, and Marica birthed the female I'd hoped for. I named her foal Alteza, the Spanish word for "highness," because of her high-stepping dashes around her mother. Marica was nervous and protective of her baby at first, but I caught the filly and petted her every day until Marica relaxed with me and her filly grew friendly.

In September, I packed my suitcases for college and said goodbye to my Alteza, by then a leggy six-week-old turning reddish gray like Lynn Unger's strawberry roan that I'd once admired. Driving away with Dad to begin my first year at Central Washington State College, I looked back at Mom waving and hoped her happiness for my college opportunity could overcome her sadness at my leaving.

Busy as I was with my classes, homework, new friends, dorm activities, and part-time work that first quarter, I sorely missed my horses and the vivid colors and activities of the autumn season on the ranch. When I wanted to feel closer to the ranch and everything about it, I reread one of the poems Mom had shared in her annual Christmas letter four years before.

OCTOBER IN THE OKANOGAN
Zelma Carson Lockwood

Our majestic river flows onward,
    Ever toward God's open sea;
Flanked by shrubs in gorgeous hues,
    Autumn's beauty for you and me.

The scattered aspen thickets
    Turn now to yellow gold.
Occasional flakes of fluffy snow
    Crown sentinel mountains old.

Beef cattle wend their way lower
    To the greener pastures of home;
It's roundup time in the mountains;
    Noisy cowboys the high hills comb.

It's apple pickin' time in the valleys;
    Frost greets each sunny morn.
To pick the red and luscious fruit
    Roaming fruit tramps were born.

Our little town bustles with people
    Pickers from far and near.
Come to help us harvest our crop
    Climaxing a busy year.

Herders have counted their sheep,
    Brought them home to the winter fold.
Rams are eager and full of fight,
    Their battles a sight to behold.

Hunters are ready with bullets and gun,
    To stalk mule and white-tail deer.
To flush up the king of all game birds,
    Has been their dream all year.

Winter will come with its blanket of snow.
    This we love rather than fear.
Spring will burst forth with strength anew
    To inspire us again next year.

In her poem, Mom had captured everything I missed. I could barely wait for the upcoming October weekend when I'd head home for a few days to see my family and ride my horses.

I rode home with another student who dropped me off late Friday evening. The next morning, I waited for the horses to come down the hill to drink at the creek crossing, and when I spotted their dust and commotion, I ran to catch them for riding. Most of all, I wanted to see the pert little filly.

Marica was with the other horses, but the filly was missing. When I saw Marica's udder swollen with milk, I knew something had happened to Marica's filly. Alarmed, I caught Prince and rode up on the ranch to search for Alteza. I let Pepper, Lucky, and Marica follow along with us so Marica could call for her baby. Hearing the long, anguished whinnies that rang out from deep in her chest wrenched my heart.

When we neared the upper end of the big field, all the horses began acting skittish. Prince fought against veering left, so I directed him that way as the others hung back. That's when I found her. The little filly lay on her side with her legs splayed as if she were sleeping. The breeze caressed her soft, short mane. She'd been shot in the chest and probably died instantly.

My devastation was as deep as Marica's chest-deep whinnies. With tears streaming down my face, I kneeled beside the dead foal and ran my fingers through her baby-hair mane, trying to understand what had happened. October was deer hunting season. In my head, I pictured the little filly frolicking around the other horses, holding her white-fringed tail up and her nose in the air. Bounding along like that, she'd have looked like a deer about the size of a white-tailed doe. A trigger-happy trespasser must have shot first and found he'd bagged something he couldn't take home.

I returned to college two days later, still sick about the loss of my spirited filly. I felt responsible for her tragic shooting because I should have noticed how much she looked like

a deer when she frolicked around her mother. My eyes welled
with tears each time I thought of her. I should have expected
hunters on the high ridge. I should have kept Marica and her
foal in the pasture near the house during the hunting season.
I should have kept them safe.

I vowed never to let anything like that happen again.
Marica went on to birth two more foals with coloring similar
to Alteza's, and they pranced around as she had. Each September when I left for college, I reminded Mom to keep the
mare and foal near the house until hunting season ended. I
couldn't bear another gut-wrenching lesson in the brutality
of human predators.

◆

My role as a ranch rider had given me freedom and joy, but
my lonely country days and lack of connections with my peers
meant that I'd missed opportunities to develop social skills.
In college, my awkwardness and social discomfort were soon
apparent. I was also wearing glasses I hated, which seemed
uglier now that I was surrounded by the beautiful young
women on campus. Dad had refused to pay for contact lenses,
which I'd begged him for because many of my high school
friends wore and loved them. "Those are just cosmetic," he
said, "and I can't afford luxuries." I couldn't afford them either,
but I vowed to find a way to ditch the glasses. I signed up for
part-time jobs through the college work-study program.

Throughout my freshman year, I scrimped and saved
from my dollar-an-hour campus jobs until I had $200 to buy
contact lenses from an optometrist in Ellensburg. During the
spring quarter, with my thick brown hair in a shoulder-length
flip and my glasses banished, I had a professional photo taken.
For the first time since second grade, I liked how I looked.

In May 1965, with my freshman year of college soon

ending, I yearned to go home to the ranch. I'd already missed my spring rides to find the fuchsia shooting stars, yellow bells, and lavender camas blossoms among the greening clumps of bunchgrass. By now, their blooms would be gone.

With only two weeks left in the semester, I received a formal invitation to the dean's annual awards ceremony, although I had no idea why. On an early June day, I sat in the audience watching scholarships being announced. Could I be getting a scholarship? I hoped so—financial aid would certainly relieve Dad, who was now struggling to pay college expenses for both Bill and me. I leaned forward on the edge of my seat.

The next speaker was Dr. Robinson, the chair of mathematics, and my mind wandered. No chance of a scholarship here. I barely heard him say, "This year's award for outstanding freshman mathematics student goes to . . ."

Did he just call my name?

Heads turned as I walked to the front of the room, forcing a smile. Dr. Robinson held out a book with gold embossed lettering on its shiny green-and-black cover. He said, "We hope you'll go on in mathematics and that you'll find this useful."

I thanked him, took the book, and slinked to my seat. The handsome cover said, *Handbook of Mathematical Tables.* The inside cover carried the signatures of the department's three male professors. I had no idea why I was the one receiving this book. I hadn't expressed any particular interest in math. I'd finished the introductory math series designed for freshmen entering college from smaller high schools like mine where there might have been only one teacher teaching all the math classes. I'd completed trigonometry and algebra II in high school, but calculus hadn't been offered, and the advanced students entering my college from other schools had already taken it. At Central, I'd breezed through the basic math sequence with three As. I thought I was done with math and ready to focus on other subjects. Apparently, Dr. Robinson had other ideas.

When the school year ended, I carried home the book with the impressive inscription and showed it to Dad.

"Well, Cookie, what did you get this for?" he asked.

"I guess it's because I got As in all the math classes I took."

"That's a pretty fancy book. Good for you."

Dad's response worried me. I'd always shown my grade reports to Dad to justify his financial support, the same way I reported my work hours to the college to receive my meager paycheck. He praised my As in math but never my other As. Once, he even remarked, "Why would anyone take poetry, music, or psychology if they could get As in math?" I had a niggling worry he might not pay if those were the subjects I chose to study. I wasn't ready to choose a major, and I wanted to explore the offerings to find what I liked most. It wasn't math, but what if Dad didn't want to pay for college if I studied something else? I needed his help to pay for my college beyond what I could cover with scholarships, loans, and my scant earnings from campus jobs. I worked as many hours as I could manage (at two dollars an hour the second year) while juggling a heavy load of classes. But I couldn't cover it all. So far, Dad had been willing to fund my shortages in exchange for my summer help with the ranch chores and the aviation business bookkeeping.

I held the nagging feeling those math professors, along with my father, were expecting me to take calculus next. But I didn't have to decide until September. First, I would enjoy the summer with my horses.

CHAPTER EIGHTEEN

The aspens were turning gold and apples were being picked when I returned to Ellensburg to begin my sophomore year. I caved to the expectations and registered for calculus. Dr. Robinson was the instructor.

My difficulties began the first week. Robinson's homework often included story problems that involved electricity or physics, both of which operated in a world foreign to me. I learned best by seeing pictures in my mind of how things worked, but now I couldn't visualize what was happening in the story problems. I did the electricity and physics problems by rote, applying the rules, but I couldn't grasp what went on in the physical world behind the numbers. As the second week began, Robinson wrote a problem on the board, and I had no idea what he was talking about. My scowl attracted his attention. He called on me, and the outstanding freshman mathematics student had to say, "I don't know."

He was surprised. He'd expected me to have the right answer or work with him to derive it. He tried to help me by repeating the question, but the figures on the board dissolved into a fog. I shook my head and lowered my face, which was probably scarlet. *What just happened to me?* The bell saved me, and I rushed for the door.

That night, I tried the ten homework problems but couldn't solve more than one or two.

Within a few days, my struggle to understand the material spread from calculus to my other classes. I lost confidence in myself and felt like a failure. I shared my troubles with my closest friends in the dorm, who urged me to write home and let my parents know what I was experiencing. On October 6, 1965, I did.

> *Dear Mom, Dad, and Gram,*
>
> *I feel pretty bad about not writing like I should have and wanted to, but the past week and a half has been one of the most trying I've ever spent. You may have sensed this from my last letter. My mind has been in turmoil constantly ever since registration. I've talked to my professors and friends and lived a week of indecision and misery. I couldn't study. . . .*
>
> *I'm afraid one of the biggest single things bothering me is, "What will Dad say?" Is it right that this should be so extremely important and binding to me now? I don't know. At any rate, yesterday morning I changed my mind for the last time. I dropped calculus. I'm taking an accounting course instead. I feel much better, and right now I'd like to forget that calculus ever existed, but time will tell, and I can take it winter quarter if I change my mind.*
>
> *I have felt sick today in a very strange way. Since about 10:00 I've felt dizzy, and when the dizziness got worse, I was all shaky and fluttery inside and somewhat nauseated. I skipped class and lay down for an hour and a half this afternoon and also this evening after dinner. I still feel dizzy, so I'm going to skip the dorm meeting and go to bed. I've never felt like this before, and I don't know*

*what it is unless maybe a nervous reaction from the
strain I've been under. I'll probably feel better in
the morning after a good night's sleep. I think I'll
feel better after writing this letter, too, and letting
you know. . . .*

Love,
Linda

⬥

The next morning, I felt worse, so I went to the student health
center. The nurse on duty took my pulse and temperature and
asked, "How long have you been feeling dizzy and lightheaded?"

"For a week," I said, "and it's getting worse. I think it's
because I'm anxious about failing calculus. It's the first time
I've ever failed in anything, but I can't think because my head
just whirls, and I want to lie down, but then I can't sleep very
well either."

"Take a Tylenol tablet," she suggested.

"I already did, but it had no effect."

"I can't prescribe anything stronger. I recommend you
see a doctor for something to help with your anxiety."

"I don't have money or insurance to see a doctor here in
town. And I don't think I can ride home in a car or bus to see
my family doctor without getting nauseous and throwing up."

"I'm sorry," she said. "There's nothing more I can do
to help you."

I was sick and scared, and I made myself feel worse by
thinking about when Mom denied she needed help during her
manic episodes. She'd said there was nothing wrong with her
and that she'd just needed a vacation to get away from my
father, who was imposing too much work on her. Then she'd
grown worse, attacking Dad and blaming him for her problems
until she'd ended up in the hospital for psychiatric treatment.

I didn't want to be like Mom, denying the issues and refusing help. There *was* something wrong with me, and unlike her, I wanted someone to help me. I thought I might need to talk to a therapist, but I had no way to pay for counseling from a professional, especially a psychiatrist. It was terrifying even voicing that foreboding word, *psychiatrist*, but I was determined to get the help I needed.

I schemed to see the only psychologist I knew, the one who'd taught my Psych 101 class the year before. He told us to call him Mr. Brown because he only had a master's degree. He was stern and a bit remote, but I couldn't think of any other options for the help I needed.

On Thursday morning, I trooped to the psychology building and stood in front of Mr. Brown's office door. I knocked, and when the wooden door opened, he towered before me, tall and gangly with dark curly hair, a short beard, and kind eyes. I was heartened he remembered me from his class, so I dove in. "I need to talk with someone about a problem I have."

He invited me in, pointed to a chair, and then sat down behind his desk, which made him look less intimidating. I shifted in my chair and said, "I'm feeling sick, and I think it's about uh-mm . . . I'm having a crisis, and I think it's from my emotions, and I need to talk with a psychologist."

He said, "Linda, I'm an experimental psychologist specializing in research, not trained in counseling. I'll be glad to refer you to my colleague in town who's more qualified to help you."

I interrupted him. "No, please, I need to talk now, and I want to talk with you."

"Well then, I'll see if I can help you. What's been going on?"

I blurted it all out between sobs, the expectations of my father and the math professors, my failing calculus and dropping it, my fear of disappointing them, and my sickness.

He handed me a box of tissues, saying, "You need to go home and have a talk with your father."

"I'm afraid to talk to him. I'll start crying, and I won't be able to explain myself, and he won't understand."

Mr. Brown suggested we pretend he was my father so I could practice saying aloud what I needed to say. He moved to sit on the front corner of his desk, and we began, me sobbing, with him prompting me to go on until I wrenched out the words. After we'd finished role-playing, Mr. Brown said, "I can see you're scared, but what do you think your father will do?"

"He'll listen, I guess."

"Sounds like he's very important to you."

"Oh, yes. He is."

"Will he try to help if he knows you need him?"

I thought about that. There was the broken pitchfork, the new eyeglasses, and the new saddle. I said, "He's always come through for me when I've been in danger or have needed something important."

"Do you think you can go home and tell your father what you just told me?"

"Yes, I can try. Thank you—this has helped a lot. But I'm not sure how to get home feeling like this. I can't even travel very well."

He asked if Dad would come and get me if I told him how sick I was. With his encouragement, I marched back to my dorm, picked up the phone in the hallway, and called home. I hated to bother Dad, knowing October was his busiest flying season. But I had no other option.

Mom answered, and when I immediately asked for Dad, she sounded concerned. But she called Dad over, and I asked him to fly me home.

I could almost see his reluctant frown as he replied, "I have a lot of orchard work lined up right now. Why don't you get a ride home this weekend?"

My stomach dropped, but I gulped and plunged ahead. "I can't wait until then, Dad. It's getting worse every day, and I don't think I could stand riding in a car or bus. I'm already nauseous all the time, and I'd get really carsick."

"Well, let me see, Cookie. I think I can get away at noon tomorrow and fly down to get you. Can you get to the airport there?"

"I'll call a taxi. It's only a short way from my dorm. I think I can make it."

"Okay, I'll give you a call when I'm ready to take off from Okanogan. I should be there an hour after that."

We said goodbye, and I lay back down on my dorm bed. He was coming to take me home! I knew I could survive nausea for a one-hour flight in my father's plane easier than I could for a six-hour bus ride. And I'd never felt nervous flying with my father, who was the best pilot ever.

The next afternoon I took a cab to the nearby airport and hurried to meet my father when he winged in and taxied up in his brown-and-silver Cessna 180. He opened the passenger door and handed me a small package. "Gram sent some of her Dramamine. She said it would help with the airsickness."

My sweet Gram! Her pills were a godsend. I took two. The dizziness I'd felt for over a week was gone by the time we touched down at the Okanogan airport.

The next morning, Mom drove me to Brewster and waited in the lobby while I saw Doc Lamberton, my family doctor since I'd turned fourteen. I told him about my crisis and the dizziness, and he offered me a mild tranquilizer.

I almost shouted, "No, I'm not like my mother!" Instead, I squirmed in my seat and said, "Do I really need to take a tranquilizer?"

This doctor had earned my trust. I'd started seeing him after my previous doctor proved useless in helping me with my painful periods; in my presence, he'd turned to my mother and said, "She'll grow out of it." But when I consulted Doc Lamberton, he'd offered solutions, like thyroid pills and soothing medicines to keep me from throwing up, and some of them had helped. He also understood my aversion to tranquilizers because he knew about my mother's illness.

"This is a very mild tranquilizer," Doc explained. "It will help you feel like you can conquer your problems. Within a week, you'll be feeling better, and then you can stop taking them."

I nodded and told myself I'd give it a try but would quit as soon as I could.

I filled his prescription for two weeks of Librium in a low dosage, and within two days, I felt normal again—no longer dizzy. I was ready for my talk with Dad. Mom said she'd given him my letter, but he hadn't yet asked me about it, probably because he was waiting for me to bring it up. I waited until after supper, then approached the faded red davenport where he reclined, scanning his *Trade-A-Plane* newspaper.

"Dad," I said.

No reply.

"Dad," I pressed.

"What?" he said, lowering his paper.

"I need to talk with you. It's what I came home for."

"Okay, I'm listening."

Afraid again, I started to cry.

Dad sat up and leaned toward me. "What's wrong, Cookie?"

I didn't know where to start, but picturing my psychology professor bolstered me, and the words tumbled out. "Dad, I'm having trouble with calculus," I sniffed. Then I took a deep breath and delivered what felt to me like a bomb: "And I've dropped the class."

"Okay."

"I know you want me to take math . . ."

"It's up to you what you take."

What? Did I hear him correctly? "But you told me that anybody who can get As in math should take it, and when I wanted to take music and literature classes, you said something about those classes not being worth paying for, so I kept taking math to get your approval."

He furrowed his brow and said, "Of course I'm proud that you get As in math. I always had a hard time with math when I was in college. But I never said you had to take math or I wouldn't pay for your college."

"I'm sure you did, Dad, last winter quarter when I was going to take those other classes."

"I don't remember saying that, but look, Cookie, you're doing a great job, and you can figure out for yourself what you want to do in life and how to prepare for that."

I was flooded with relief and wondered how I could have misunderstood Dad so completely and let my fears grow so huge. Maybe he had been joking about not paying for music and poetry classes, but I hadn't heard any humor in it, so I'd selected classes to satisfy him. All these months, I'd been making myself sick with worry about what he'd do if I quit taking math classes. But here he was, proving he loved me and would always be there for me. He'd proven it by picking me up and bringing me home. And now he was proving it in a way I needed even more by letting me choose my own path.

"Oh, thanks, Dad," I blubbered. I moved closer to the couch, and he opened his arms to me. I leaned against him and rested my head on his chest. Then he held me and said, "You're going to be all right." I knew it was true. He was my rock of safety and protection, and I needed him for that because I'd felt as if I was on my own for so much of my life. My mother hadn't always been there for me, though I didn't understand why.

I returned to Ellensburg the following Monday, ready to work. And work I did. I had to make up for the missed days and regain my stride. Right away I felt like myself again, and at quarter's end, I earned all As. I visited Mr. Brown and thanked him for showing me how to talk with my father and giving me the boost to do it. He said, "Congratulations, Linda! Thanks for coming in to let me know you did it. I'm glad I could help."

I decided to continue my accounting and business courses the next quarter because I wanted to be proficient in subjects that would support a practical career. But my failure at calculus still nagged me. I didn't want to feel like a failure in anything, so I decided I'd try it again when it was *my* choice and mine only. In the spring of my sophomore year, I took calculus, this time with Dr. Dale Comstock, a professor whose teaching style was a fantastic match for my learning style. He drew precise pictures on the board to illustrate how to integrate the area under a polynomial curve by taking thinner and thinner slices all the way to infinitely thin, and I could see it happening in my mind's eye. I finished his calculus class with a splendid A, then signed up for more of his classes and went on to earn an eighty-credit major in mathematics.

I repaid the math professors for their early recognition with the fancy book award by becoming their first student to earn a math degree with honors. Dad was pleased and proud about my decision to return to math, but he kept his word that I could chart my own path. Through it all, I learned how and why to base decisions on what I wanted and needed rather than what would earn approval from others.

Out of this frightening, emotional experience came another lesson. I'd always experienced strong emotions while growing up but had no one to talk to about them. My brother taunted me until I exploded at him, and I coped by running up the creek and climbing to my secret place on a little hillock ringed by trees, where I cried until I felt calm again. Or I mounted my horse and rode into the sagebrush with my dogs running alongside. But the calculus block and panic attack weren't things I could run away from. They were happening *within* me. My anxieties made me sick, and the parallels I saw with my mother's episodes worried me tremendously. I needed help, so I called on friends, family, a psychologist, and my family doctor, and each contributed until I'd gathered enough support to resolve my issues.

Now I had a new strategy to use when I was anxious or upset: reaching out to people I trusted and asking for help. It made me feel stronger, like being part of a brigade or team. And in learning to voice my emotions, I felt better about my chances of avoiding my mother's fate. I believed her emotional isolation was an enemy, and I would do anything I could to keep that enemy from crossing my front line.

CHAPTER NINETEEN

In June 1966, I finished my sophomore year of college and came home for the summer. Right away, I could tell that life on the ranch had changed.

Only our seven horses and the forty cows with their spring calves remained. In the seasons when native grass swept the hillside, they could fend for themselves, and in snowy winters, Dad would be home to give them hay. All the other animals were gone now—no more sheep, no more chickens, and no more cow to milk—leaving Mom with no daily chores for animal care and no one to cook for except Dad, and then only in winter. I could tell from her letters that she was growing increasingly lonely and depressed, and when I came home for summer break, I found nothing had changed for her.

During the break, I helped with whatever the family and ranch needed, which included spending a lot of time at the Tonasket airport to help Gram keep the business accounts and prepare meals for Dad, Bill, and the hired pilot who often ate with us. I preferred being at the ranch with Mom and my horses, but Gram was overloaded, so I stayed at the airport night after night.

One morning in early August, I said to Dad, "I'm caught up with the business books. Would it be okay for me to spend a couple days at the ranch with Mom?"

"Yes, go check on your mom," Dad said. "She probably needs some company."

Driving the farm truck, I set off for the ranch, eager to see my horses and ride up the hill to check on the cattle and fences. For me, being with the animals and getting out onto the property was the essence of the ranch experience, and I was antsy to get back to it. Besides that, I felt sorry for Mom being left by herself with no transportation when the rest of us were together at the airport.

I pushed the old truck at fifty miles per hour through the punishing August heat, hot air blowing through the open windows. It rattled up Chiliwist Road and finally roared up the hardened dirt lane to our home. Crossing the yard, I stepped around the usual clumps of horse manure and the yellowed spots of dog urine, then tripped up the back steps into the kitchen and paused in the dining room. Something felt strange, tense. It was as if the house was holding its breath.

"Mom, are you here?" I called.

No answer. No sign of any activity. The sun was high, and Mom should have come inside by then, her morning chores done. This was weird. Maybe she was taking a nap.

Still calling her name, I turned down the short hallway and entered my parents' bedroom. A rank smell hit me like a tidal wave. The offending smells were as strong as the stench in the maternity ward during lambing time. I saw an unmoving shape under the covers. Was Mom sleeping? I walked to the side of the bed.

"Mom? It's me. Wake up." I said it again, louder.

I leaned down and touched her shoulder. She was warm and breathing, but something seemed very wrong. "Mom, wake up!" I pushed at her, rocking her.

She stirred and moaned. Then she mumbled, "Ahm-moh-kay."

The bed was yellow, soaked with urine and reeking of ammonia. What was going on? My mother was barely conscious.

I rushed to the telephone on the dining room bureau. The nearest emergency responders were the volunteer firemen in Malott, five miles away, three of those on a bumpy rural road. Calling them wouldn't get help here fast enough. I had to act on my own right now. I'd call her general doctor.

Raising the handset, I heard voices on the five-party line. I broke in.

"I need to make a call. Please hang up. It's an emergency."

"What's wrong?" asked Vern Cox, our nearest neighbor.

"I need to call the doctor."

"What happened?"

"It's my mom. I just came home and found her in bed, and I need to talk to her doctor."

"We'll hang up," Vern said.

I dialed the doctor's office in Omak, and when the nurse answered, I blurted, "My mom is in bed, and she won't wake up."

As I waited for the doctor to come to the phone, my thoughts raced. *Will I have to rush her to the hospital in Omak? What if she's dying in there while I'm standing out here? What's wrong? She's never been sick in bed like this before. What is this? What's happening?*

The doctor came on the line and asked, "How long has she been like that?"

"I don't know. I just came home, but she's been here alone for several days."

"So she's been like this for at least a day?"

"I think so. More than a day. The bed is soaked with urine."

"Did she take an overdose of her medication? What did she take?"

To both questions, I had to say, "I don't know." That made me feel incompetent, like I didn't even know my own mother.

"She'll be all right," the doctor said. "Just get her up and moving around and get some coffee and liquids into her."

I found his apparent lack of concern jolting. "Really?" I asked. "That's all?"

"Bring her in to see me in a day or so."

I hung up and dashed back into Mom's room. She still hadn't moved and was mumbling incoherently. I was in the kitchen plugging in a coffee pot half full of stale coffee when Vern Cox knocked at the kitchen door.

"I heard," he said, "and I thought you'd need some help."

We went into the bedroom and threw off the covers, and then Vern helped me lift Mom out of bed. We led her out to the living room and made her walk back and forth, still in her urine-soaked nightgown. Every few minutes we asked her to sip the warmed-over coffee.

"I'm all right," she stammered in a slurred voice. "I'm tired. Just put me down." We refused. I insisted she swallow more coffee, and Vern kept her walking.

It sickened me to think she might have been in this state for several days at this point, alone and suffering. On a hunch, I slid open the lid of the Franklin woodstove, and there on the old coals was a pill bottle. I lifted it out and found it empty. The prescription bottle read, "Take one at bedtime as needed for sleep." It had her name on it.

I held up the bottle. "Mom, what's this? Did you take all these pills?"

"I don't remember," she said.

"How long were you in bed like that?"

"I don't know."

We let Mom sit down, and I called Dad at the airport. He said he'd be home in an hour. With the emergency apparently over, I thanked Vern and let him go home.

I urged Mom to sip chicken noodle soup, then I had to get her cleaned up. In the bathroom, I pulled up her soaked nightgown and helped her into the bathtub, trying to avoid looking at her naked body. I'd never seen her naked before, but I realized I was more embarrassed than she seemed to be. I rummaged in her dresser, found a clean nightgown, and laid it beside her towel.

The next day, Dad and I took Mom to her family doctor. Dad showed him the empty bottle. The doctor said he'd prescribed the pills because Mom had complained she was having trouble sleeping. Knowing her history, he hadn't given her enough barbiturates to kill her in case she took them all at once.

This overdose was something new, and it scared me. Usually, Mom carried out her cooking and chores and seemed okay if she took her "tranquilizers," our family's code name for the Mellaril and Artane prescriptions she'd been taking since her last hospitalization. But it appeared she'd intended to overdose. Whether it was an intended suicide or a cry for help, I didn't know. Both possibilities made my heart ache.

On the way home, Mom and I waited in the car while Dad went into a store. I leaned toward her and gently asked, "Why did you do that, Mom?"

"I don't know," she said, turning away toward the window.

"No, really. Why did you take so many sleeping pills?"

"You wouldn't understand."

I gave up and leaned back in my seat. I wanted to understand, but I couldn't. She'd never shared her feelings with me, even during good times, and now I was left to speculate. Did she feel guilty she'd let the family down, unable to do her chores? Did she think she had no other way out of her pain and confusion, and had she asked for the sleeping pills with that goal in mind? And now was she ashamed of failing to end her life and being caught trying?

Dad didn't have any better luck than I did in getting Mom to talk about it. On the drive home, she met his questions either with silence or "I don't know." I never talked to Dad about it because I assumed he didn't understand her reasoning any more than I did. Bill stayed at the airport with Gram, avoiding everything.

Everything about Mom's illness was a mystery to me, and if her act was a cry for help, I didn't know where to get it. The summer before, I'd reached out to her family doctor. She'd complained of arthritis pain in her back, and I could see she had the beginnings of a dowager's hump. Wanting to get her some relief, I took her for a checkup.

After a physical exam, the doctor said, "How much pain do you have in your back?"

"Oh, I don't know," Mom said. "Most days it's not bad, but it really aches if I try to plant flowers or weed the garden, so I can't do much."

"I'd like you to get more exercise. Walk as much as you can and get adequate sleep at night."

"It bothers me in bed at night too," Mom said.

I broke in. "Would you consider changing her meds?" I asked him. "They seem to be degrading her physical health over time. I see her doing less and less activity."

He shook his head. "I can't change them. I'm not a psychiatrist. You need to talk to a psychiatrist about that."

There were no psychiatrists or family counseling services in our rural county. The psychiatrists at Eastern State Hospital had stabilized Mom and discharged her with the two prescriptions she had continued taking. Now I wished we could work with someone at the mental hospital to deal with Mom's overdose, but ESH didn't offer outpatient treatment. I seemed to hit nothing but dead ends when trying to help with my mother's health.

For the rest of the summer, I stayed with Mom at the ranch or brought her with me when I went to the airport. I didn't know what else to do for her, and it made me feel ignorant and helpless. My other family members were busy with summer crop dusting work and didn't seem interested in helping, so it was up to me. I encouraged Mom to find things to do in her spare time, like crocheting, sewing, or gardening, which she used to enjoy. I suggested she learn a new craft, but she wasn't interested. When I thought about how lonely her life had become, my stomach rattled with anxiety. I understood what a lonely place the ranch could be, but it also held many charms for me because I could play with my horses and ride on the ranch and the surrounding lands. I loved spending time alone in nature, adventuring with the horses and the dogs. But Mom just stayed in the house, more and more isolated.

As the summer of 1966 ended, Bill and I planned our returns to college in early September. He would drop me off in Ellensburg and continue to Seattle. On the day we were to leave, I looked at Mom across the breakfast table. She looked weary and much older than her fifty years, with her near-black hair fading into salt-and-pepper.

"Thanks for breakfast, Mom," I said. "I'm sorry we have to leave today. I know you get lonely here without us."

"I'm proud of you and Bill for going to college, and I'm glad you can," she said.

I knew that was a shorthand reference to the sacrifices she and Dad were making to pay for our educations. "Thanks for your support, Mom," I said, wracked with guilt over leaving her.

When we shared a goodbye hug, I said, "I love you, Mom." She said, "I love you too," but her arms were loose, and there was no light in her brown eyes.

At school, I mailed Mom a letter every two weeks asking how she was feeling and telling her about my classes, the fun I was having with friends, and my experiences being assistant to Mrs. Bailie, the head resident of my women's dormitory. Mom always wrote back, telling me about Dad's current flying work, how my horses were doing, and what she'd heard from

Bill, but she never wrote about how she was feeling about anything beyond looking forward to my next visit home.

During my junior year, I stayed at school for the summer quarter to pick up the advanced calculus classes I needed for my math major. When I came home in August of 1967, I felt run-down, and Doc Lamberton performed surgery to remove my tonsils, which had become infected with strep. I went home that evening. By the following day, my throat felt so good that I was swallowing ice cream and the delicious tapioca pudding Mom made for me. But when I awoke the next morning, it hurt to swallow, and I had a fever of 101 degrees. The doctor had said I should call if I experienced increasing throat pain or a rising fever.

"Mom," I said, "I think we should call Doc Lamberton. My throat really hurts today, and my temperature is up."

"Maybe it will get better," she said. "Let's wait and see."

I asked her again to call the doctor, and again, she said it wasn't time yet. This was a repeat of when she'd delayed getting me to the doctor for two days after the sledding accident, which left me with a permanent scar. I was frightened because I knew I couldn't trust my mother to make the right decision when it came to my health care. Why didn't my mother want me to get the medical attention I needed?

Crying from pain and frustration, I threatened, "I don't feel like getting up, but if I have to get out of bed and crawl to the phone, I will, and I'll never forgive you for forcing me to make the call."

That did it. She called Doc, who told her to bring me in. He prescribed an antibiotic, which reduced the pain and fever. From then on, I knew the responsibility for my health care was mine.

After my 1968 college graduation, I spent the whole summer at the ranch and experienced yet another example of Mom's aversion to seeking medical attention. One day in late

July, my right eye felt so scratchy I couldn't wear a contact lens. Two days later, I felt stabbing pains in that eye, and it worsened in sunlight. Terrified it could damage my eyesight, I called my doctor and described the piercing pains.

"I need to look at that," Doc said. "Come right in."

I hung up and said, "Mom, he wants to see my eye. You'll have to drive me to Brewster."

Earlier, Mom had urged me to see if my eye got better. Now she said, "Maybe you can drive yourself there."

"I can't drive. It hurts in sunlight, even if I cover that eye."

"Now?" she asked.

"Yes. Now."

Mom drove, and I ducked down in the back seat, covered both eyes, and tried to endure the piercing pains.

When Doc Lamberton finished his exam, he said, "Don't worry. It's just a small corneal scratch, but it's infected and needs treatment to help it heal. Use these drops, and it will heal in no time."

I vowed that would be the last time I'd let Mom delay my trip to a doctor. Why was she so afraid of doctors?

———◆———

Bill and I received our college degrees in June 1968. (He required an extra year after transferring from Central to the University of Washington.) Then I went on to the University of Michigan with a scholarship to earn my master's degree in economics while Bill joined the army and served a year in Vietnam. In 1969, we both married and moved to Seattle, officially leaving Mom with an empty nest. Our departures spelled new beginnings for us but boredom and loneliness for her.

In January of 1970, Tony and I were living in Seattle when Dad called to tell me Mom was back in Eastern State Hospital.

She'd flown with him to a pilot's convention in Los Angeles, stopped taking her meds, and become psychotic. During their flight home, she became paranoid about his Cessna crashing and demanded to take the bus home. He gave her cash and bus tickets, and she made it to Eugene, Oregon, where she ended up in a psychiatric ward because she was wandering the streets, not knowing where or who she was. Someone called Dad. He picked her up and then drove her to Eastern State Hospital, where psychiatrists stabilized her using antipsychotic medicines. This episode was a strong reminder to all of us that Mom could never stop taking her meds.

In November of 1971, Tony and I drove to the ranch for Thanksgiving with Mom and enjoyed her delicious full-course turkey dinner.

By the next spring, we were ready to start a family. We'd just learned I was pregnant when my father called on April 13, 1972, and said, "Your mom is dead."

The next two weeks were a fog of grief that overwhelmed what should have been happy news when I told Dad and Gram of my pregnancy. When Tony and I got home from Mom's funeral and burial on the Oregon coast, I went back to work and tried to focus on the future we'd planned. Now, that future would be without my mother.

CHAPTER TWENTY

Six weeks after my mother's suicide, the awful waves of morning sickness had passed, and I felt well enough to drive to the ranch and spend Memorial Day weekend with Dad and Gram to sort through Mom's belongings. When I called Dad with my plan, he said, "I'm glad you can come, Cookie. You take whatever you want, and I'll dispose of the rest."

It was late when I arrived after the five-hour drive from Seattle. I had only enough energy to hug Dad and Gram and then crawl into bed. I lay in the darkness of my pink bedroom, but my thoughts drifted when sleep didn't come. Lying awake, I compared this neglected old ranch house to the home Tony and I had recently bought near Seattle, a well-maintained rambler with two bathrooms. On the ranch, our family of four, sometimes five with Gram, made do with one bathroom, no shower, and everything in constant need of repair, like the stopped-up toilet and the rotting linoleum under the leaking bathtub.

In this poor old house, nothing was fixed until it was completely broken, and sometimes not even then. Money was short and came in unevenly through the year, so Dad prioritized fixing the things that could help earn money. Comforts and luxuries, like a properly functioning bathtub or a toilet that didn't have to be flushed with a bucket or an interior stairway to the basement to retrieve Mom's food stores—these things had to wait.

I thought of the years when I'd dressed and slept and read into the night in this little bedroom in the double bed that nearly filled the room. I'd been lying awake for more than an hour, and I'd run through all the memories and nostalgia I could. But the core emotional issue I'd been avoiding wouldn't leave me alone. Why didn't I tell my mother about my pregnancy when I first found out? After her suicide, I'd been filled with guilt and regret, thinking the news I'd withheld for four days might have changed her decision. But that night, a new understanding dawned on me. Maybe I'd delayed out of a subconscious need to protect my baby from the dark shadow of my mother's illness. Maybe by not telling her, I thought I was already being a good mother. That possibility gave me some comfort, and I eventually drifted to sleep.

I woke up the next day hearing the familiar morning sounds of birds and frogs outside my window vent, and it was strange, almost eerie, not to hear Mom's morning sounds along with them. The house was quiet and cold, and on cold mornings, she was always the first one up. She'd open the lid of the black Franklin stove with a loud scrape of metal on metal, then crumple and stuff newspapers inside, pick a double handful of kindling from the woodbin, lay it on the crumpled paper, strike a red-and-white-tipped wooden match on the metal stove with a scratch and snap, light the paper in several places, and slide back the complaining stove lid. Soon came the welcome crackling and popping as the pitchy fir kindling caught and blazed.

My bedroom door was near the stove, and the fire-starting always woke me up. I'd always resented the ruckus but was grateful for the warmth. If I snuggled in my bed until the stove radiated heat, I could spread my cold jeans and coveralls on the nearby settee to warm them. Then I'd pull on my barn clothes and milk the cow before changing into my school clothes to eat breakfast and catch the bus. That had been my routine from the time I was thirteen until we sold the milk cow when I was sixteen.

Every morning from now on, the house would stay quiet and cold until Dad rose and started the fire. No more warm mornings, no more warm, yeasty bread, no more warm venison mincemeat pies, no more full-course dinners. The house itself seemed dead. It was as if the place had lost its heart.

Even in her later years, my mother lived for her children. Bill and I were her remaining hope—our visits brought her joy, and she took pride in our careers when her crazed outbursts stifled her ambitions for publishing her writing and an apple recipe cookbook, thanks to numbing drugs and treatments at mental hospitals.

During Mom's last two years, Dad lived at the ranch year-round. In 1970, he lost his pilot's license because of diabetes and hired other pilots to fly his planes and the helicopters he flew for the orchard work. He was devastated because he'd always loved flying. The business became less profitable because it was more efficient and productive for him to fly than for anyone else to. It pained me that Dad's passion was taken from him. I knew how much he loved being a pilot, and I'd always been proud of how good he was at it. In his many thousands of hours of hazardous flying, he'd never made a landing he couldn't walk away from. Even after Dad's flying career ended and he lived on the ranch full-time, he left each morning to farm or pursue business deals, so Mom still spent her days in the isolated loneliness of the ranch house. With Bill and me out of the house and visiting infrequently, I'm sure Mom felt no one needed her, which must have been depressing.

Now I had to live with the fact that I'd missed the chance to bring light to her life by sharing the wondrous news that she would be a grandmother.

I huddled with these morning thoughts in the little bedroom only ten steps from where my mother had sat on the faded maroon davenport, pointed the revolver at her forehead, and pulled the trigger.

Gram made breakfast, and Dad left for work after we ate. I went to the basement where I'd slept as a child and peered through Mom's canning stores to load a box that I'd take home for meals with Tony, knowing that each bite of fruit and jam would remind me of Mom preserving it. In the dim light of a bare bulb, I saw Mason and Kerr jars filled with the sunny peaches, pale pears, purple prunes, and golden apricots Mom bought every summer from friends in the Okanogan River Valley. There were pint jars of red raspberries that went into the canner when the lush bushes in her garden bore more than we could eat fresh over our breakfast cereal and on our ice cream. After Bill and I left home for good, Mom stopped canning. The dates written on the jar lids were now several years past.

When the cramps began, the discomfort drove me out of the basement and back upstairs to the bathroom. I'd had cramps in my belly while driving from Seattle the day before, but I'd tried to ignore them, and they'd eventually subsided. Now they were back, and I saw blood spots in my underwear as if my period was starting.

I'd always had painful periods. Sometimes the cramps had grown so severe and unrelenting that I'd turn pale, break into a sweat, and vomit. The pains would last all day, and the only thing that helped was a sleeping pill if I could keep it down long enough to work. Hours later, I'd wake up feeling exhausted but no longer in pain. Every month, I suffered a lost day of agony.

But why now? I was pregnant—there should be no cramps, no blood. And to protect the baby's health, I'd refused to take any drugs, so that ruled out the relief I usually found in sleeping pills. I crawled into bed to rest, but the cramps grew stronger.

Now I was really getting nervous. I called out to Gram, who was reading in the living room.

"Gram, would you come in here, please? I need you," I said.

Gram came into my room and said, "Oh, my dear, what is it? You look like you're in pain."

"It's cramps like I used to have, and it's getting bad."

"My goodness, can I get you something for it?"

"I don't know what I can take that won't harm my baby. I need to call my friend from college, who's now a nurse at the doctor's clinic in Omak."

Gram looked up the phone number for the doctor, and I dialed it, my finger shaking.

The clinic receptionist who answered didn't want to bring Sharon to the phone, but I said it was urgent. As I waited for Sharon, I leaned over the bureau and rubbed my abdomen, silently begging the woman to hurry. Several minutes passed. Then I heard, "Linda, it's Sharon. What's happening?"

My voice quavered from the pain. "I'm at the ranch. Sharon, I'm pregnant and having cramps, and they're getting worse. I'm scared."

"How many weeks since your last period?"

"About twelve."

"Is it the time of month you'd be having a period if you weren't pregnant?"

I thought for a moment. "Yes, it is."

"Now, don't worry, Linda, some women have break-through bleeding or even continuing periods, and they still carry to term. Have you taken anything for the pain?"

"No, I was afraid it might harm the baby."

"If you come in, the doctor can give you some Darvon. It's a mild painkiller that won't harm the fetus."

"I'm cramping too much to drive. I might throw up or pass out," I said. "Gram never learned to drive, and Dad left for town. I don't know how to reach him."

"I'll bring you the Darvon," Sharon said, "but I can't leave until my shift ends at four. Take five hundred milligrams of Tylenol, lie down, and don't worry about the baby."

I staggered back to bed. Gram brought the Tylenol tablet, but it didn't ease my pain, and the cramps grew stronger, hour by hour.

Four hours later, the dogs barked as Sharon's Volvo rolled up the lane. She handed me two small yellow tablets and watched me with concern. "It's the strongest thing I can give you," she said. Sharon stayed and watched as I writhed with pain. After an hour passed, she said, "The Darvon should have helped by now."

"It hasn't," I said, grimacing.

"We should get you to the hospital before it gets worse," she said. "They can give you something stronger there. Can you walk?"

By now, I was mumbling more than speaking. I got out of my bed, hunched over and grasping my stomach, and stumbled to the car. Sharon helped me lie down in the back seat. Gram handed me a pan in case I threw up, and then she shut the car door and waved us off.

Sharon drove—it seemed forever—five hundred feet down our lane, two miles down the jarring washboard of Chiliwist Road to the highway in the Okanogan Valley, three miles north to Malott, nine miles upriver to Okanogan, and four more miles to the hospital in Omak.

The pain broke across my body in waves that issued from the core of my belly and spread until I tensed from head to toe, unable to relax. I rolled on my side, dug my feet into the car's floor, and willed the medication to stop the curling, crashing waves that battered my midsection.

When we arrived at the hospital, people dashed out with a stretcher, lifted me onto it, and wheeled me into an exam room. The pain was grinding at my belly, but I was afraid it might mean the worst if it stopped. The people in white asked me questions and busied themselves with procedures while I rode the waves of pain. Finally, a nurse came toward me with a shiny needle in her thin, white hands and injected cold liquid into my vein.

In that instant, at the threshold between pain and relief, I glimpsed why my mother might have turned the pistol to her forehead and pulled the trigger. She'd suffered years of complicated psychic pain, and perhaps it had become so excruciating she would have done anything to stop it. My pain was physical and my circumstances very different, but it had become so agonizing that I thought, *Just end it.* Even though I knew the medication going into my vein risked the pregnancy, I was desperate for the relief I knew it would deliver. I wondered, *Was Mom's desperation so acute she saw no other way out?*

Then I slipped into unconsciousness.

◆⋙⋘◆

When I awoke and began struggling back from nothingness into stark white light, there were no more people in white bustling around me, but all around was white, white, white. Light bounced from white sheets to white ceilings to a white blanket to a white floor scrubbed clean of dirt, bacteria, and life. That's when I had a flash of dread, sensing there was no other life in the room. I looked down and saw my body wrapped in a white blanket, a mummy's wrapping.

Just then, a white-clad woman bustled in and chirped, "Oh, you're awake. How are you this morning?" She pressed a cold, round sensor against the inside of my elbow and squeezed a rubber ball until the inflating blood pressure cuff tightened around my arm; then she listened and watched as the pressure released. She pressed my wrist with her dainty fingertips, and her warm touch comforted me as she counted my pulse against the passing seconds.

"Feel like sitting up?" she asked in that perky voice that made me wonder why she was in such a good mood. "Your breakfast will be coming in soon."

I shifted in bed, and my elbows rasped against the starched cotton sheet as I tried to rise for her pillow plumping. Too weak, I gave up and slumped back onto the bed.

She lifted my shoulders and propped me up. "There you go, dearie." She padded away so focused on her duties I didn't have an opening to ask what was going on with me. I flopped back against the pillow, surprised by how weak I felt. I felt as if something had changed. What had happened to me besides a night of drugged sleep? The pain was gone, but my strength was also gone, stolen by the pain and later by the drug that eased it. Then I had a jolting moment of clarity. *Was I . . . ? Did I . . . ? Oh, God, no.*

The chirpy nurse shuffled in, carrying breakfast. She set it on a bed tray, plumped up my pillows, and left me to eat. It was gelatinous eggs and mush, but I resolved to eat half of the cold, repellent food for the baby's sake. Then, exhausted, I fell back onto my pillow.

Nurse Cheery padded back in, whisked the breakfast tray to a cart in the hallway, and returned to ask, "Would you like to use the bathroom?"

"Yes, thank you." I tried to sit up and quickly collapsed again with a sigh.

She suggested a bedpan. "Lie back and lift up," she said.

"Oh! Ooh—it's cold!" I winced.

"Sorry, dearie," she said. "It always feels a bit cold at first, but you'll warm it up. Just take your time, then ring me when you're done."

My bottom rested on the silver shell, and I relaxed when I felt the warm liquid streaming into the pan. But then I felt a smallish lump slip from my vagina.

My thoughts raced. Could it have been a blood clot?

Might it have been some distressed tissue that had acted to protect my baby but was now being cast out, its work done and the crisis passed?

Fear surged through my chest and neck. *Please, God, don't let it be my baby.* I flashed through denial, fought off fear, and realized I could look into the bedpan.

I hesitated, wanting to look and not wanting to look. By then I'd already begun to register the nauseating reality of why I was in this hospital and what had just slipped from between my legs. But nothing had been confirmed. I had no evidence yet. Maybe I was wrong.

I needed to look. If I didn't look now, I'd probably have no other chance to see for myself what had come out of me. When the nurse came, she'd take it away, and I'd never have the chance to see it, to understand what happened, to say goodbye.

I pushed up on my raw elbows, then slid the bedpan out from under me. I curled into a fetal position, clutching the bedpan, and eased it closer to my face. The steamy smell of ammonia assaulted my nose. I steeled myself and slowly looked down. What I saw was, at first, horrific. An elongated lump of flesh smaller than my own thumb floated next to blood clots in a shallow sea of red urine, swaddled in membranous tissue. It had an eye socket and tiny ear on its large, domed head; on its tiny body were a budding arm and leg. Overcome with sadness, I squeezed my eyes shut against the welling tears. Then I looked again, this time with wonder, at the new life that had been repelled from its place within my womb. Why did this happen? What had I done?

I looked through the hospital window at the white sky. My thoughts wandered to the ranch, to the time I'd discovered the foal Pepper had aborted. I'd walked across the frost-hard hillside near the barn and nearly stumbled over the tiny frozen figure. It looked like a miniature ghost-horse. Pale and partly decomposed, it would have stood only twelve inches high at the shoulder.

Surprised and saddened by the abrupt and tragic ending of Pepper's third pregnancy, I looked around the barnyard and found her standing nearby. When I approached her, she seemed nervous and upset, walking away from me at first. There was bloody discharge under her tail, but otherwise, she looked okay. A few minutes later, I went to open the pasture gate, and next to it, I found another corpse lying in the snow. I gasped. Twins were unusual for horses, and the second one didn't match the first. Pink instead of gray, it was larger by half.

The vet who came to treat Pepper told me the small, pale one had been dead for weeks while the other continued to grow until the mare's uterus expelled the living fetus along with the dead one because of the contamination. The vet gave Pepper penicillin shots, and the infection in her uterus healed, but from then on, she was sterile.

I gazed at my own lost fetus and knew from its pale, purplish color that it had perished before my uterus expelled it and long before I'd received the narcotic injection for the painful cramps. But I still wondered if I'd done something wrong to harm it. I'd been so careful with my nutrition, my sleep, my physical activity. I couldn't think of anything I'd done wrong, but I still ached with guilt.

"Bye-bye, baby," I said to the tiny form in the bedpan. Then I turned away from the silver coffin and pressed the call button.

When Nurse Cheery came in, I said, "I'm through."

She reached for the bedpan and then stopped. I didn't meet her eyes, but I could tell she wasn't cheery now.

"Looks like you've passed a bit of tissue here," she said, suddenly businesslike. I'll take it to the lab. They'll want to examine it." Then she marched out.

An hour later, another nurse treaded in and woke me from a half-sleep. Her tag read *RN*. She said, "I'm Jane, the head nurse. How are you feeling? Do you still have any pain or cramps?"

"No, none since I woke up. Everything since the shot last night is a blank."

"Did you know you were pregnant?"

"I've known for six weeks," I said, heaving a sigh.

"I'm sorry," the nurse said softly, "but you've lost the baby."

"I know. I looked in the bedpan." My voice broke, and I could barely croak out the rest of the words. "I saw it."

She looked at me with kind eyes. "Did you want this pregnancy?"

"Yes, very much. Why did I lose it? Was it malformed?"

"We couldn't tell for sure. It was somewhat decomposed—sorry for the rough terminology." Then she went on to say what I needed to hear. "There's no way to know why the fetus died, but early miscarriages are more common than most people know. It happens around fifteen percent of the time. One theory is that it could be nature's way of getting rid of a defective fetus. Another theory is that your hormones weren't strong enough to support the pregnancy."

"Will this happen again next time?"

"Having a miscarriage this time doesn't mean you'll miscarry next time."

"So, I should try again?"

"Yes. A lot of women have a miscarriage during their first pregnancy and then carry the next one to term. I did that myself."

"And you have a child now?"

"Two children."

I managed a weak smile, and she tenderly patted my arm. "Rest now. You need to build up your strength. You'll probably be going home tomorrow."

Going home. Tomorrow I'd be going back to the ranch, but right now, the ranch felt like so much emptiness. Mom gone. Baby gone. At least Dad and Gram would be there, and I warmed a bit at that thought.

I looked at my watch. Tony would be home from work by now. I picked up the phone by my hospital bed. He answered, and I said, "I have some bad news. You'd better sit down."

"Okay," he said. "What is it?"

"I just had a miscarriage. We've lost our baby."

"Oh, no. Are you all right?"

"Yes. I'm going to be fine now, but it was very painful, and I'm still in the hospital in Omak."

"I'm sorry, honey. Do you want me to head there now?"

"No, I'm being discharged tomorrow, and Dad will take me back to the ranch. I'm being well cared for. I should be home in a few days."

"Is there anything else I can do?"

"Not now. They said I'm fine, and we just need to wait a while. Then we can try again."

"Okay. You rest now, and call me tomorrow. I love you."

"Thanks, I will. I love you too."

Later in the evening, Dad brought Gram to visit me in the hospital. They tried to be upbeat, talking about the weather warming and asking me what I'd like to eat once we were back at the ranch. No one mentioned the miscarriage. Then they left me to rest another night in the hospital.

That night, I felt empty and alone. I fell into an exhausted sleep after taking a sleeping pill, and just before waking the next morning, I had a vivid dream.

I was in an orchard harvesting some kind of round, brown nuts. They'd all fallen to the ground, looking fully ripened and unblemished, but I couldn't find any good ones. Each time I picked one up, I tapped the shell with my hammer and cracked it open. I searched for the kernel that should have filled the cavity, but there was nothing inside, or there was something small and shriveled. I went on cracking shells and searching through the contents, looking for a good one.

CHAPTER TWENTY-ONE

I was discharged two nights after the miscarriage, and Dad drove me back to the ranch. At the entrance to our property, I opened the gate and pulled back the wires, then closed and fastened it, something I'd easily done many times before. This time, I climbed back into the pickup, exhausted.

I called Tony, and he agreed that I should stay at the ranch through the week, using my sick leave to regain my strength. I rested and turned to my beloved Lucky for comfort. At thirteen years old, she was now the age I'd been when she was born. She looked wonderful and healthy, glossy-coated and fit from grazing the native bunchgrass. I sat near her in the green pasture and watched her crop the grass. She rolled in the dry, dusty corner that hot afternoon, and I later used a brush to clean her coat.

On my second day back, I mounted her bare, sleek back and guided her around the pasture with my hands on her neck, no reins. On the third day, we galloped the pasture, again with no saddle, jumping over the creek as we always had. I felt my strength returning and my spirits lifting. Soon I was ready to saddle up, so I led her to the chicken house tack room and lifted the saddle onto her back. It took effort, but by now I was just strong enough. We headed out to ride the sunny hills and fields where the meadowlarks called from fence to fence.

Each day after that, we shared long rambles over the ranch and around the valley roads.

Those rides helped heal my wounded spirit and fortified me to sort through my mother's closet and dresser, choosing which belongings I wanted to keep.

Mom's worn, faded clothes were out of style and didn't fit me—at five feet, seven inches, she'd been almost two inches shorter than me and was much heavier, with larger breasts. Still, I tried on several of her flower-print blouses and the housecoat I'd given her just to be inside the garments she'd worn. I slid hangers to the side and came upon the red plaid jacket she often wore for 4-H meetings. Red was her best color. She wears the wool jacket in a photo of the four of us that was taken in 1962 at the ceremony when Bill was awarded his Eagle Scout badge.

Mom had often complained that she could never afford nice clothes, but I told her, "You always look great in that red jacket." While I was glad to have the photo of her wearing it, I didn't take the threadbare jacket.

In a small box in my mother's dresser drawer, I found her homemade wedding dress and veil. I recognized them from my parents' wedding picture, in which Mom looks young and beautiful. I kept the picture along with the dress and veil.

I gathered the scrapbooks her mother and grandmother had kept, both stuffed with old photographs of family and community gatherings and news articles of events they'd participated in. It was like sifting through a collected history of my people. I also found Mom's scrapbook in a desk. She'd pasted poems and stories she'd penned through the years, mostly handwritten, and the annual Christmas letters she typed and mimeographed to mail to relatives. She'd stored her poetry and letters in this small black writing desk with the hinged fold-out cover, its paint now old and cracked. Mom had told me this desk was the one thing she'd asked for after her mother passed away. Mom's father had built it himself, and Mom remembered him seated at it when she was a child, writing his own letters and poems. I was delighted to inherit my grandfather's writing desk as well as some of the poems he'd written while sitting at it. I wanted to sit at it and write stories, too, to continue the family tradition.

Dad said I should have Mom's jewelry, which consisted mostly of costume pieces. Tears welled in my eyes as I sifted through the jewelry box on her dresser and found the necklaces, brooches, and rings she'd worn to school events and other meetings. I found her wedding ring, its gold band worn thin and its little diamond missing. I was nineteen when she lost the stone. She told me the diamond had fallen out. She'd already looked all over the house for it, but I helped her look some more, all the while hearing the sadness in her voice that she'd waited too long to take it to a jeweler to repair the loose prongs. We didn't have money for such things, so she'd kept wearing it. One day, the diamond was gone.

Mom economized to help when Dad's business wasn't profitable, but her regret over the lost diamond was tinged with resentment. There was never enough money, and I knew she blamed Dad, who consistently invested his profits into planes for his expanding flying business or fences and livestock on the ranch. Mom lost faith that she'd ever see any of the rewards. That resentment fueled the blame and anger that erupted during her psychotic episodes.

I tried on some earrings, but their awkward screws or tight clips were uncomfortable in my pierced ears. Some had stories behind them, like the rhinestone brooch my brother's Cub Scout pack gave her for being den mother and the painted doll earrings her younger brother sent when he was stationed in Japan after the war. I put the jewelry back in the pink box to take home and sort later.

Next, I retrieved the wooden box of silver flatware from

the buffet. Mom had told me she'd collected the eight place settings, piece by piece, from years of couponing, first as a young woman and then as a wife with little means. One dinner fork was missing because the coupon offer was discontinued before she'd had a chance to add it to the set. She always brought out the silver collection for holiday meals at the dining room table, and it was the only thing my mother had owned of lasting value. For me, it carried warm memories of the food she presented on those special occasions, including the last Thanksgiving dinner we shared before she died. That night, as I dried the silverware and stored it in its wooden box, I'd asked, "Mom, can I inherit your silverware someday?" She'd said, "Yes, honey, you should have it."

I paged through Mom's old *Good Housekeeping Cookbook*, which was stuffed with recipes cut from newspapers and magazines and peppered with her notes about how well the recipes had worked and what kinds of adjustments she'd made. I thought Dad should have a cookbook in the house, even though he told me he probably wouldn't use it, so I left it with him, along with all the kitchen items.

I'd regret that decision a few years later when I asked Dad for it and he told me it had disappeared. With it went Mom's venison mincemeat, apple swirls dessert, date pinwheel cookies, and other family favorites. I was the one who'd valued those recipes, so I should have claimed the cookbook when I was going through Mom's things, but all the losses and all the memories, good and bad, had borne down on me so heavily that week that I didn't make good decisions.

The day before I returned to Seattle, I stood at the kitchen sink in a sunbeam that shone in from over the steep hill that was fringed with firs. Little shelves at the corner of the window held a jumble of knickknacks, and I caught sight of a small, dusty plaque with a faded picture of a rose on its round, smooth face. I knew what was on the other side. I turned it over and nestled it within the palm of my hand, looking at my own tiny handprint.

Gazing at the plaque took me back to my first school years in Issaquah. I thought of my mother's hands braiding my hair into pigtails and tying red bows around the rubber bands. I didn't complain when she pulled my hair to make the braids because I loved to wear it that way. That's how I looked in my second-grade photo, with brown bangs cut evenly across my forehead and a mischievous sparkle in my eyes. I wore a matching top and skirt handed down from my cousin Kathy, who was a year older. Her clothes were nicer than mine, and she had more of them. Every year, Aunt Eva mailed an exciting box of outfits Kathy had outgrown. That stopped when I reached third grade and grew taller than Kathy and nearly all my classmates. The sailor dress in my second-grade photo, navy blue with white piping and buttoned front, had been my favorite.

I'd made the plaque with help from my first-grade teacher and had nearly burst with pride to give it to my mommy that Christmas. Now, standing in the kitchen, I marveled that Mom had kept it all those years. Looking at it, I was reminded of the innocent child's love I'd felt for her then, but heat climbed up my neck and face as I grew angry thinking about her betrayal of that love. My anger grew hotter until, in one fraught moment, I dropped the plaque into the trash can.

Years later, I'd regret that decision too. As with the cookbook, I'd made an impulsive choice at an emotional moment, a choice I eventually ached over.

But I kept her poems and stories, and nothing could make me feel as close to her as reading the words that came straight from her experience, from her imagination, from her heart. In one of my favorites, she wrote of ranch work with love and vibrancy.

JUNE AT THE SKY RANCH
Zelma Carson Lockwood

The sun's shining brightly,
    A light breeze is blowing.
When cottonwood trees shed,
    It looks like it's snowing.

Strawberries are rip'ning,
    Scarecrow Sue stands on guard,
The iris and roses
    Gaily brighten the yard.

Three horses graze calmly,
    A new colt follows one.
Linda's proud of her horses,
    "Best under the sun."

Beef cattle come daily
    To the pond for a drink,
Their calves gaily frisking,
    They sure look "in the pink."

Hay crops lie in windrows
    'Til the baler comes round—
Hardest work on the ranch,
    The Al Lockwoods have found.

Bill rides the Cat once more,
    Just to conquer the weeds;
Preparing the fallow ground
    For the planting of seeds.

June's "weed time" for Linda,
    Poison weeds she must spray;
With equipment tied on,
    She rides her horse each day.

Al's off spraying grain crops,
    Hither, thither, and yon;
He flies in now and then,
    His long days start at dawn.

The air's full of bird songs,
    Chickens cackle and crow
Each farm has its "music,"
    We enjoy it, you know.

The poem was written in 1963, the last summer Bill and I were both at home. All of Mom's poems were upbeat like this one because she only wrote poems when she could feel and express joy. I've kept them to remember who she was in the good times. Maybe that's why she kept them too. I embraced the hope that as she descended further and further into depression, reading the sunny poems of her own creation offered some relief.

CHAPTER TWENTY-TWO

A month after my miscarriage, my next period arrived on schedule. My body was in sync with its natural rhythms, and my doctor gave the go-ahead, so we tried again for the baby we wanted. In mid-July of 1972, my second pregnancy was confirmed. For Tony and me, this thrilling news meant another chance and renewed hope. My mother's suicide had left a void in my life, but my guilt and grief began to recede as we planned, once again, for an addition to our family.

When the morning sickness arrived, I accepted it as my taxed body's natural reaction. I researched which foods to eat and how often, then listened for my body to tell me what it liked and needed, like yogurt and graham crackers, at least every two hours in between three regular meals. If my body wanted it, I ate it. I'd learned the importance of this kind of cooperation with my natural tendencies by working with animals on the ranch.

No one taught me to train horses or dogs; the animals themselves did. Pepper showed me the importance of a good saddle for restraining a bucking horse and controlling a runaway. Thanks to her, I learned about grit and resilience. Gypsy was a perfect model of passion and zeal as she circled the escaping sheep and hustled them back to me. And with Lucky's consistent responses to my voice, hands, and legs, she showed me how to communicate with a horse. I thought about those animals often, such wonderful teachers and friends, and I committed to keeping their lessons in mind as I made decisions about my body and motherhood.

By August, the morning sickness had abated, and I was enjoying my workdays in the Heart Lab, where I felt productive and at home. By then, I'd spent eighteen months working in Dr. Harold Dodge's cardiovascular research lab. He was a pioneer in the early days of heart research, measuring blood flow in the left ventricle, the pumping chamber of the heart.

His researchers injected dye into a beating heart while an X-ray recorded the heart's action. My job was to view the movie in the lab and select the frame showing the outline of the left ventricle at its most relaxed and full moment (diastole) and another showing its most contracted or emptied moment (systole). As I traced these outlines, the movement of my handheld digitizer fed data into Dr. Dodge's algorithms to compute the ejection fraction, the percentage of blood being pumped out during a contraction. If the heart wall had sections of dead muscle from a heart attack, my tracing showed it bulging outward when the rest of the heart muscle contracted.

I liked learning new things and helping with an important research project. Dr. Dodge was a willing teacher, even for lab techs like me, whom some doctors seemed to view as servants.

One morning in the Heart Lab, my ringing desk phone startled me. Dad was calling with bad news. "Your grandmother is in the hospital," he said, his voice heavy with despair. "She's had a heart attack."

My stomach clenched. Gram had survived a heart attack when she was sixty-five, but now she was eighty-one.

"She's pretty weak," Dad said, "and I'm sure she'd like to see you."

As I hung up, I pictured my grandmother's damaged heart contracting, part of its flaccid wall bulging out, unable to pump enough blood to feed oxygen to her body.

On Friday after work, Tony and I left our home to drive over Stevens Pass to the ranch. During the five-hour trip to the home where I grew up, I thought about how much Gram meant to me. Like a second mother, she had stepped in to fill the gaps when Mom failed me with her emotional distancing and sudden absences for hospital treatment.

When Gram came to see the lambs in 1955 and help Mom in our first hard winter, I was eight and she was sixty-four. She'd been widowed for nine years. Her siblings, friends, and others had known her as Mary—a vibrant girl with a lilting soprano voice, then as a beautiful auburn-haired young woman, and later a wife.

Mary evolved into the woman we introduced as Gram, a soft-spoken, silver-haired, essential member of our family. She eventually qualified for a monthly social security check and moved into low-income housing in Omak, where she lived at peace in a small cottage, reading library books and growing beloved petunias in bright profusion beneath her window.

During our first three years on the ranch, Gram had been in her late sixties, and she often delighted me with surprises that showed another side to her I hadn't previously imagined.

I saw Gram shoot a gun only once, but that one shot left me awestruck. One sunny morning, Gram was washing dishes at the kitchen window when a China pheasant strolled across the hillside and paused on the trail. Gram spotted it. "Look," she called. "There's a rooster over there that would make a nice dinner."

We came running from the living room to see it.

"Don't make any noise or you'll spook him," Bill said. "But he's too far away for the shotgun."

"Not for the .22," Gram replied.

"The .22? You can't hit him with the .22 at that range."

"Maybe *you* can't. Let *me* have the gun."

With that, Gram picked up the bolt-action rifle, loaded the shell into the single chamber, and cocked the hammer. "Now you just watch." She stepped quietly out the screen door onto the back porch, raised the gunstock to her shoulder, took aim, and fired. *Bam!* The rooster went down.

Bill and I couldn't believe it. The bird barely flapped as we ran across the creek plank and up the hill. Bill grabbed the rooster to wring his neck and finish him off. But no! The pheasant was limp and unblinking and didn't even look wounded.

Bill exclaimed, "Look at that! She shot him right through the eye at that distance!"

"Gram, you got him," I screamed. "He's dead!"

I was always sad to see a beautiful creature die, but of all the game birds we ate on the ranch, pheasant meat was our favorite, its white breast tasting like chicken and only slightly gamey.

We feasted on pheasant that night, and from then on, I looked at my grandmother differently. If Gram was around when our family had visitors, I'd always find a reason to tell them about my grandmother, a sharpshooter.

Now Gram was in the hospital where I'd been rolled into the emergency entrance just two months earlier. I shoved these thoughts aside as Tony drove us to Omak on Saturday morning and we entered the hospital. In her hospital room, Gram was propped on white pillows, her frizzy white hair surrounding her face with its lovely smile-wrinkled skin. Several cards and a pink azalea sat on her side table. I looked at her smiling face and gray eyes behind trifocal lenses. She held up her hand, and I squeezed it as she said, "I'm very glad to see you, Linda."

I took the chair beside her bed and asked, "How are you? What happened?"

"I went out to dinner, and I guess I ate too much rich food. I had a steak and baked potato. On the way home, I started feeling awful and having pains, so we came here. They say I've had another heart attack. I just know it was bad. The pain was terrible."

Gram's first heart attack was in 1956, back when they called it "a coronary" and the only treatment was bed rest. She spent nearly six weeks in the hospital and was advised to stop taking care of others and to take better care of herself. After that first heart attack, Gram worked to put aside her widow's fears of being alone in the world. She gave her worries to God and counted her blessings.

To deal with her high blood pressure and high cholesterol, she adopted a careful low-fat diet. Regardless of what the rest of us had for breakfast, she ate Special K cereal with nonfat milk and half a banana.

Gram had often told me about her fear of seeing her cardiologist. She tried to keep her blood pressure under control, but over the years, the doctor prescribed stronger drugs with worrying side effects. At every doctor visit, as she waited to have her blood pressure taken, she felt her heart pounding and her blood pressure rising. She had a severe case of white coat syndrome.

For sixteen years she'd lived in fear of this second heart attack. I wanted to give her something to look forward to, so I told her my good news. "I'm pregnant again, Gram."

"Isn't it too soon for that?" she asked.

"Not according to my doctor. He said I should wait a month and try again."

"I'm not sure about that. It seems too soon to me."

"I'm sure it will be fine, Gram. I'm rested and feeling good."

"Well, you better take good care of yourself."

We chatted until she grew tired, then I kissed her and said we'd visit again the next morning before returning to Seattle. That night, Tony and I talked about what we might do to help Gram. The next morning, I told her we wanted her to stay with us when she felt better.

"I don't want to be a burden on you," she said. Then she reached out and held my hand between hers. "I'm not sure I'm going to get well enough to do that."

I didn't like the sound of that. I looked into her eyes. "Sure you will."

"No, dear, you don't understand. This heart attack was extremely painful, so bad that if I have another one, I don't want to live through it. I'm ready to go on to be with God. I'm the last one left of my generation, and I'm ready to go."

"But Gram, I don't want you to go. I'm sure you're going to be okay."

She shook her head. "I'm scared of another attack. The doctors say they want to get me up to walk soon, and I'm afraid of that. I don't think I can do it."

I couldn't accept that my grandmother might be near death, so I failed her. When she needed me to really hear her, the best I could say was, "Gram, I'm so sorry you have to go through this. I love you very much, you know."

I leaned down to kiss her pale, soft cheek, then turned back to wave as we left the room. Gram looked frail and alone.

Four days after our visit, Dad called me at work. "Cookie, it's Gram. She had another heart attack, and this time she didn't make it. She's gone."

I gasped. His voice cracking, he said, "The doctor wanted her to get out of bed and walk. But when the nurses got her up, she had a massive heart attack and died."

I was stunned. It was just as Gram had predicted. She knew her body. She knew what was happening, and I'd dismissed it.

"Should I come to the ranch?"

"No, meet me in Oregon. We'll have her funeral in Corvallis."

After we hung up, I buried my face in my hands. I hadn't listened when Gram warned me that the end was near. I hadn't told her how much I loved her, how much I'd miss her. I hadn't said the things I would have said if I'd known I'd never see her again. As my second mother, she deserved to hear those words. Now she never would.

I squeezed back tears and ran out the office door to the back corridor. I sank down the yellow wall onto the cold tile floor to huddle with my grief and muffle my sobs.

Tony and I drove to Corvallis for Gram's funeral. I grieved for Gram, I grieved for Mom, and I grieved that neither of them would see my baby. And I grieved my own self-centered stubbornness, which made me selfishly dismiss Gram's wish to let go.

To offer Gram solace, I should have remembered what I learned from my ewe, Trixie, when she taught me how to companion a dying creature.

In 1958, when Dad began converting our flock to registered Suffolk sheep, Bill and I had each asked for a purebred ewe as payment for our help. When Dad said yes, I chose a young ewe that had just birthed twin females. I named her Trixie and her lambs Pixie and Dixie. I kept an eye on their activities in the herd but was careful not to turn them into pets.

One day in 1961, I hiked up to the creek from the house and came upon Trixie lying beside the stream. She was alone, which was unusual for a sheep because they feel safe only within their flock's protection. She didn't move to get up when I approached her. I looked her over and saw no reason for her malaise, but her woolly body concealed its secrets. "What's wrong, Trixie?" I asked as though she could understand. She lay on her belly with her legs tucked under, her head stretched in front, and her chin resting on the ground.

I had seen sheep mired in mud give up their struggles and wait to die, so I tried to get her up, first by rocking her from side to side and then by lifting her rump to free her hind legs. She sank back on limp legs and made no effort to rise. Was she in pain?

I stroked her black face to reassure her that I was friendly and wouldn't harm her. Then I sat a few feet away to keep watch so she'd know she wasn't alone. She seemed to be peaceful and wanted only to rest. Then I realized she might be dying and might need me to do nothing more than stay nearby. As I waited, her breathing slowed, and something changed in her eyes—they lost focus and then glazed almost imperceptibly as light and breath left her. Trixie had died peacefully, and I had companioned her simply by staying near and sitting quietly.

Like Trixie, Gram had needed and wanted me to stay by her side and be her companion in her final days. She'd often confided her worries to me on nights when she was feeling alone and couldn't sleep. This time, she'd had no one else to call upon, and I'd failed her.

CHAPTER TWENTY-THREE

A month after Gram's funeral, I was in my third month of pregnancy. Early one morning, Tony dropped me off at University Medical Center on his way to work. I had several new heart films to trace, so I started working.

The ache began in my abdomen.

Oh, God, no. I shuddered. *No.*

I rushed to the restroom and saw blood spots in my underpants. Back in the lab, I checked my calendar to confirm how many weeks along I was. Then I slumped in my chair, horrified at the realization that I was exactly as far along as I'd been when I'd had a miscarriage only months earlier.

I wanted to go home and rest, but I couldn't reach Tony. He'd be delivering freight around Seattle and the outlying area until his truck was empty or his workday ended. I called his supervisor and left a message for my husband to call me as soon as possible.

The door opened, and Dr. Dodge sailed in behind two white-coated doctors. He was excited to show them his heart research lab. This was the last thing I needed. I thought that if I could just rest, I'd avoid an ER visit and what it had led to back in May.

"This is the Heart Lab," Dr. Dodge told the visiting doctors. "Here we digitize the heart films taken in the cardiac

catheterization procedures like the ones you saw yesterday."
He pointed to the digitizing table and said, "Linda, would you
show us the films for yesterday's heart attack patients and the
normal heart film you showed me last week?"

I was cold, sweaty, and trembling from the cramps gnaw-
ing in my belly. Dr. Dodge didn't appear to notice.

"Maybe you can show them? I'm not feeling . . ."

"You draw them better than I do, and I want you to
show these doctors how we do it." Smiling, he said, "They're
cardiologists from Vienna, and they want to see what we're
doing here in Seattle."

Steeling myself against the cramps churning in my
belly, I loaded the 16mm film, took an awkward perch on the
high stool, turned on the projector, and showed them how I
located the frames with the maximum and minimum volumes
of blood, then stopped the action to draw the heart chamber
with the digitizing pointer. Drawing the outline involved both
art and accuracy for the chamber's shady areas. Dr. Dodge had
trained me, and he liked my results.

The cardiologists compared the shapes of the normal and
damaged hearts that I showed them. I tried to keep my voice
steady as I answered their questions.

As Dr. Dodge explained his formulas and responded to
his colleagues' questions, my cramps became harder to with-
stand. At last, he checked his watch and announced, "It's time
for our next meeting. Thank you, Linda." The doctors nodded
and thanked me. Then they all left.

I stumbled back to my desk chair and dropped my damp
forehead to the desk. That first miscarriage was etched in my
memory. It had begun with cramps just like these and had
ended with a tiny gray embryo slipping from my body.

I couldn't stand the thought of another loss, and I knew
I needed to control the fear that was beginning to wrack my
body. I needed to convince my body there was no danger

to fight or flee from, the way I used to gentle my newborn horses. The greatest danger was the fear itself, which was rational given what happened before, but fear wasn't helping my baby.

I settled in my chair to calm down and think. When my lab partner Lois arrived, my lips were parched and I was still cramping.

"You look very pale," she said. "What's wrong?"

"Lois, I'm so glad you're here," I said as I tried to steady my breathing. "This morning I started having cramps and spotting. I'm really scared. It's the same way the first miscarriage started."

"Oh no! How can I help?"

"I need you to take over the lab for the rest of the day."

"I can do that."

"Thank you so much. I need to lie down somewhere until Tony can pick me up."

Lois furrowed her brow. "Call Sheri in Cardiology. She can find a bed for you down there."

Sheri answered and I explained the situation. "Of course," she said. "Come down. You can use one of the on-call beds."

When I walked into her office, her smile vanished, and she said, "Oh, my dear, you're pale. You need to be home in bed. I'd take off and drive you, but I'm typing a deadline project that's due today." She showed me to a bed and pulled the curtain around it.

Lying in bed helped. The pains kept coming but didn't grow stronger. I tried to calm myself by focusing on breathing and letting my body go limp. It helped.

Four hours later, Sheri pulled the curtain aside and asked, "How's the pain?"

"It's still there, but it's not as bad."

"I'm done with my project, and I can take you home now if you like."

"It'll be a long round trip for you. I should wait for Tony."

"I know what you're going through, and I want to help," she insisted.

Sheri brought her red Volkswagen Beetle to the back door of the research wing, gathered me in, and motored north to my home in Edmonds. On the way, she told me of her own painful miscarriage. "We women need to support one another," she said.

I paused at my door to give Sheri my heartfelt thanks, and then I went straight to my bedroom and crawled into bed. An hour later, Tony called. I told him I had cramps and he should stop for a take-out meal on his way home. I'd be glad to have him home, with our car, if I needed the ER.

I managed to sleep through the night and then woke to find the spotting and cramps were gone. I stayed home for another day of rest, then returned to work.

In mid-November 1972, I reached the fourth month of my pregnancy, and during an ultrasound, the technician reported all was well and said I was most likely having a girl. She turned the screen to show me the blurry form, which I could barely make out, but I saw the little blur make a sudden movement like a swim stroke. Most thrilling was the fast, swishing sound of her tiny heart.

By five months I felt pulses inside me as if a little fish was flicking her tail against the soft bowl of my womb. "Hello, baby," I said. "You're healthy and safe."

CHAPTER TWENTY-FOUR

B y the winter of 1973, I'd become extremely anxious because
I had so many unanswered questions about my mother's
mental disorder, the greatest of which was whether it could
transfer genetically to my child. I also feared the pain of childbirth. Would it hurt as much as my miscarriage had? It seemed
unlikely that the pain would drive me into psychosis as it had
my mother, but I couldn't be sure.

When my ob-gyn offered three options for pain management, I chose the strongest one. "With the saddle block, you'll
feel nothing below the waist," he said.

I asked, "What's the effect of the anesthetic on the baby?"

"It shouldn't be a cause for concern."

On April 6, Tony drove me to the hospital to have my
labor induced. The nurse helped me into bed and inserted a
needle into my arm. The oxytocin hormone in the intravenous
drip caused contractions that were hard and regular. The pain
increased for nearly six hours, and as my cervix slowly dilated,
I began wondering how much longer I could endure it without screaming. At last, I was wheeled into the delivery room
and given the injection for the saddle block. As the numbness
spread from my waist down, my legs turned wooden and no
longer seemed to be a part of me.

When it came time to push, I couldn't feel the contractions, but Tony and I knew what to do, thanks to our childbirth classes. The nurse helped me roll up while Tony braced my back and urged me to push or breathe as the nurse called out, "Here it comes, push—one, two, three . . . now breathe." My doctor watched until the head crowned, then gave me directions until announcing, "You have a girl!"

The nurse cleaned and swaddled my tiny daughter and brought her to us. She was sound asleep, and we stared at her in my arms, admiring her flushed face, round cheeks, and dark, fuzzy hair. Little Deanna looked like Tony.

I held her for only a few minutes before the nurse whisked her away for medical checks and a bath. When they brought her to my room for nursing, she wouldn't rouse from her sleep. The delivery room nurse said, "She's fine. Just a little sleepy from the anesthetic."

My plump full-term infant appeared healthy and normal, but she spent two days in the neonatal intensive care unit because she wasn't maintaining her temperature. I regularly went to the NICU to breastfeed her, but each time she fell asleep.

On the third morning, she was sleeping in my arms when I asked the nurse, "How can she go so long without nursing?"

The nurse picked up Deanna's chart. "It says here that she woke up crying and hungry at two a.m., and the night nurse gave her formula."

"*What?* I was told if I expressed my milk into a bottle and stored it here in the freezer, she'd be given my breast milk if she woke up when I wasn't here."

"I'm sorry. I guess the night nurse didn't see the note in her chart," she said.

After all my efforts to breastfeed, I felt betrayed. I knew Deanna needed the rich colostrum in my first milk, not the formula.

After three days in the hospital, Deanna's color and blood tests improved. She began nursing, and we took her home. However, she didn't nurse for very long before falling asleep, and I was having second thoughts about the anesthesia I'd agreed to.

She slept soundly those first days at home and didn't cry when I roused her. I was acting like a mother ewe who nudges her wobbly newborn lamb onto its feet to nurse.

Two weeks later, I'd not yet heard her cry as I'd seen most newborn animals do when hungry. I wondered what was wrong until Deanna woke by herself one day and cried lustily until I came to nurse her. Thinking my worries were over, I rejoiced to hear her cries.

After another two weeks, she developed colic and howled in pain for hours every afternoon and into the evening. I held her and walked or rocked her all afternoon, then passed her to Tony while I prepared dinner. After six weeks, her desperate colic days ended, and we settled into a regular routine for the summer. I'd quit my job to stay at home for six months to nurse and enjoy my baby.

On sunny days, Deanna napped and played in her play-pen nearby while I spaded a grassy area and planted a large garden. The twenty pounds I'd gained melted away, and by the end of the summer I was slender and strong again. Life was good despite my ongoing sadness that Mom and Gram would never see my beautiful baby or watch her grow.

CHAPTER TWENTY-FIVE

In the idyllic summer of '73, with Deanna healthy and thriving, I felt able to look open-eyed into what had gone on with my mother, and questions began to haunt me. I wanted answers about her schizophrenia.

I dug out Mom's scrapbook and began to read it. The book held many poems, some written by her father and grandmother. During her teens, she'd also clipped poems from newspapers or hand-copied ones she liked. Those were the 1930s Depression years, yet she collected upbeat poems as if being cheerful despite one's hard work and pennilessness was a critical element of finding a better future.

In her late teens, Mom began writing her own poems and kept them in the same scrapbook. Sifting through them, I marveled at her creativity. Mom had told me about her desire to publish her poems, and the scrapbook held many rejection slips. Only one poem made it into print. She wrote it in 1934, at age eighteen, and it ran in the *Oregon Sunday Journal* on October 4, 1936.

TO AN AUTUMN LEAF
Zelma Carson Lockwood

Oh, tell me, little autumn leaf,
    Where are your high hopes bound?
You flutter by so gracefully,
    Where will you reach the ground?

Your home has always been a tree,
    Up on a branch, so high;
All summer you have faced the sun
    As it sailed across the sky.

Now, autumn cool is in the air
    And you have left your home.
Oh, tell me, little autumn leaf,
    Why do you choose to roam?

If you are seeking adventure
    You'll surely have your fill,
For Mr. Wind does like to play,
    And you are at his will.

As I read my mother's poem, it evoked the same feelings of hope and uncertainty I'd felt as I finished high school and looked ahead to an unknown future. But the poem seemed more poignant now that I knew the course her mental illness would take. It served as a reminder that we never know what's ahead—that the present moment is utterly precious.

Then, deep within the pages of the bulging scrapbook, I found a snippet of an autobiography my mother had written in 1937 at age twenty-one. As I read it, my pulse began to race. This was a clue!

STORY OF MY LIFE
By Zelma Carson Lockwood

In the midst of a beautiful little valley known as the Yachats River Valley, I first saw the light of day on February 24, 1916.

My first recollection dates back to 1920, when I was four years of age. While the family and relatives were spending a Sunday at the beach, on August 8, I was one of five who had the misfortune to be in an automobile accident in which the car, a Chevrolet touring model belonging to my uncle, rolled over a bluff 157 feet to the beach sand below. But it was our lucky day in that the tide was out, or we would have rolled in the ocean surf. My mother had all the ribs on her right side broken, my grandmother had an ankle broken in five places, my younger sister Blanche received a couple of little cuts on her head, my cousin of my age had a fractured skull, which left her unconscious for two days, and I almost lost an ear besides being unconscious for four days. But we were fortunate in getting immediate expert medical aid, and ten days later my father drove us home in the wagon. My memory goes back to the time I became conscious four days after the accident.

In the following September, we left Oregon and spent about three months in Salt Lake City, where another sister, Eva, was born. I can remember my trips to the doctor every other day and the little "butterfly" dress that I wore. My grandmother had made it for me from flour sacks and embroidered it with butterflies.

She went on to explain that during that accident, she'd suffered a concussion, and one ear had been torn off and then sewn back on. Later, she referred to having nasal surgery at age eighteen to remove "crushed and decayed bones."

When I finished reading, I thought back to what Dad had said about the mental breakdown during the delivery of her first child, marking the beginning of her mental illness. But reading Mom's own words about the terrible head trauma she suffered as a little girl made me think those injuries were the underlying cause. I now suspected something deep and long-lasting had happened to my mother in that car accident, something she didn't remember and didn't know she carried with her. The surgical removal of the "crushed and decaying bones" in her nose was a clue. What if the surgeon hadn't removed all the decaying bone matter? And was it possible something else from her childhood concussion had remained behind, waiting to ambush her? What if the psychotic break during her first childbirth was simply the first outward sign of her incipient schizophrenia? I didn't know enough to piece it all together, but I tucked away the clues and vowed to follow their trail to learn more—somehow, someday.

Some of us cling to our grief long after loved ones pass on, perhaps as a way of keeping them with us. I did that after my mother's and grandmother's deaths, probably because I felt guilty about the mistakes I'd made and the opportunities I'd missed just before their deaths. But mistakes have a way of teaching us to choose differently when we face similar experiences again. Many years later, I'd have another chance.

CHAPTER TWENTY-SIX

After losing both his wife and mother in 1972, Dad met and married Rosemary, a woman whose love for adventure matched his. They built a home in central Washington fronting the Pacific Ocean, and he drove the sandy shore on every sunny day, happily riding in his beat-up four-wheel-drive pickup, mouthing an unlit cigar, his two Weimaraner dogs running alongside as he looked for driftwood to saw into chunks and haul back for the fireplace. He also drove their motor home on trips up and down the West Coast, from California to Canada, fishing the rivers and exploring gold mines in the mountains, sometimes frightening Rosemary by taking on rough, narrow mountain back roads with the large RV.

When cancer began invading the bones in his back, he refused to see a doctor and lived in denial, believing it was old back pain or bouts of flu as the disease laid waste to his once-strong body that used to lift and fling sixty-pound hay bales. He was a courageous, gutsy man who wouldn't give up, so he made several last motor home trips with Rosemary, including the long journey to Florida in what would be his last winter. He'd always wanted to see the Florida Keys, and he pushed on with Rosemary and his dogs despite feeling "rocky" on many days.

In January 1988, they made it to Key West, but as they came back up the Florida peninsula, he was too nauseated to drive farther. He entered a hospital in Kissimmee, where the doctors balanced his salt levels and advised more tests, but Dad chose to get back on the road and make his way back to Seattle for treatment.

The return trip was hellish because he insisted on taking the motor home with the little Datsun towed behind, and Rosemary didn't drive the big rig. That meant hours of daily driving for Dad, who called his brother Ray for help. From North Florida to Seattle, Ray drove the RV while Dad rode shotgun or reclined in the bed when the nausea and back pain became too much. Finally, when the RV engine broke down in Nevada, Rosemary convinced Dad they should fly to Seattle. Ray and the dogs continued on in the little Datsun.

An X-ray taken at the Seattle hospital showed that cancer metastasizing from his lung had dissolved pieces of his ribs—the unmistakable cause of his excruciating pain. For the next five months, Dad went through chemo and radiation, but by then it was too late. In June of 1988, he halted the painful treatments and planned for hospice care.

One morning while Dad was still in the hospital, I was about to leave him and head to work. Rosemary stopped me. "You put your briefcase down and get back in there," she said, her expression as serious as any I'd ever seen on her face. "He's dying, and now is your chance while he's still lucid. You go in there and say what you need to say to him."

Thanks to Rosemary, I didn't make another enormous mistake before the death of someone I loved dearly. I went back to my father's bedside and pulled up a chair. I held one of his thin, frail hands and told him how much I loved having him as my dad. I told him how grateful I was for all he'd taught me and for always coming to my rescue when I needed help. He held my gaze and gave me a simple, heartfelt "Thank you."

As I sat with my father on his deathbed, I realized I wanted to know more about his faith. When I was eight or ten, I'd heard him say, "I believe the Great Outdoors is the church God built for man, and it's greater than any church man has built for God."

I knew what he meant. We didn't attend church on Sundays, but we were outdoors every day. In Dad's hospital room, I realized I'd grown up in God's church on Sky Ranch. There, my observations of the natural world and life and death, along with my narrow escapes from disaster, had led me to faith in God as creator and protector. But I wanted to hear more from him, so I asked, "Dad, do you believe in God?"

For a man who seldom spoke of his beliefs, his response was quick and emphatic. "Yes! I believe in God. And I believe in Jesus Christ, and I love Him!"

Amazed at his forthright reply, I blurted, "And I know you're going to be with Him soon!"

"I hope so," he said softly, flashing that grin I delighted in.

"I know so," I replied.

Out of words, I shifted into being his little girl again. All I wanted was to curl up in his arms, to hug and be hugged, but the best I could do was cuddle next to him on the hospital bed and rest my head on his shoulder.

He started to wrap his arm around me for a homecoming moment, but then he winced. "Sorry, Cookie. That hurts."

Grateful he'd given me a hug despite his pain, I rose from his narrow bed, leaving him to the embrace of the narcotic, and he slept.

Two days later, Bill flew to Seattle in his four-seat Cessna, settled Dad into the plane, and reclined his seat to help make him comfortable, then flew Dad and Rosemary over the Cascade Mountains. As they approached the Okanogan airport, Bill raised Dad's seat so he could see the view and the landing at the airport where he'd landed his own planes and helicopters a thousand times before.

At Bill's home in Okanogan, his wife Donita ably managed Dad's care. Following their local doctor's orders, she gave Dad his pain medication and a hospice nurse visited regularly. At first, Dad could sit in a recliner in the midday sun and visit with friends who came by, but his energy diminished day by day. He needed more painkillers and slept after each dose.

At the end of one of my weekend visits, I sat beside Dad's bed for a long time before my drive back to Seattle. After he swallowed the narcotic solution Donita gave him, I talked with him until he fell into a drugged sleep with me holding his hand. An hour passed before he opened his eyes and focused on me beside him, clasping his hand. "I fell asleep," he said. After a few seconds, his face brightened. "You're still here."

I nodded, sending my love into his gray eyes.

He smiled and simply said, "Thank you." He'd always accepted a gift or a compliment by speaking those words with finality and grace. I understood the full meaning behind them now.

Those were my father's last words to me. I drove back to Seattle that evening, and he died the following morning with Rosemary, Donita, and the hospice nurse by his side.

At their beach home a few weeks later, Rosemary held a memorial gathering filled with memories of my father and their sixteen years together. Rosemary gave Bill two containers containing Dad's ashes and declined her seat on his plane. He and I drove to the local airport at Ocean Shores and climbed into Bill's plane. Bill took off, banked toward the ocean, and flew north a few miles to the beach house. He circled the Cessna over the house twice, and below, I saw Rosemary and the family had come out to watch us.

Through the plane's open window, Bill streamed one box of ashes in line with the cresting white waves of the Pacific Ocean that Dad loved so much. From the passenger window,

I dropped handfuls of flowers from the memorial, along with stalks of the dune grass we'd gathered from the yard.

The next morning, I walked the flat sand beach to find white daisies, red roses, and dune grass stalks washed in along the tide line. My tears mixed with the wind and waves that had given this parting salute to my father. I marveled at how he'd spent his lifetime understanding and harnessing these same natural forces for aerial flight and to coax crops from an arid land.

One month later, I returned to the Chiliwist with Deanna, now fifteen. My daughter, a confident rider, happily joined me on this deeply meaningful pilgrimage to the ranch I so loved. I visited Paul and Eula Stout, who still lived down the road from ours. I asked them if I might borrow two horses to ride up on the ranch. Paul immediately agreed and went to gather two of his horses from the herd on the nearby hillside. He came back with a gentle young horse named Scout and an old horse I recognized. Red was the first horse I rode for sheep-herding so many years earlier, and now he was over thirty-five, ancient for a horse. Once the horses were saddled, I wrapped the container of my father's ashes in a jacket and tied it behind the saddle, then Deanna and I mounted the horses.

We rode the mile up the Chiliwist Road and entered the Sky Ranch gate. Dad didn't own it now, but Paul knew the renters who lived in our old house and said, "I don't think they'd mind." In my youth, I'd been permitted to ride anywhere in the valley if I closed the gate after myself, and I counted on that custom. Deanna and I turned to the shallow creek, splashed across, and headed up the steep hillside road to the first cultivated flat. We stopped, and I waved my hand to show Dad's landing strip along its outer edge. "That's where Pepper bucked me off again and again until Dad brought home the new Western saddle."

Deanna had heard those stories before, but she never seemed to tire of hearing about my wonderful, wild childhood.

"What happened to Pepper after you all moved away?" she asked.

I thought about the wonderful horse that had been my introduction to riding and how mellow she'd grown over time. "About the time you were born, we gave her to a family with young children, and she grew old giving gentle rides to their kids."

We rode past the wheat field and into the bunchgrass pasture. I said, "See that sagebrush? That's where the rattler was when Spot attacked it and got bit."

We rode up the two-track road through the bunchgrass to the ridgeline. "I used to gallop Lucky right down this slope," I said, pointing to the incline scattered with trees, sage, and rocks.

"Wow, that looks pretty steep and rough," she said.

"But Lucky was so sure-footed, I always felt safe," I said, recalling our thrilling descents toward home.

At the top of the ridge, we dismounted beside our landmark, the Big Rock. From there we could see the farm road continuing down through the fields on the south slope and ending where it met the county road that descended through Davis Canyon to the Okanogan River. We looked up to Dent Mountain, and I helped Deanna spot the golden eagles' brown nest. "Look halfway up the gray rock face," I said, pointing.

"I see it!"

I climbed to stand on the Big Rock, its ten-foot diameter nearly split in two from decades of freezing and thawing in winter. The wind tore off my hat, and I turned my face to the wind—wind that seemed to belong to my father. He flew in these winds, landing and taking off from his little airstrip on the first flat, following the hilly contours to spray weeds or spread fertilizer.

Like my father, I was part of this land. With my horses and dogs, I roamed and explored and protected it. My roots were here, and now part of my father would be here forever.

Deanna took photos as I opened the container and hurled his ashes into the wind that swept the Sky Ranch.

We mounted our horses and walked them down the ranch slopes and past the crumbling old barn to the creek and out the front gate to the county road. When we reached the flat stretch of the road where I had enjoyed so many wind-rushing runs with Lucky, I asked my daughter, "Do you want to gallop?"

"Yes! Let's do!"

Off she went on eager young Scout, looking back with a laugh, and I had to urge old Red to keep up. I hated to ask him to gallop, but he managed a stiff canter with his old willingness.

When we arrived at the Stouts' ranch, we helped Paul unsaddle the horses, and Eula invited us to warm up with coffee and cookies. We talked for several hours, catching up and reminiscing as Deanna sat quietly, listening. Eula said, "You kids had a hard time," and I knew what she meant. She'd been around us enough. She'd gotten to know my brother and me as we rode with her on the little school bus. She'd also been a friend to my mom and had seen her change over the years. She'd been the one Mom came to the day she was paranoid because voices told her something had befallen my father. Eula had called the sheriff for help, and her son Stan had helped my father drive Mom to Eastern State Hospital to be committed.

I hadn't told Paul and Eula the real purpose of our ride that day, but she'd always been a sharp one. She said, "I saw you tying something behind your saddle. Was that your father's ashes?"

I couldn't hold back my tears as I told Eula how I'd released Dad's ashes into the wind at the top of the ranch. She hugged me and then Deanna, and I was grateful Deanna could experience the warmth this woman had so often brought to my childhood. What wonderful friends this family had always been. Now, sitting next to my daughter at their cozy kitchen table, I felt the significance of that.

For Thanksgiving that year, we gathered in Seattle at the home of Nannette, the eldest of Rosemary's five children and the one nearest to me in age. It was the first family gathering since my father's passing, and Nannette wanted to host their traditional event with extended family and friends because Rosemary was grieving too much to attempt it. Now that both my parents were gone, I felt strongly that I wanted to be part of Rosemary's welcoming family. By then, Tony and I had divorced, and I'd been married to my second husband, Bill, for five years. Bill and I were parenting three children: Deanna, his son, and our daughter, Rosemary, named for my beloved stepmother.

As we sat at long tables for the feast, with grace said and food being passed, I looked around and thought about how much my father would have loved this gathering. I thought, *Dad will never have another Thanksgiving with us, ever.* Then a piercing wail rose in the room. It seemed more animal than human, and it startled me until I realized it had come from *me*!

Everyone turned to look at me, and from across the table, my husband exclaimed, "What the hell?"

From my right side, I felt arms wrap around me as his sister Jan pulled me into her hug, saying, "There, there, it's all right. You go ahead and cry." I pressed my face into her shoulder and released my sobs. Her permission to cry made my keening feel natural—a clean and complete release of pent-up grief, publicly and openly.

When I stopped sobbing, I thanked Jan for her empathy. Then I stood and apologized to everyone. I shared the thought that had triggered my outburst. Everyone nodded and voiced understanding. Then the feast went on.

With that wail, I released my father. He'd always been the one I could count on, but now he'd gone to be with God and gifted me his faith. From then on, I counted on God as my rock.

But I still hadn't released my mother. I had far too many unanswered questions. And I knew there was only one place where I might find answers.

CHAPTER TWENTY-SEVEN

My mother never talked about what she felt or experienced during her psychotic episodes or her treatments in psychiatric hospitals, but she wrote about her February 1962 commitment to Eastern State Hospital. I'd read that story when she finished it five months later. After that, she hid it away in her scrapbook.

After Mom's death in 1972, I found her "Admittance" story again and recognized its importance. I wanted to understand more about the schizophrenia that led to her suicide and how it had affected her, me, and our family. But I delayed my investigation. More than forty years later, each rereading of Mom's "Admittance" story made me want to learn more about her illness and what had happened to her in the state mental hospital. I'd always thought of ESH as a forbidding, scary place. All I knew of mental hospitals came from books and movies like *One Flew Over the Cuckoo's Nest*, but when I grew older, wiser, and more curious, my haunting questions slowly outweighed my fears.

By 2017, I was determined to be brave enough to follow my mother's footsteps behind the locked doors and padlocked gates of a mental hospital, as I felt she'd beckoned me to do with her story. I screwed up my ranch girl courage to find out if I could access her medical record.

I began with a phone call to Eastern State Hospital in Medical Lake, near Spokane. When the receptionist answered, I said, "My mother was a patient there in the 1960s, and I'd like to see her medical record if that's possible."

"That far back, it would be in the archives, and we'd need some time to find it, but we can do it."

"I'm so glad to hear that," I said.

"We never throw anything away," she said. "You'll need to fill out a records request form, which I can mail to you. And when you come, you'll be allowed to go through the chart and make copies of any pages you like."

Amazing! They still had the chart and could produce it forty-five years later. And I could have copies to keep. It was much more than I'd hoped for.

Six weeks passed while I gathered documents and awaited approval to see my mother's medical chart. I arrived in Medical Lake on a clear, sunny day and drove up the hill to Eastern State Hospital. I was early for my 10:00 tour of the hospital's museum, so I had time to drive around the hospital campus. I entered the huge red brick building and gave the smiling receptionist a description of my red Nissan for their security team, then I asked for a map of the grounds.

"We don't have anything like that," she said, "but there are street signs with arrows."

Is it for security reasons, I wondered, *or because not too many visitors want to drive around the grounds?* I exited the lobby into the bright sunshine and headed for my car.

I grew up exploring the Sky Ranch and its surrounding country, led by my curiosity. I summoned the same spirit of discovery as I drove around the campus where my mother was treated for schizophrenia three times. I left the visitor's parking lot and slowly cruised along the main four-story building. The arches above the windows and the designs in its red brick gave the venerable old building a surprising classic beauty. But its old brick window casings held modern white-vinyl window frames, and all the windows had the same white coverings on the inside. What secrets were hidden behind them?

At the next intersection, I turned right and could see the back side of the long building recessed between two wings, one on either end. Halfway across the back, I stopped beside a sign that read *EASTLAKE ADMITTING.* Beyond the sign was a corridor lined by chain-link fencing leading to the entrance door. I realized this view was probably much the same as when my mother was escorted in and passed to a guard, and the sense of proximity gave me a chill.

I continued driving to learn the lay of the land, just as I had when I roamed the roads and hills around our ranch to fill in the details of my surroundings. Down the hill, beside the western twin lake, was the modern Westlake Campus. Its main structure was a two-story white building, and a sign said *MEDICAL RECORDS.* I'd return here for my afternoon appointment.

Setting aside my trepidation about what I'd find in those records, I drove back to the main building, where Mom had been admitted. Driving along the long east wall of the Eastlake building, I spotted capital letters embedded in the brick: *WOMEN.* My mother had written about being in the C-1 ward. Was this where she was kept, in this *ward*? I fixated on that word, *ward.* Something about it gave me a feeling of dread, and for a moment, I thought about how much I'd give for a time machine so I could step back four decades for just an hour, maybe even just five or ten minutes, to walk those halls and witness my mother's demeanor in this institution, to hear her voice, to see what her eyes might reveal.

I wondered, *Would such a perspective give me more peace or more pain?*

I noticed two deer grazing peacefully next to the wall on a rich, green lawn beneath a row of leafy shade trees, and I sat in my car for a few minutes to observe their tranquility. The tension in my shoulders began to release. Then it was time for my appointment with the hospital's historian.

In the visitor's lobby, a nice-looking woman with shoulder-length blonde hair greeted me with a smile. "I'm sorry," she said. "The museum area is closed today for unexpected repairs. But I can tell you the history of the hospital and how psychiatric treatment has changed over time, as you would have learned in the museum."

"Sounds good," I said. We sat in adjoining chairs as she showed photos and I took notes.

Dr. Thomas Kirkbride designed the original building as an asylum, or "sanctuary," and it opened in 1891 as the Eastern Hospital for the Insane. At its opening, the four-story building was described as one of the finest structures on the Pacific coast. Patient treatments involved resting, working in the gardens, or taking part in crafts like sewing or furniture-making. Many patients recovered and returned to their families. After the turn of the century, interventions—many cruel and medieval—were introduced to the United States, often brought over from Europe. These included cold baths, insulin shock, electroshock, and even lobotomies and sterilization. I took notes and tried not to imagine what those "treatments" were like for the patients.

I learned that my mother's psychotic episodes spanned two different eras of psychiatric treatment practices in US hospitals. Physical interventions, like shock therapy, were the standard treatment in the '40s and '50s. Her first psychotic episode occurred in 1944 during my older brother's birth, and the hospital used shock treatment to "bring her back to reality," as my father had put it. In 1951 and again in 1955, she was voluntarily hospitalized in Spokane and again received shock treatment. As far as I could tell, Mom had seemed like her usual self when she came home from the hospital after those treatments.

For the next four years, Mom worked hard at the ranch and got along with my father. But in 1959, her verbal attacks began in late summer and lasted three months. The pattern repeated in 1960 and 1961, and for those three years, she refused treatment even though it was clear her condition was worsening. By February 1962, she had become overtly psychotic and was involuntarily committed for treatment at Eastern State Hospital. By 1962, the standard therapy for psychiatric treatment favored antipsychotic medication over dramatic physical interventions, and Mom came home from the hospital with a prescription for Thorazine.

After an intense two hours with the historian, I emerged into the high noon heat with my emotions churning. But my overwhelming emotion was gratitude that my mother escaped the barbaric treatments others were subjected to.

I drove down the hill into the town of Medical Lake, where I bought a tuna sandwich and an iced tea, and then found a green hilltop park with a shaded bench.

Across the valley was a hillside with scattered pine groves, golden wheat spreading up the slope and over the top, and areas of sagebrush dotted with clumps of yellow sunflowers. The hillside reminded me of Sky Ranch with its high desert terrain and dryland wheat fields. A half-century ago, I'd been in a similar scene when I sat atop the ridge on my horse, protecting the wheat crop from our hungry sheep and protecting the sheep from coyotes. The sight of the ripening wheat brought back a vivid memory of riding my horse through a field of ripe golden wheat, enjoying its warm, yeasty smell while staying alert for the slither or buzz of a nearby rattlesnake.

I'd spent my youth protecting the ranch and its animals, domestic and wild, and my mother as well. Now I needed to do what I could to protect my offspring. And that meant gathering information. It was time to take a deep breath and drive back for my afternoon appointment with the medical records person.

I drove to the modern Westlake building and checked in at the lobby desk for my appointment with someone named Ellen. In walked a short, plump blonde woman in her late fifties. She greeted me with a strong, friendly handshake, and her hazel eyes looked warm behind wireless glasses. She welcomed me into her office, and I sat before her desk as she took her seat. She picked up a thick packet of papers bound with two wires at the top edge. From my early work in cardiology research, I recognized it as a medical chart.

"I've had this record pulled from the archives where it rested for forty-five years."

The chart looked well-preserved, and I wondered if it'd been touched in all this time.

Ellen looked at me with a serious expression. "I glanced through it. Your mother's chart has something in it that not all our charts have. Sometimes family members are surprised to find it, and I hope you won't find it upsetting."

The chart would be full of our family secrets, but that would be true of most charts. What kind of surprise was she warning me about?

She handed me the inch-thick packet and led me to the empty chair at the corner table in her office. She gave me a pad of yellow Post-its to stick on the pages I wanted her to copy, then pointed out a Kleenex box nearby. I shrugged, not yet knowing how much I'd need it.

I knew that medical charts are organized by reverse chronology, so I flipped to the back and began with my mother's first admission to Eastern State Hospital in February 1962. The chronicle of Mom's diagnoses and treatments through her three admissions unfolded in these pages, narrated by the doctors and nurses who treated her.

I scanned the first few admission pages, and then my mother's face popped up in glossy black and white. This photo was Ellen's surprise, and I was stunned. Then I launched back to 1962 when I was fifteen, Mom was forty-six, and she'd just been committed to this place against her will. I'd felt concern and shame for her because she'd spent a night in jail and was then driven here by my father. At that time, I knew only that she'd been taken away to make her well, and all I wanted was for my mother to come home and for life to go on as normal.

Years later, I looked at the face of the mother I loved but also resented. I resented her inability to parent and protect me. I resented her crazy, unpredictable behaviors. I resented that I had to take over the sheepherding, assume many of her chores, and watch over her when I was so young.

The portrait shows her face and shoulders against a white background, and I was immediately reminded of school picture day. Her dark brows lower into a slight frown, and her lips are pressed tight. I studied her expression and wondered if she was angry about having this photo taken. Then I wondered if my mother's obvious unhappiness was why Ellen thought I might be upset.

I turned away and breathed deeply, reaching for a tissue to dab my tears. My throat ached as I pressed a yellow Post-it square onto the page and continued turning pages. I found a second close-up that was taken five months later, during a readmission to adjust the meds that had caused her muscles to stiffen and clench. There were few photos of her during our ranch years because she was usually the one behind the camera. Certainly, none were this close-up, this intense—none so clearly trying to tell a story. They were painful to see, but I wanted the copies, so I applied the yellow stickies.

Moving through the chart, I marked the commitment documents from the Okanogan County Superior Court, the admission and discharge summaries, doctors' progress notes and clinical summaries, and the nursing record detailing her days and nights. I was astounded to read my father's voice in three letters to the ESH doctors, giving them his version of the events leading up to her admissions.

Two hours later, I'd marked almost half the chart for Ellen to copy. When she saw all the stickies, she said, "Are you sure? The copies cost a dollar a page."

"It's worth it to me," I said, and she started copying.

When Ellen handed me the copies, along with a bill for fifty dollars, I said, "My mother's mental illness began before I was born, and even though I saw it progressing, nobody told me her diagnosis was schizophrenia. It was never talked about in the family."

"That wasn't uncommon in those days," she said.

"That's why it's so important to me to have the truth."

She teared up and gave me a sweet hug. We both grabbed Kleenex and shared a smile.

"Thanks very much for your help," I said, "and for your empathy."

She nodded. "Helping people get the answers they need is one of the best parts of this job."

Clutching a bulging brown envelope, I walked out of the building and into the hot, thick air, daunted by what I knew I was carrying.

━━◆◆━━

The next day, I sat at my desk and opened the envelope, but within seconds, my throat constricted, my eyes filled with tears, and I slid the pages back into the envelope. I tried again a week later, approaching the task with a deliberate, objective mindset, as if I was about to research a stranger. By sticking stubbornly to this mindset, I was able to type out a transcript of the copied pages with relatively little emotion so I could preserve the originals and make notes on my typewritten version.

Even though I tried to stay distanced, I knew those pages revealed the truth of what happened to my mother—what her mind did to her, what doctors did to her—so as I typed, I reminded myself that I was investigating. I was looking for facts. I was simply completing a research project. But when I sat back to read the finished transcript, the enormity of what befell my mother sank in, and I cried again.

After each of Mom's six hospitalizations, Dad had told me little, and only when I asked direct questions like I did during our only long talk after Mom died in 1972. But in '72, I didn't even know what to ask. And for the next sixteen years before he died, I missed chance after chance to ask him more about what he witnessed, what he feared, and what he thought was wrong with his beloved.

So there I was, left with only pages from a medical chart to finally help me understand my complicated and long-suffering mother, a woman who was deeply misunderstood.

CHAPTER TWENTY-EIGHT

The transcript I typed revealed what I'd always wanted to know: what had led up to my mother's commitments at Eastern State Hospital and what had happened during her treatments there.

The first thing I read, again and again, was my father's letter to the ESH doctors:

> *In the fall of 1959 for about a three-month period, Zelma became very critical of my business abilities. Everything that I do is wrong, and everything if left up to her would be successful. Very belligerent, lacked ability to reason.*
>
> *She would cause severe emotional upset at the table at meal times, and the rest of the family would leave and skip the meal and she would finish her meal with an excellent appetite. Some improvement the rest of the year. This was repeated in the fall of 1959, 1960, 1961.*
>
> *In the past year of 1961, she did not improve and continued the belligerent attitude toward me and then added my mother and my son Bill. She took some medicine the first part of 1961, and we thought that it was helping. All summer she refused medicine.*

As I read, I clearly recalled the events Dad referred to. But deeper into his letter, I read about events I'd never heard about, and his words chilled me.

> *Approx. Dec. 1st I took her to [her family doctor] at Omak and advised Zelma and the Dr. that either she get proper medical attention and take the medicine as directed, or I would leave the Dr. office at that time and go to my attorney's office and ask for a divorce. Zelma agreed to go and see [her psychiatrist] in Spokane, which she did, and took her medicine OK until the week before her arrival at the State Hospital.*

What? Divorce? I'd never heard a word about divorce from either parent. If I'd known about Dad's threat, I'd have been very, very frightened, both for myself and for Mom. He must have been desperate to get Mom to accept treatment, and this threat was his last resort. It worked for a month or so until her paranoia led to a crisis witnessed not by her family but by the neighbors she visited.

> *At this time she quit taking her medicine and claimed she was alright. Also refused to comply with [her psychiatrist's] directions, whom she visited in Spokane by herself on Feb. 9, 1962. Sat. AM Feb. 10, she started to have a persecution complex. These were of short duration. By Sunday night she suddenly wanted to take her medicine, and I called [her psychiatrist] to get the OK on the medicine Monday AM.*

As I read Dad's account, I couldn't figure out how I'd missed all of that. How had they both kept such extraordinary problems secret?

I then went to Brewster in the afternoon, and when I came back in the evening she was in the hands of the county sheriff. The persecution complex had taken over shortly after I had left her and was rather severe and continued for a couple of hours. She then became very quiet with a very fuzzy mind and was in this condition when placed in your hands.

The chart also contained a letter written by a private psychiatrist in Spokane who had seen my mother five times over the four months leading up to her admission to ESH. He described Mom's symptoms and his attempts to treat her:

Mrs. Lockwood first consulted me on October 23, 1961. When seen, she showed the typical symptoms of a schizo-affective psychosis and seemed extremely paranoid and set in her opinion and showed very poor reasoning. She rationalized and projected a great deal and claimed that most of her difficulties were due to the poor marital relationship and was quite paranoid toward her husband as well as toward her mother-in-law. Although I saw her on four more occasions at fairly regular intervals, she did not follow through, especially with regard to her medication. When last seen on 2-9-1962, she was extremely paranoid and did not want to continue with further treatment.

I didn't know about Mom's trips to Spokane to visit a private psychiatrist. She must have driven there and back while I was in school.

I also read about what happened after I left for school on February 12, Mom's last day before her involuntary commitment. Two local doctors had examined my mother for the

Okanogan County Superior Court. They reported her medical history:

> ... *acute and recurrent ... progressive mental illness ... present for three years ... Increasing problems during the past three months—much worse during past two days.*

The doctors also summarized witness statements taken from three neighbors, including Eula Stout:

> *[Mrs. Lockwood] visited all of these people expressing paranoid thoughts and delusions.... Very upset with neighbors—feels they're all against her.*

The two doctors found that my mother was

> ... *uncommunicative, very quiet, slow to answer questions—seems unsure of answers when she even responds.... Paranoid delusions—feels things are missing and that someone trying to take personal belongings.... Felt certain papers and articles of clothing had been stolen even though present.... Patient disoriented—not responsible for acts toward self or others.*

On February 13, the Court found Zelma Lockwood *mentally ill and unsafe to be at large and should be hospitalized ... at Eastern State Hospital until released by the superintendent thereof.*

Wow, I thought as I read. My mother was judged "*unsafe to be at large*" soon after she'd made my brother and me breakfast and sent us off to school. How had she managed to keep the voices in her head at bay that morning when they told her she was being persecuted? I'd spent that day at school, completely unaware that my mother was being kept safe in jail and would be sent to a mental institution the next day.

Returning to the medical record, I learned about Mom's experience inside the mental hospital. I'd hungered for that information. For the forty-five years since her suicide, I'd felt I owed it to my mother to look straight into the truth, to open my eyes and learn everything I could about what she went through. I'd already read Mom's account of being admitted. But her attending physician's description told a different story:

> *At the time of admission she was extremely careless in her habits of dress and her personal hygiene. Her mood was one of excitation, and she was very easily agitated. She refused food and drink for the first twenty-four hours of her hospitalization, and it was necessary to seclude and restrain her for her own protection. . . . Her activity was markedly hyperactive, and she was very noisy.*

Very noisy? The nursing record revealed that she spent the first night screaming. But Mom's story had glossed over those first two days, saying she spent them "resting." Maybe she didn't remember them.

> *Emotionally, at the time of admission, she was sarcastic, irritable, and very suspicious . . . the patient was completely disoriented and . . . actively hallucinating. She would not answer questions and was very uncooperative.*
>
> *On the second day she began to take food and liquids and was placed on Thorazine 100 mg three times a day.*

Within three days there was almost a complete change in this patient's behavior and attitude, except at that time, there was considerable rambling and evasion . . . and paranoid ideas relative to her husband and her family. However, within a week, most of this disappeared and the patient's affect became quite appropriate . . . and she was spontaneous, relevant, and cooperative.

Amazing! Within a week, she'd made a complete turnaround. That's when she was allowed to make the phone call home that had surprised us so much.

From that point forward, Mom's written account agreed with the activities mentioned in the nursing record: going to church services, movies, a dance, and working in the dining room. The nurses wrote she was pleasant, sociable, and liked by others.

On March 17, she was released to my father. Her discharge diagnosis was "schizophrenic reaction, acute undifferentiated type." She had a prescription for Thorazine, 200 mg per day at bedtime, to take "for many months."

After she'd been home for a month, I'd seen Mom pacing the house and walking stiffly. After many weeks of restless days and sleepless nights, she grew desperate for help and asked Dad to drive her back to ESH, where she voluntarily signed herself in on June 2. It turned out that she'd had a reaction to the Thorazine. Her chart includes the letter her attending psychiatrist wrote to my father on June 27:

Mrs. Lockwood has been changed to a new type of medication. . . . Mellaril 50 mg four times a day plus Artane 5 mg four times a day. These will be her only medication, and we feel that she will do well on them.

Mom was discharged on July 9, and the chart held the letter she'd sent to her attending doctor at ESH: *I have been home now for two weeks and am feeling fine. The medicine prescribed there seems to be fine, and I have no complaints.*

During those two weeks at home, she penned her "Admittance" story, showed it to me, and then buried it in her scrapbook.

Mom's last hospitalization at ESH occurred in January of 1970. That was when she went with Dad to a helicopter convention in California. Sometime during the convention, Mom stopped taking her medications and became psychotic. In the chart, her ESH physician summarized the ensuing events:

According to information received from . . . a Eugene, OR, psychiatrist, this patient was flying back with her husband from a helicopter conference in Los Angeles when she became obsessed with the idea that a plane crash was about to take place. At the next stop she refused to go further with him. She went into town to take a bus back to Malott and ended up in Eugene, OR, where she showed up at one of the local hospitals . . . quite obviously disturbed, and a psychiatrist was called. According to [the Eugene psychiatrist], she was disoriented in time, place, and person. She had to look through her purse in order to find out who she was. Her husband was contacted, and the patient was then brought to ESH, where she signed in as a voluntary patient on January 26, 1970. She was given some medication [by the Eugene psychiatrist], which was probably Thorazine, which seemed to help her a great deal because she was not obviously psychotic when she arrived at this hospital.

Mom was rational enough to sign in voluntarily to ESH. Her admitting physician continued the Thorazine, and her thinking stabilized after two more days. Then her attending physician, knowing her previous reaction to Thorazine, changed her antipsychotic prescriptions to Mellaril (100 mg three times per day) and Stelazine (5 mg three times per day). On February 16, 1970, she was released to my father with the discharge diagnosis of "acute schizophrenic episode."

That time, her rapid relapse had made clear to the entire family—and Mom herself—that she could never stop taking her antipsychotic drugs. The medications kept her from becoming psychotic but not from sinking into depression and, finally, the despair in which she ended her life in 1972.

CHAPTER TWENTY-NINE

After typing the key parts of the hospital record, I was puzzled by some of its medical language. Some handwritten notes in the nursing record were indecipherable abbreviations, and many of the medical terms were a mystery. I recognized the names of the prescriptions Mom took at home, but I wanted to know more about these drugs.

At my writing group's monthly meeting in September, I talked about the medical chart and my difficulties interpreting some of it. One member, Abby, offered to decipher the abbreviations and explain the unfamiliar terms. She was a highly trained, experienced behavioral therapist. Abby proved to be the guide I needed, truly a godsend.

On a sunny Saturday in late September, I drove to Abby's home with the envelope of chart copies on the seat next to me. She served me tea and said, "If it's okay with you, I want to read through all the pages of the chart before we talk about it."

I said, "Of course." I handed her the envelope. "I'm so grateful for your help." Then I sipped my tea and waited.

After thirty minutes, Abby said, "Your mother was really crazy!"

No one had ever put it to me so bluntly. Once I got over the shock of hearing someone speak so boldly of my mother's mental illness, I understood that her words were a gift. After all the years of avoidance and camouflaged references to my mother's condition with words like "mental illness" and "tranquilizers," Abby's unvarnished truth was refreshing.

She started right in. "You were a child struggling through long, hard years while a core member of your family went in and out of mental illness episodes. Even on a normal day, your mother was a bit paranoid about socializing or talking to a doctor. This is who your mother really was, and when you can understand the whole picture of who she was as a mother, then you can understand yourself."

At last, I knew why Mom had delayed and resisted when I needed medical care. It was because of her own paranoid fear of doctors. Was that the legacy of months of painful doctoring after the car accident?

Next, Abby said something that took me a while to process. "Children of a bipolar or schizophrenic parent experience difficult childhoods because that parent is inconsistent in an intermittent way."

This immediately helped me understand how my mother's behavior had affected my sense of security growing up. Sometimes she was able to respond and comfort me, but other times she was emotionally distant and seemed not to care about me, like when she refused to call a doctor when I was in pain. When I went through puberty, I talked with her about my needs, like wearing a bra and a sanitary pad, but she gave me very little support and never shared her own feelings and experiences. I felt closed off from my mother when I needed her most, which left me feeling motherless and insecure. The worst times were when Mom became psychotic and irrationally attacked my father. During those episodes, I couldn't rely on her for anything.

"When your mom was becoming this difficult person," Abby said, "the best you could hope for was her becoming emotionally flat. You'd wonder what you were doing wrong. You concluded you had to be a good girl, help your dad and mom, and not make any trouble. Effectively, you didn't have a mother."

Effectively, you didn't have a mother. I let her words sink in.

I pictured myself as a little girl growing up without a mother I could rely on to defend or soothe me. I felt anxious and angry when Mom wouldn't or couldn't intervene to shield me from my brother's harassment. I felt alone when she didn't talk about her feelings or mine. I felt unloved and unsafe when I was in pain and she didn't call a doctor. It all made so much sense now.

"I can relate to this," Abby said, "because I grew up that way too. Children like us, who feel abandoned by their parents, bond with animals and give them our affection. Our animal friends show us how to do things."

I thought about the times when I'd brushed Lucky and she stretched her nose around to rub an itch on her rump or back. As I brushed the itchy spot, she'd reach her muzzle toward me and rub me back with her strong upper lip. Once I learned more about horse behavior, I realized that by grooming me in return, Lucky was showing me acceptance as a friend, as horses do when they stand head to tail and scratch each other.

Abby went on to say, "Normally there are ages when kids need to develop a sense of mastery of things like reading, social adjustment, or a desired skill. Your parents weren't present to guide you during these important times, so you had to figure it out on your own, learning how to take care of yourself, your mother, and your horses."

As I listened, I wondered, *Is that the silver lining of all this? Am I as capable and self-sufficient as I am because my parents were absent?*

"When you grow up as you did," Abby explained, "with no one showing you how, you attempt something in steps or stages, come back, get praised and soothed, and then try the next step."

I didn't remember anyone praising or soothing me. When Pepper kept bucking me off, I climbed back on and tried again, day after day, ashamed of my failures, until Dad noticed my injuries and brought home the new saddle. What did it mean that my parents skipped the praising and soothing parts?

"Children like us," Abby continued, "become little heroes and learn on our own, but we also learn falsely that we'd better try to fit in and be good and not attract attention. As a result, we hold the fear of not being competent, not being good enough."

These words went straight to my heart and resonated with what I'd learned in therapy: I'd always secretly believed I wasn't good enough. When Abby pointed out how that untruth originated in my childhood, the revelation washed over me like outgoing waves revealing a rock embedded in the sand.

Because neither of my parents was present or emotionally equipped to give me the support I needed, I turned to people who were, like my high school English teacher, Mrs. Voelckers, who called on me to babysit her little boys. And I worked to excel in school, where teachers paid attention to me and where I could prove my competence by getting As. By working to excel academically, I played my best card while burying my tender heart and emotions.

Next, Abby explained how my family coped with my mother's illness. "When a person is as crazy as your mother was, the family constellates around that person and tries to compensate for her and get along. As you've demonstrated in your writing about all this, each person in your family experienced what happened through a different filter."

She was right. As a child and then an adolescent, I was uninformed about Mom's mental illness and unprotected from her manic moods, but I was still expected to watch over her, make sure she took her tranquilizers, graze the sheep, and move the sprinklers each day. Feeling responsible for my mother was an emotional load too heavy for my age, and the burden grew heavier with time. What a dramatic event to find a parent after an overdose! I'd helped my mother recover from that attempted suicide, and after that episode, I felt she should never be left alone again, especially by me, the only one who could get along with her when she was ranting about my father's treatment.

"Did your mom ever attack you?" Abby asked.

"No, she never did. Not verbally or physically."

As I responded, I wondered why. Maybe it was a conscious choice. Maybe she was clearheaded enough to realize she didn't want to alienate the one person she could talk to. In the summers, when she and I were often alone at the ranch, she needed my companionship and help, and she had no problem venting her personal problems to me despite how young I was and despite ranting about my own father. And I didn't dare challenge her. Usually, I'd slip away to do a chore, preferably one on another part of the ranch.

Through the years, I'd had relatively little awareness of the root causes of my mother's confusing behavior, but I was aware of my own fierce emotions. As early as age eleven, I began to worry I might one day become irrational like my mother. But I had no one to talk to about it, so I quietly harbored that fear until my college years, when I learned, during my calculus panic attack, that I could find help by reaching out to others. For years, I'd lived with the silent fear that I might develop a debilitating mental illness, and I had nobody, *not one person*, to ease my fear.

Abby moved on to my father. "He gets martyr points," she said, "for sticking with your mother through their difficult marriage, but he didn't bear the brunt of it—*you* did. You were always left with your mother, and he wasn't there to support you. He couldn't be blamed for leaving when he had to fly, but it was bad judgment to leave you to take care of your disturbed mom and the ranch animals. Your parents were the grown-ups, and it was their job to take care of you, not vice versa."

That was true, although my dad might not have realized how hard it was for me or that he shouldn't have put it on my young shoulders. Once, when he was in his eighties, he acknowledged my efforts, saying, "You always stayed and helped with your mom, and I want to thank you for doing that." It wasn't much, but it was something.

"Then there was your brother," Abby continued. "He coped with your mother by distancing himself from her as much as he could."

"Yes," I said. "He was able to get away, especially once he could drive. But from the beginning, he teased me to the point of making me cry and then laughed at my tears and called me a crybaby. I never understood why he was so mean to me."

"There are two kinds of teasing," Abby said. "The first runs from humorous to sarcasm, and the second is bullying, which is intended to undermine the person, like mocking your intelligence."

Once again, Abby was right. Bill didn't just tease me; he bullied me. He mocked my level of common sense, which he maintained was more important than good grades. His favorite put-down, which he carefully launched only when our parents were out of earshot, was, "You haven't got sense enough to pound sand in a rat hole." He was wrong. I had a lot of sense—that I knew—including the sense to feel demeaned by that old saying.

Decades later, once we both had children of our own, I bared my heart to my brother. We were on a car trip to visit Dad and Rosemary at the beach. Bill was riding in my car, and his wife was driving their van with our four young girls playing together. Along the way, I said, "Bill, I want you to know how much you hurt me by teasing and belittling me through all those years when we were growing up."

Bill turned to look at me with surprise in his eyes. "What do you mean?"

"Remember how you teased me when Dad killed my Easter bunny for the dinner table, and you called me a sissy for my tears?"

He looked puzzled, so I went on. "And when we got to the ranch, you forced me to do the hard chores, like filling the sawdust burner when it was actually your turn to do it."

He thought for a minute, then said, "I do remember being surprised that one time when you refused to do it, and you slapped me so hard it really hurt."

How interesting, I thought. *He remembers his pain but not mine.*

"What about that time when I was in seventh grade and you were in eighth, and you changed my homework answers on the school bus?"

"I kinda remember doing that." He wrinkled his brow, trying to think back.

"And you made fun of me on the bus, refusing to give back my paper. And then I was embarrassed again, in front of my class, when I got a failing grade on my math paper."

"I just barely remember that," he said, beginning to look sheepish.

"All your belittling and bullying was really hurtful. It reduced my self-confidence, which held me back in college, and it took me a long time to build it back."

He was silent for a minute, then said, "I didn't mean to hurt you."

I drove along, not answering for several minutes. How could I believe him? Back then, his goal was obviously to hurt me. Maybe he just didn't realize how deeply he cut.

Then Bill turned to me and said, "I'm sorry. I apologize for hurting you."

His tone was sincere, and I believed him. I also realized I could use his apology to free myself. The resentment I'd held all these years, justified as it was, could only hurt me. I decided to let it go.

"I forgive you," I said. We drove quietly for a while, but at the next stop, we came together for a warm hug. It was an immensely powerful moment—since that conversation and the hug that followed, I've felt free to love my brother.

Abby interrupted my musing to invite me to a late lunch at her favorite local bakery, followed by a walk in the woods with her dog. As we talked and walked, she said, "I know this has been a lot to absorb today. Feel free to call me any time you have more questions or need to talk further."

I smiled and thought about what a friend she'd been in all of this. How extraordinarily helpful. As I processed our meeting over the next several days, I realized that the understanding, support, and communication I was deprived of in childhood was bountiful in my adult life. And for that, I was immensely grateful.

CHAPTER THIRTY

B ecause I gained access to my mother's medical records and my friend Abby shared her invaluable insights, I could piece together the story of my mother's mental illness, at least in part, and how it affected our family. But a few big questions lingered in my mind. I wanted to know what caused my mother to develop schizophrenia. What did her paranoid episodes feel like? What was it like for her to undergo shock treatments and then need antipsychotic medications for the rest of her life?

To understand Mom's plight, I turned to books and articles on mental illness. I read memoirs written by people afflicted with schizophrenic illnesses or memoirs by their family members. My empathy for her grew as I learned more.

One evening after our writing group met at her office in Seattle, Abby gave me a book, saying, "I've used this for a long time with my clients. I think it will help you understand more about your mom. It has sections about schizophrenia."

Lloyd Sederer's *The Family Guide to Mental Health Care* is intended for friends and relatives of people with mental illnesses. It offers simple, helpful explanations of what's happening to their loved one and what family members can do to help. I wish my family and I would have had a book like that back in the '50s and '60s. We couldn't understand my mother's behavior, and we couldn't help her because we had no idea what we were dealing with. In those days, schizophrenia wasn't commonly understood. Today, the norm is family therapy, which includes everyone.

After my mother died, I clung to the hope that she didn't actually have schizophrenia. *Maybe Dad has it wrong*, I thought. Schizophrenia carries great stigma and underlies deeply frightening stories in books and movies, so I'd hoped and hoped that Mom had suffered from something less dark, less sinister. Her medical chart ended that hope. Armed with my new knowledge, I worried that I or my children could inherit her schizophrenia.

Three more years passed as I read and studied more about Mom's disorder. And once again, a friend in my writing group heard my struggle and came to my aid.

Patricia was a retired medical doctor, and she pointed me to the most recent medical research on schizophrenia. There, I began to find authoritative answers to the questions that haunted me. For a very long time, I'd wondered, *What is schizophrenia?* Thanks to Patricia, I learned that it's a general term for a group of psychotic illnesses characterized by disturbances in thinking, emotional reaction, and behavior. Typical symptoms include hallucinations, delusions, disorganized speech or thought, a lack of insight about having the illness, and cognitive impairments in attention, memory, and thinking processes for controlling decisions and behavior.

Negative symptoms—such as a flat affect, loss of motivation, and poverty of speech—usually develop in the illness's later course, and I saw them in my mother during her last ten years. When she prepared a meal and sat down to eat with me, it was as if she wasn't there, and I often felt like I was sitting at the table with a near-wordless robot. She'd listen to me talk and briefly respond to my questions, but she didn't initiate conversation. I'd wondered about her lack of emotional response because I couldn't seem to reach her.

In addition, Mom often displayed a lack of insight about her condition. When her psychotic symptoms were clearly escalating, she was certain she wasn't ill. Sometimes she was malleable enough to be convinced to voluntarily sign herself into the hospital, but at other times, she refused treatment. At home, she sometimes wouldn't take her medication.

The worst aspect of Mom's psychotic escalation between 1959 and 1962 was the three-year delay in treatment while her illness progressed. Untreated psychosis leads to a loss of brain cells and a decline in logical thinking and decision-making. When Bill and I were young, Mom enjoyed PTA meetings. She also volunteered as an assistant leader for my brother's Scout pack and our 4-H Club. But during our high school years, she avoided social interactions. She must have become aware that her thinking and behavior weren't normal.

By 1970, it became harder for her to hide the cognitive toll of her illness. At my wedding rehearsal that summer, she had trouble following the directions for her role as mother of the bride and became visibly agitated. During the wedding ceremony, she hesitated when the minister asked the question she was to answer: "Who gives this woman . . . ?" Finally, the minister fed her the words: "Her father and I do." She repeated her line, but I saw she was anxious and stressed. As always, her discomfort pained me.

At the reception, after the guests finished flowing through the receiving line, I said to Mom, "You did just fine," but she frowned and shook her head.

My biggest question was what had caused my mother's illness. After reviewing the recent studies my physician friend had recommended, and after finding countless resources on my own, I unearthed a lot of truth about why my mother was the way she was.

I learned that there's a strong genetic component to schizophrenia. I couldn't know for certain whether my mother inherited a genetic vulnerability, but her immediate family history shows no evidence of mental illness—not in her parents, grandparents, siblings, or children. This information was a relief, but it also made me sad to know how my mother had to go it alone.

There are also environmental factors involved in the illness's development, which points me back to my mother's traumatic car accident in early childhood. Was that horrific experience the start of it all? I can't know for sure, but my research told me it was quite possible.

Or was Mom's illness due to the other environmental factors I'd read about? Were its roots in a childhood bacterial infection? Inflammation? Stress? Concussion? It could have been any of these, and she'd had them all. Throughout her life, she had periodic drainage from her partially blocked ear canal; its foul smell meant it was inflamed or infected. But if Mom did acquire DNA cell mutations due to these damaging environmental factors, the mutations couldn't be passed to her children.

Comforted by my conclusion that my mother's schizophrenia wouldn't be passed on to my children, I went on a mission to learn more about what Mom might have gone through as she experienced different treatments.

I don't know what type of sedative Mom had when Bill was born, but when it was applied, she was screaming from pain and fear and struggling against the doctors, and she woke from the sedative screaming and dissociated. Dad told me they used shock treatments to "bring her back to her right mind." That could have been either insulin shock or electroshock therapy—both in common use in 1944. Either way, it would have been harsh treatment for a new mother who'd suffered a physically and emotionally traumatizing labor and delivery.

Mom also received shock treatment twice in the '50s. By then, electroconvulsive therapy was the common treatment for mental disorders, although without the safety features now used, such as muscle relaxants. Memory loss and cognitive difficulty were common side effects. Mom never confided to me about these treatments, but her reticence could have stemmed from her wish to hide the severity of her condition or from her memory being erased by the treatments—or both.

By 1962, antipsychotic drugs were the standard treatment. Thorazine was marketed as a cure for schizophrenia, but that claim was never proven. Mom came home from her commitment to ESH with a prescription for Thorazine, and when she proved unable to tolerate it, the doctors switched her to Mellaril and later added Stelazine. According to Abby, these drugs would have made her feel tired and dull with an absence of normal emotions. No wonder she tried to stop taking them.

Today, antipsychotic medications are the first-line treatment for schizophrenia, and better ones have been developed. In conjunction with these medications, community behavioral health providers can address schizophrenia with case management, self-management, problem-solving therapy, and cognitive-behavioral therapy. But my poor mother's only therapy was medication. Today's services could have helped her cope with the medicine's side effects and overcome her lack of insight about being ill. She might then have taken the meds more consistently and avoided the relapses that were triggered when she stopped taking them. But these services weren't available yet in the 1950s and 1960s.

For my mother, it was a perfect storm: mental illness, isolation (increasingly self-imposed), a deteriorating marriage, an absence of community care providers, and a family unable to understand and support her.

People afflicted with schizophrenia experience higher rates of depression, anxiety disorders, substance use disorders, and suicide than those who don't. Mom always avoided alcohol and other addictive substances, but late in her illness, depression's grip on her was merciless.

I wondered if Mom's untreated depression led to her suicide. I returned to her chart, looking for clues that the ESH doctors might have recognized and treated her depression. Mom's medical record for her January 1970 admission doesn't mention her 1966 suicide attempt. My father must not have reported it to them. And I don't know if the ESH doctors ever discussed suicide prevention with him when Mom was discharged.

In March of 1966, as the weather changed from a long winter slog to the hopeful signs of spring, my mother sent her family and friends a poem that she had first written during our early years on the ranch:

ADVENT OF SPRING
Zelma Carson Lockwood

After our long cold winter days,
    How we welcome each spring!
All life throbs and wakens now,
    It's such a gorgeous thing!

It's meadowlark and sparrow songs
    And noisy killdeers too,
And all the other songs of birds
    Returning from the "blue."

It's baby calves and little lambs
    Cavorting all about,
Horses and colts feeling their grain
    Letting extra steam out.

It's muddy lanes and slip'ry roads;
    But this we must endure,
And messy barnyards where we feed;
    Spring days will be the cure.

It's daffodils and bright tulips,
    And hyacinths so gay,
And pussy willows filling out,
    Each bright sunshiny day.

It's spray planes and helicopters
    Flying the orchards low,
Spreading death on bug pests
    Everywhere they go.

Spring brings so many lovely things;
    We're glad that winter's past.
Brown hills will turn to vibrant green
    As spring arrives at last.

This poem reflected what springtime had once meant to her. I can imagine how hard it was for her to emerge from the winter doldrums with her emotions and creativity muffled by the drugs she had to take. I picture her grieving that she couldn't feel the enchantment of daffodils on a spring day or the hope of new life awakening.

Four months later, Mom swallowed all of her sleeping pills. In 1970, four years later, she stopped taking her anti-psychotic medications and ended up wandering the streets, not knowing her name or who to call. After that, she realized she could never stop taking them. Two years later, she ended her life.

AFTERWORD

I couldn't save my mother when she aimed the pistol at her forehead, but I can express the respect and honor she deserves for the person she was despite the profound challenges she encountered.

As she battled the perfect storm of her illness, Mom had a home to return to, a family to care for, and daily tasks to sustain her. She could feel needed and useful, and her efforts contributed to our daily life and livelihood. In fact, I now realize that even in the last year of her life, when she seemed emotionally remote, she still rallied to express her love for me with that wonderful Thanksgiving dinner. Food was her love language, spoken through all the wonderful meals and desserts she made for her family over the years.

Because my family lacked any other explanation for Mom's psychotic disruption of our lives, we believed it was her fault. We didn't blame Dad for his broken leg, Gram for her heart attack, Bill for his rheumatic fever, or me for my painful periods. Each of us received care and support, and we recovered. Yet we blamed Mom when her illness recurred and worsened. How unfair that was. None of it was her fault.

I talked with Abby again after having this revelation. "It's time to let it go," she counseled. "You'll never know for sure what caused your mother's illness. Now you need to focus on yourself, complete your healing, and move on."

She's right. Too many of my questions are unanswerable. During my childhood, we lived a family myth that Mom's illness was episodic and that she was fine again between hospitalizations. And we acted as if the farm would keep Mom safe, but we showed little appreciation for her hard work and no understanding of her struggles as her illness advanced. We kept our feelings of love under wraps of shame that isolated her. In that way, we all played a role in her illness.

It's time to stop blaming myself and bargaining for a different outcome. I'm ready to complete my mourning. And so I begin.

I mourn that I had to grow up without a mother who could protect me and give me emotional comfort and guidance. In my high school years, I visited a few times with friends whose mothers chatted with us over nice meals or snacks. Those mothers were interested in their children. I felt their support and wished I had a mother like that.

After Mom's suicide, I felt angry that she hadn't given me a chance to say goodbye, and then my anger grew when I realized she'd been leaving me gradually for years. My anger dissolved into sadness and regret when I understood how desperately she must have worked to stave off her psychotic thinking and paranoia and how hard she must have fought to give my brother and me as normal a home life as she could.

I'm grateful she married my father. Together they taught me their great appreciation of the outdoors and reared me on the ranch, where I learned perseverance and how to be responsible for myself. I'm also grateful for the gift of intelligence that she handed down to me. She was a straight-A student through high school, and so was I. She attended my graduation from Central Washington State College and watched the college president place the valedictorian's medallion around my neck. She was proud of my honors and awards, and I think she could have done as well if she'd had the chance.

When her illness knocked her down, she got back up and did the best she could until she made her final, fateful decision. I respect her choice.

By honoring my mother, I forgive myself. But it doesn't end there. It ends with acknowledging the love that was always between us.

Every year, my Carson relatives gather for a family reunion in the Yachats River Valley, the valley my mother called home. On a tree-lined hill next to the former site of her family's home, dairy barn, and sawmill is the Carson Cemetery. I visit that cemetery each time I attend the reunion. I wander up the rise to find the graves of my grandparents, aunts and uncles, and other family members. Among them lies my mother's grave, marked by the marble gravestone my father made for her, engraved ZELMA CARSON LOCKWOOD, BELOVED WIFE AND MOTHER.

I kneel to clean the marble and linger beside it. I leave a red rose, a lock of my now-silver hair, and a few tears. I ask her to forgive my ignorance and accept my love as I pledge to love her forever. I look up through the tall firs to the sky and say, "See you on the other side, Mom."

ACKNOWLEDGMENTS

I would like to thank the mentors who first encouraged me to write: Robert Ray and Jack Remick, who were instructors for the University of Washington Certificate in Creative Nonfiction in 1998 and then for years held weekly writes at local coffee houses.

At Hugo House in Seattle, I was inspired to write a memoir, first by John Marshall and then by Christine Hemp, Theo Nestor, Steve Almond, and many others. With classmates at Hugo House, I enjoyed the writing support of a group that evolved into the Lake Forest Park Writing Group: Sara Kim, Patricia Sparks, Helen Wattley-Ames, Anu Garg, Connie Ballou, Mercedes Nicole Elessa, and earlier members Abby Smith, Don Normark, and Jennifer Hopkins.

I would like to acknowledge the online memoir writing classes taught by Brooke Warner and Linda Joy Myers, the story-writing classes taught by Nicholas O'Connell and Scott Driscoll, the Kachemak Bay Writers' Conference, and the Pacific Northwest Writers Association.

Thank you to the She Writes Press staff, including Brooke Warner for her steady guidance throughout the publishing process, and Shannon Green, Krissa Lagos, Signe Jorgenson, and the designers for helping me publish. My special thanks to developmental editor Jodi Fodor for crafting my words into a memoir and teaching me along the way.

I thank Nan Lockwood, JoAnne Bailey, Abby Smith, Stanley Stout, and Robert Klug for their feedback on drafts of my manuscript, Kathy Lee and Jan Baker for emotional support as I visited Eastern State Hospital, and the staff there who were so helpful.

I thank my husband, Robert Klug, for his love and patience with me during these last ten years of my journey into the past to understand my mother and finally reveal my story to the world.

ABOUT THE AUTHOR

LINDA M. LOCKWOOD is the author of *Sky Ranch: Reared in the High Country.* Following her youth riding horses on a sheep and cattle ranch in the Okanogan Highlands of eastern Washington state, she made her home in the Seattle area, pursued a career in heart research and health planning, and then served customers of Seattle's electric utility. Linda lives in Seattle with her beloved husband, and she enjoys neighborhood walks, joyous times with her children and grandchildren, and her lifelong pursuit of learning.

Author photo © Seattle Headshot

Looking for your next great read?

We can help!

Visit www.shewritespress.com/next-read
or scan the QR code below for a list
of our recommended titles.

She Writes Press is an award-winning
independent publishing company founded to
serve women writers everywhere.